BUSHI

The Way of the

BUSHIDO
The Way of the Warrior

Bohdi Sanders, PhD

First Edition

Published by Kaizen Quest Publishing

Printed in the United States of America

Library of Congress Cataloging-in-Publication Data
Sanders, Bohdi, 1962-

BUSHIDO: The Way of the Warrior

ISBN - 978-1-937884-20-8

1. Martial Arts. 2. Self-Help. 3. Philosophy. I. Title

Endorsements for *BUSHIDO*

Doctor Sanders has done it again with this inspirational new book, *BUSHIDO*. As you might guess, it gives a new quote for each day of the year for the warrior spirit within us all. With each page and each thought, comes a pattern or process that each person with this birthright of passion can relate to.

As you delve into the written word, almost scripture-like in nature, you start reflecting on your own personality. You begin to examine your actions and reactions to events in your everyday modern world and realize that something old is new again.

Sometimes we forget that those who walked before us had all the same issues that we have today, even though we have advanced technology. We are still human and have the survival gene that all living beings have. Those who are chosen to be warriors by DNA selection are unique in the way they respond and react to challenges in life.

The Bushido scriptures are like a flow chart of that process. I highly recommend that everyone, warrior or not, give this book a read, since it will shed light on that driving spirit that makes a warrior thrive!

Dan Tosh, PhD, JD

Grandmaster Dan Tosh has been training in Shorin-ryu Karate since 1958 and now holds the rank of 10th degree black belt. Dr. Tosh has a Ph.D. in economics, as well as a law degree, and has served as an adjunct professor for Novus Law School. Grandmaster Tosh has been involved in choreography, movie production, stunt work, workshops and tournament competition for many years.

Endorsements for *BUSHIDO*

Dr. Bohdi Sanders has done it again. This time, he has provided a daily tool for the warrior to stay focused and forward-looking, through daily reminders about what it is to be a warrior, in his book, *BUSHIDO*. *BUSHIDO: The Way of the Warrior* provides a timeless lesson for each day of the year.

These lessons are golden nuggets of struggles and triumphs experienced by masters, leaders, and others through the ages, and collected as an aid to all who seek warriorhood. Our passions and our way of life can be challenging enough without the aid of tools. *BUSHIDO* is a visionary tool that assists today's warrior in maintaining his or her perspective on his or her chosen way of life.

Warriorhood is timeless and placeless. Although we associate many warriors with specific times and specific places, warriorhood is really a state of mind. It is the mindset of one who lives by a code that is based on a moral way of life, an unshakeable moral compass.

Today's warrior is a chivalrous, self-reliant, protector, a sheepdog, with a confidence borne of mastery of self and the tools of life. The warrior remains on a path of continuous improvement and seeks tried and true methods to maintain that forward momentum of improvement. But, as in any sport or way of life, we do not reinvent the wheel; we use the tools available to help us achieve our goals. *BUSHIDO* will become one of the best tools to stay focused.

I enjoyed reading *BUSHIDO: The Way of the Warrior* and it will remain in my library. I am confident others will enjoy reading it also and allowing it to assist them as they move forward.

Phil Torres
Colonel of Marines, Retired

Phil Torres rose from Private to Colonel in the U. S. Marine Corps and retired after an illustrious career lasting more than 34 years of active duty. He served in Vietnam and was awarded the nation's third highest combat decoration, the Silver Star Medal, for actions as a Platoon Sergeant. He is a lifelong martial artist with over 53 years in the martial arts. He currently holds the title of Kyoshi in Okinawan Shorin Ryu Kenshinkan Karate, as well as the title of Hanshi. Phil is also a competitive shooter in the action shooting sports.

Endorsements for *BUSHIDO*

Dr. Bohdi Sanders is a rare individual. I enjoy his championing of warrior spirit and how he weaves the aspect of heart throughout his teachings. Warriorship is all about lifestyle, and as a warrior, one must be certain that the battle is one that needs to be fought.

Anger and revenge need to be overcome inside you and not just in the world. Give me another man to fight and I have no problem; that is much easier. The toughest battles that we will ever fight are the ones between our own two ears – the internal battles.

BUSHIDO: The Way of the Warrior beautifully shares deep insights from many masters that have walked the Budo and/or spiritual path. Bohdi takes their statements, koans, proverbs and sayings and expands on them with his thoughts and wisdom in the form of transformational lessons or stories.

Bohdi will lead you and provoke you to think and act beyond your current perception of yourself, so that you can be more. He wants you to excel in your life.

It takes a warrior to be courageous enough to overcome the inner battles, fight the outside ones with honor, and maintain a balanced heart and life. Dr. Sanders does just that in his life lessons presented in *BUSHIDO: The Way of the Warrior*, as well as all of his other great books.

Grandmaster Richard Van Donk, Ph.D.

Dr. Van Donk has been studying Budo for 50 years. He is an inheriting Grandmaster in DeCuerdas Eskrima, a senior Bujinkan Shihan 15th Dan, and Bushindo Ryu Sword Grandmaster. Dr. Van Donk has authored and published over 100 books, DVD's and courses on martial arts, spiritual awakening, and personal transformation. Richard is the founder of the *Empower Yourself Teachings* available on Bushindo.com.

Endorsements for *BUSHIDO*

Dr. Sanders' book, *BUSHIDO: The Way of the Warrior*, is simply amazing. It is an extraordinary book which will guide you in your journey to be a better martial artist and warrior. But don't be mislead, this book is not just for martial artists. This is a book that everyone, whether they are a martial artist or not, will benefit from.

It's a must read for those who want to live a fuller life in the martial arts. It is also an amazing book for anyone who wants to live a life of character and integrity in a world where many sorely need instruction on living a better life.

Don't just read through this book. You will get more from it if you follow the wisdom and incorporate it into your own life. Own it and live by it! If you do this, your life will change for the better.

Dr. Sanders is in the business of life transformation and this book is nothing short of amazing. I highly recommend this book to everyone who wants to be motivated and inspired to live a better life!

Grandmaster Eddie Mapula

Grandmaster Eddie Mapula is the founder of The United Kick Boxing Arts Federation and the United Boxing Arts Federation. He is also a two-time World Kick Boxing Champion and a one-time World Champion in Karate. Eddie worked in the Chuck Norris organization for 27 years. Today, Eddie works as a life coach and a personal martial arts trainer.

Endorsements for *BUSHIDO*

Dr. Sanders obviously put a lot of thought into this amazing book, both in his teachings and in the great quotes that he has included throughout the book. The wisdom and teachings in this book are invaluable and something that seems to have been lost in our modern day culture. I can't recommend this book highly enough!

Hanshi Frank Dux

Hanshi Frank Dux is immortalized by the motion picture based upon his life – *Bloodsport*. Jean-Claude Van Damme played the role of Frank Dux in this amazing tale of Hanshi Dux's life. From the years 1975 through 1980 he was the World Full Contact Kumite (no-holds-barred) Champion. He holds 16 world records which have been standing for little over a quarter of a century and has been inducted into five martial arts Hall of Fames as a *"Living Legend."*

Endorsements for *BUSHIDO*

I love Bohdi Sanders' *BUSHIDO: The Way of the Warrior*! This daily devotional helps in the process of balancing and improving every aspect of the Warrior's life. It is a must read for the martial artist who has a warrior's heart, the martial artist who wants to live life with honor, justice, and with a code of ethics that does not change with circumstances. It is also great for the warrior who wishes to stand firm and fight when others won't be inconvenienced to do so.

Reading *BUSHIDO: The Way of the Warrior* brings daily encouragement to the warrior with thoughtful insights about warriorship, insights that make the warrior more attentive to strengthening the mind and the soul, while still encouraging the warrior to strengthen the body.

The insights shared in *BUSHIDO: The Way of the Warrior* help the warrior live a more balanced life, increasing the chances of winning life's physical, mental, and emotional battles.

While it encourages the building of strength, stamina and martial technique, *BUSHIDO: The Way of the Warrior* really encourages the warrior to continue to develop character, to know and stand firm for what is right, for truth, justice, and the martial way of Bushido. It also encourages the warrior to forgive mistakes made and to move forward with more fortitude to do better at the next opportunity.

I highly recommend *BUSHIDO: The Way of the Warrior* to every martial warrior. It will help renew your mind and your spirit daily, and I guarantee you will see growth in your martial walk.

"True karate is this: that in daily life one's mind and body
be trained and developed in a spirit of humility, and that in
critical times, one be devoted utterly to the cause of justice."
Gichin Funakoshi

Dana Stamos

Dana Stamos has studied Tang Soo Do Karate, Danzan Ryu JuJitsu, Goju-Shorei Karate, and many other styles of martial arts. Dana has also been inducted into the Masters Hall of Fame and the Universal Martial Arts Association Hall of Fame as "Woman of the Year." She is also a member of the Martial Arts Magazine Hall of Honors.

Endorsements for *BUSHIDO*

This work by Dr. Bohdi Sanders was a pleasure to read. His ability to clarify a salient objective is very lucid. There are not many who have this ability; although there are several that are attempting to match his wit and objectivity.

I find it a joy to read his work and always look forward to his keen insight into needed subject areas. Too often we as martial artists forget that it is not just the work that we do in the dojo or school, but it is the mentality of our efforts that must be defined before the real training begins.

I have seen individuals, who become very proficient at the physicality of varied martial arts, but who have no honor, no integrity and no instilled spirit of what is right and what is wrong. They are petty and instead of trying to elevate themselves, they find it more expedient to try and drag others down to their level of mediocrity.

This book helps us to keep focused on doing the harder thing, the right, instead of the easier, wrong thing. Tulach Ard!

Chaplain Billy B. Martin

Chaplain Billy B. Martin has been involved in martial arts for over fifty years. He first became involved at West Point. Chaplain Martin has trained, coached and been an operator with the military and other entities for five decades. He has trained many world champion military sniper teams and wrote the Department of State's ATAP for snipers. He also has a degree in English and has taught at the university level. He is a USA director for WASCA (two million plus members) and the USIMAA.

Endorsements for *BUSHIDO*

I'd like to personally thank Dr. Bohdi Sanders for another outstanding book on the ways of Bushido and principles of Zen. It is a highly effective book and gives well thought out principles in our daily walk in life.

It gives renewed hope to anyone, whether you're a warrior or just have a curious interest in how martial arts are still such a driving and popular force in the world today. The majority of us started out not knowing where we would apply our talents in life, whether in competition, movie stunts or just in dojo participation. Even then, not knowing where we would end up in our lives.

For those of us that have made it our careers, and a lifetime of learning, we knew it was much more than just a way to stay in shape. Martial arts are definitely a never-ending way of life, which is the way it should be.

To all who partake on the life long journey of learning, this latest book, *BUSHIDO: The Way of the Warrior*, will definitely enlighten your daily life and is one I'm sure you find hard to put down once you start your journey.

Dr. Bohdi has meticulously put so many great words of wisdom on paper for each to follow. Your warrior spirit will definitely be renewed. It is my honor to have the opportunity to endorse this great "Warrior of Wisdom."

Shodai Soke Richard E. Hallman

Soke Richard E. Hallman holds the rank of 10th Dan and is the founder of Aido-Ryu Jiu-Jitsu. He is the vice president of The United States Soke Council and a member of the Shinja Martial Arts University Hall of Honors. He has also studied Northern Shaolin Kung Fu, Kodenkan Dan-Zan Ryu Jiu-Jitsu, Tang Soo Doo, Tae Kwon Do, and Okinawan Ryu-Kyu Kempo. He may be reached at: unitedstatessokecouncil.com and also on Facebook.

Foreword

It's ingenious how Dr. Bohdi Sanders has managed to put tons of quotations from throughout the world into this one book. Once you pick it up, it is hard to put down, as the words of wisdom permeate your mind, your neurological pathways come alive with his superb and articulate writing style. Dr. Sanders bravely engages everyone, including the common man that is not involved in martial arts, to help enlighten them with his masterfully integrated philosophy, theories, and mindset in the ways of the modern and ancient warriors.

Throughout my travels, I have had the opportunity to meet many masters and men of wisdom in various cultures and different countries. What Dr. Sanders has done is to collectively put my many years of traveling into a compact, dynamo of philosophical strategies that fit right into my personal, technical, and fighting principles. I am in awe that, even when you think you know, you know that you don't know, especially when the wisdom in this book hits you like a sledgehammer. Some of the things that I have long forgotten have been rekindled after reading this amazing book.

You can pick up this book at any time, flip to any page, put your finger down on it, and no matter where your finger lands, the quotation will somehow affect some part of your day. And the explanation that follows enhances your ability to grasp the meaning and essence of the quote. You could read the wisdom in this book, one quotation and one explanation each day for the next year, and still you will come back for more. This book is that packed full of wisdom.

This book is superbly and articulately written. Dr. Sanders enlightens us as he masterfully integrates philosophies, theories, concepts, and mindset that allow the martial artist, and even the common man, to understand the pathway to achieving the code of ethics of the warrior.

I know that different countries and cultures have their own philosophical teachings to govern everyday life, but none has impressed me more than the Bushido spirit of the samurai and the Japanese culture. I am armed with my Bible and with Dr. Sanders' book, *BUSHIDO: The Way of the Warrior*; together they give me a philosophical and spiritual edge which greatly enhances my emotional and physical ability to gauge my day. This is one book that absolutely will change how you look at your life!

The virtues and ethics outlined in this book, such as integrity, loyalty, trustworthiness, honor, and being honorable are made simple, understandable, and are easily absorbed and digested. The true lesson learned here is the true essence of the heart and spirit of the warrior that lives within every warrior. It is inside every soul to cultivate and become a warrior of honor and to follow a code of ethics and virtues. This is the difference between a warrior and a fighter without a cause.

Dr. Sanders' teachings are a must for the advancement of every martial artist who wants to achieve the greatness of a sage. One piece of wisdom comes to my mind concerning this book. A wise man learns by his own mistakes, a wiser man learns from the wise man's mistakes.

We can learn by self-discovery or we can learn to improve ourselves with these teachings in which Dr. Sanders has so masterfully combined his experience and wisdom in his excellent philosophical, motivational, and just plain extraordinary book. The inspiration in this book will put you on a path to a higher standard and will set you apart from the rest.

It is with appreciation and humbleness that I give praise to Dr. Bohdi Sanders, who with this book, has given each and every one of us a chance of achieving a greater level of thought. I appreciate the countless hours and hard work that it took to put together this masterpiece of quotes and commentary that is *BUSHIDO: The Way of the Warrior.*

Sifu Al Dacascos

Sifu Al Dacascos was inducted into the Black Belt Hall of Fame in 1977. He has been on the cover of over 185 National and International Martial Arts magazines and has won over 200 martial arts championships. He is also the founder of the unique fighting art, Wun Hop Kuen Do, a system that incorporates Chinese and Filipino martial arts into the traditional KAJUKENBO system. He has trained many celebrities including Eric Lee, Karen Shepard, and his son, Mark Dacascos. His book, *Legacy: Through the Eyes of the Warrior*, will be released in 2016.

Introduction

What is the warrior lifestyle? The true warrior is a rare person in today's world. He lives life with a different set of values compared with the rest of society. Even those who do share the same values, rarely live a lifestyle which adheres to those values to the extent that the warrior does. To most people, ethics are situational. They make decisions according to what is best for them, instead of what is right. This is not the case with the warrior. The warrior values honor, integrity, justice, and his sense of what is right, above all else. His ethics are not situational; they are his way of life.

The warrior lifestyle revolves around a code of ethics which is non-negotiable. The warrior's code of ethics, or code of honor, is taken very seriously. To the warrior, distinguishing between right and wrong is of the utmost importance. He sees right and wrong in terms of black and white. He knows that an action is either honorable or dishonorable. This is not to imply that honor is black and white; honor is not that simple.

Those who live the lifestyle of the warrior know that whether or not an action is honorable is determined by both one's intentions and the situation at hand. This is not to be confused with situational ethics. The warrior's ethics do not change according to the situation. His actions will change as needed, but his ethics remain set in stone. There is a big difference between ethics and actions. Ethics determine actions; actions do not determine ethics.

The warrior lifestyle is concerned with what is right and what is honorable. A warrior's ethics revolve around these two issues. Justice and honor are foremost on his mind. His thoughts are centered on "what is right," not on other people's opinions of what is right. He realizes that many people profess a belief in absolutes which they neither live by, nor truly believe in when push comes to shove.

The only absolute the warrior lives by is that which is right and wrong. If it is not right, he doesn't do it. He determines what is right and wrong by his strict code of ethics, not some arbitrary laws or the politically correct standards of the day. The warrior doesn't appear to be honorable; he is honorable. Sincerity is ingrained in this lifestyle. This is a lifestyle that is meant to be lived, not fantasized about or merely discussed.

This lifestyle consists of much more than being trained in the art of war or the art of self-defense, although these are important parts of the life of a warrior. It also consists of the challenge to perfect one's character. This is a process much like the Japanese concept of kaizen. Kaizen can be translated as constant, never-ending improvement. True warriors try to apply this concept to every area of their life. They seek to balance and improve each area: spirit, mind, and body, on a daily basis.

I am often asked whether or not I believe that the term "warrior" should apply only to military men and women who have been in war, or to trained and experienced fighters. Although I realize that this is the literal definition of a warrior, I do not believe that this is the correct definition, not according to the many accounts from past warriors anyway.

This literal definition of a warrior is not the definition that is used for our discussion of the warrior lifestyle in *BUSHIDO: The Way of the Warrior*. An ape can be trained to throw punches and kicks, a dog can be trained to fight, but that doesn't make either of them warriors. Being a warrior involves more than being trained to fight or being in the military; it involves character training as well. Character training is the true goal of Bushido, the way of the warrior.

Yes, the warrior is concerned with physical training and the martial arts, but he also knows that character training is the cornerstone of the warrior lifestyle. The true warrior should be trained in the martial arts. His ethics require that he be ready to defend his family, friends, and himself in certain situations. In today's world, you never know when you may have to use your martial arts skills.

It is essential that you have this training to be as self-reliant and safe as possible, but without a code of ethics, based on a deep understanding of what is right and wrong, there is no warrior; there is only someone trained to fight. There is a difference. Without the character traits of honor, integrity, and justice, there is no warrior lifestyle.

In short, the warrior lifestyle is for anyone who wants to live a life of excellence; a life which adheres to a strict code of ethics. You must be willing to live your life based on honor, preparedness, and what is right. This lifestyle requires that you put your ethics before your comfort, and that you put what is right before what is profitable. It requires filial duty, dedication to family and friends, and a willingness to help those in need. It requires independence in thought and action. This lifestyle is a decision, not a profession.

This is just a brief introduction to the lifestyle of the warrior. Each of these points can be greatly expanded and I understand that not everyone will agree with my assessment. Even if you disagree with my definition of a warrior or the characteristics of the warrior lifestyle, you will still find the wisdom in this book to be very useful. *BUSHIDO: The Way of the Warrior* seeks to provide the reader with wisdom from throughout the ages that will help him or her live the warrior lifestyle. This lifestyle is not a goal to be achieved, but rather a path to be traveled.

This book can be used in several ways. There is one quote, one expanded commentary, and one affirmation for each day of the year. The reader can simply read the quote, commentary, and affirmation for each day, meditate on the wisdom from that day, and reflect on what each day's wisdom has to offer. It is also useful to repeat the affirmation to yourself aloud.

BUSHIDO: The Way of the Warrior can also be used like *The I Ching*. Instead of throwing coins to determine which passage to read, you may simply ask for guidance and open to whatever page you feel led to read for that day. This is not to be confused with any mystical type of practice, but rather is merely another way to read the passages.

You may also choose to simply take *BUSHIDO: The Way of the Warrior* and read it as you would any other book. Just sit down and start reading it and read all the way through. Although it is perfectly fine to read this book in that way, you will get more out of the wisdom offered in *BUSHIDO: The Way of the Warrior* if you will take your time and reflect on each passage as you read it. But, if you are like me when I get a new book, you will want to dive in and read it all the way through. If you do this, I strongly suggest that you also take some time each day to read and reflect on the passage for that specific day.

I hope that you find *BUSHIDO: The Way of the Warrior* to be a useful guide for your quest to live the warrior lifestyle. Read with an open mind and spend time reflecting on each quote and each commentary. While you may not agree with each quote or each commentary, you will still benefit from each one as it causes you to think about and pinpoint your own beliefs. It is from these clarified beliefs that you will develop your own code of honor. So kick back, find a comfortable spot and delve into the wisdom of *BUSHIDO: The Way of the Warrior* and enjoy!

Bohdi Sanders, PhD

BUSHIDO

The Way of the Warrior

January 1

Rise from the ashes of the old year like the phoenix and become the person you truly want to be.

As we step into the New Year, take some time to reflect on your life. Examine what is working for you, what you have achieved, what isn't working for you, and what needs to be changed. Examine your thoughts and actions, and take note of how you have lived up to your principles and in what ways you need to make changes in your life.

The New Year is a time of renewal. It is a time to make firm commitments about how you will live your life, if you haven't already. It is the time to start anew. If you haven't been walking the path of the warrior, or living the warrior lifestyle as you should, this is the time to renew your enthusiasm and your commitment to the principles that you hold dear.

No matter what mistakes you have made in the past year or how you have fallen short, you now have the opportunity to start fresh, to warrior up and live your life with honor and character.

Rise above all of you mistakes and all of the things that have been holding you down. Rise from the ashes of the old year, like the phoenix, and become the person that you truly want to be. No one can stop you from being the person that you want to be.

All you have to do is make a decision and follow through with it. Change what needs to be changed and stick to your principles. Now is the time to make those changes. Now is the time to live your life with honor, character and integrity. Now is the time to warrior up and make this your best year yet!

I will make this year the best year of my life!

Beware of an old man in a profession where men usually die young.

Old warriors did not get old by accident; they got old by being wise, having the right knowledge, and by being tough. Never underestimate an old man who has grown up in a rough profession or a rough environment.

These men have been around. They have done things, and experienced things, that you have probably never even thought about. They are tough, their minds are tough, and they have the knowledge, the skill, and the will to finish you, if you force them to do so.

They are no longer interested in their image or their bad reputation. They have no time for games or proving who is tougher. They understand the aches and pains that come with old age, and are not willing to get banged up fighting to prove a point. If they have to fight, someone is going to get hurt!

My dad always used to say, "A boy will fight you, but a man will hurt you." There is a lot of truth in this. Older men have no time for the foolishness of social fighting. When they are forced to fight, they mean business. If it comes down to it, they have no problem shooting you or slicing you up with their old knife.

Always remember, they weren't always old. They have lived a long time and have probably developed a lot of skills over their years, skills which may not even be taught or used in today's society. We live in a politically correct society that waters things down; they didn't. Never underestimate an old warrior!

I respect my elders. I never underestimate them.

January 3

Don't fear the enemy that attacks you, fear the fake friend that hugs you.

Those of us who have prepared ourselves and who have experienced a physical attack, and all of the physical reactions that come with it, are pretty much ready to handle that kind of situation. We train for it, we visualize how we will respond, and we are ready to respond as needed.

However, most of us are caught completely off guard when it comes to a so-called friend who blindsides us and stabs us in the back. When we spend years developing trust in someone, it is just hard to imagine people who can be so devious, and have such little regard for honor and character, that they would betray someone who they once called their friend. But this happens virtually every day.

As a warrior, you have to be aware that not everyone lives with honor, not everyone sees true friendship in the same way that you do. The word "friend" means little more than an acquaintance or a buddy to most people. They can take you or leave you, and neither one matters that much to them. What matters to them is what they can get from the "friendship." They are your "friend" as long as it is advantageous to them.

Warriors see true friendship in a different way. To the warrior, true friendship is a sacred bond, and one which he or she would never betray. In fact, a true friendship is a bond that is almost impossible to break. And, it is exactly this dedication and bond of honor that makes us vulnerable to being betrayed by fake friends. Keep your eyes wide open and do your best to know the difference between true friends and those who only pose as friends. Don't allow yourself to be blindsided.

I am always careful when befriending someone.

January 4

A journey of a thousand miles
begins with one step.

Lao Tzu

Some journeys are harder than others. Putting off the inevitable only extends the amount of time that it will take in order for you to get where you need to be. It doesn't matter how hard, nor how long, the journey is that you have to make; it starts with the first step. Don't delay your journey because of fear or dread. If it is a journey that you have to make, just get started and take it one step at a time.

Your decisions always bring with them consequences of one kind or another. This is just the way it is. Sometimes unwise, thoughtless decisions can have far-reaching consequences which we wish we didn't have to deal with, but deal with them we must.

The consequences of our actions don't just disappear because we long for them to go away. You must take responsibility for your actions and deal with those consequences. The warrior has to take responsibility for all of his actions and the consequences which come with them.

Sometimes the journey that our actions have set in motion can be a long, hard journey, but it still has to be traveled. Have the courage to face up to the road that you choose, and walk it with honor. It doesn't matter if the road is long and hard or if the road is short and easy; your journey still begins with one step. And, no matter how many bad, ill-thought out decisions you have made, you can still change your life. All it takes is making a firm decision to live life as it should be lived; and it begins by taking that first step.

I will find the courage to travel my path with honor.

January 5

Discipline is choosing between what you want now and what you want most.

You must discipline yourself to achieve anything worthwhile in this life. An undisciplined person never sticks to anything long enough to truly become proficient or to accomplish great things. The undisciplined person will only workout when he or she feels like it, or is excited about it. Once the newness and the excitement wears off, they move on to something else.

In order to achieve a high level in your martial arts, you must be disciplined. You must discipline yourself to work on your art daily. You must workout even when you are not in the mood. You must push yourself when you had rather be doing something else.

You must learn to control your mind and force yourself to look at your long-term goals. Where do you want to be this time next month, or next year? You must discipline yourself now in order to be where you want to be later.

Those without discipline will, sooner or later, envy those with discipline. Most everyone wants to have the skills, the demeanor, and the abilities of a great, martial arts master, but very few people are willing to do what has to be done to reach that level. People in today's society have been taught to think they are entitled, but thinking you are entitled does not develop your skills.

You are not entitled to anything in this world. If you want something, you have to go out and earn it. And that takes discipline. Discipline yourself to stay the course!

I discipline myself to focus on my ultimate goal.

January 6

*I refuse to lower my standards to accommodate
those who refuse to raise theirs.*

Steve Gamlin

If your principles and standards are negotiable, then you don't really have principles. Real principles are based on a firm decision about how you will live your life. Principles are not negotiable; you can't simply set them aside or put them on a shelf like you do your coat when you no longer need it to keep you warm.

If you are willing to lower your standards to make others feel more comfortable or to satisfy those who have lower standards, then your standards are meaningless. For your standards to truly mean anything at all they have to be firm and they have to be important to you. If your standards are important to you, then you don't lower them or set them aside in order to accommodate other people.

Warriors take their principles seriously. They refuse to lower their standards to accommodate others. There is a big difference between saying you have principles and living according to your principles.

Saying that you have principles, but being willing to set them aside when you get a little pressure, is merely trying to play to the crowd. It is purely hypocritical.

Warriors refuse to be hypocrites. They say what they mean and mean what they say. If someone tries to get them to set aside their principles, that will only make their convictions firmer. The warrior will not lower his standards to accommodate those who refuse to raise theirs.

I refuse to lower my standards or my principles!

January 7

There is no greater danger than
underestimating your opponent.
Sun Tzu

Never underestimate your opponent or your enemy. Looks can be deceiving. You really don't know what your opponent knows or what kind of skills he or she may have. It is the opponent who is calm and quiet, and doesn't seem like a threat, who may be your worst nightmare.

The enemies of men of honor will most likely not be men of honor. They will be very underhanded and will not mind attacking you in dishonorable ways. Never underestimate what malicious actions such people will take to hurt you. They do not live by the same standards that you do, and it is a mistake to assume that they do.

Always expect the unexpected when it comes to your enemies. Instead of thinking that they *won't* do something to hurt you, do your best to make sure that they *can't* hurt you. Make your defenses so strong that you give your enemies no openings. Expect them to be dishonorable in their attacks and prepare for just that. Never underestimate men and women of low character.

It is always better to overestimate your enemy than to underestimate him. This simply makes sense. Think about it; is it better to be over prepared or underprepared? Is it better to show up to a knife fight carrying several firearms or carrying a small stick? Make it a point to never underestimate your enemies. Always show up to a knife fight with a gun, not a stick.

I will never underestimate my opponent or my enemy!

January 8

Warriors are not always the fastest or the strongest men. Warriors are those who choose to stand between their enemy and those that they love or hold sacred.

Not everyone can have the talent of Chuck Norris or Bruce Lee. Not everyone can be built like Arnold Schwarzenegger or is made to be a Navy Seal. But everyone can have the courage to stand between their enemies and those they love.

Warriorship is not about talent or strength, but about spirit, mind and heart. Most of us have responsibilities to fulfill. We have to work to support our family; we don't have the luxury to train as much as we would like.

What we can do though, is be as prepared as possible to meet any threat, and develop the courage to stand against those who would prey on our loved ones and the innocent. Warriorship lies in your spirit and your attitude, and everyone can develop those to the same level as the most elite warriors.

We may not always be the strongest, the fastest, or the most skilled, but we can be skilled enough to prevail and to keep our families safe. That is the attitude of the everyday warrior. It does little good to stand between those we love and our enemies if we don't have the skills to stop our enemies.

It may be a valiant gesture, but it won't get the job done. We must not only stand up to our enemies, but we must also have the skills to stop our enemies from harming our loved ones. Warrior up!

I stay prepared to protect those I love.

January 9

Don't ever think that the reason that I am peaceful is because I forgot how to be violent.

True warriors, those who have discovered what being a real, balanced warrior is all about, do not like being violent. They don't like hurting other people. They are men and women of peace, who enjoy living peaceably as much as they can, while all the time preparing for the time when they are forced to be otherwise.

But, because they love living a peaceful, quiet life with their friends and family, that doesn't mean that they do not understand violence or that they have forgotten how to be violent if they have to do so. Warriors understand that even though they love peace, there are many in this world that do not; there are those who love to prey on the innocent.

Because of this fact, the peaceful warrior continues to train for violent confrontations, even though he hopes in his heart that he will never have to use his well-honed skills. He understands that the best way to ensure peace is to be ready for war. The weak do not intimidate the strong; only the strong keep the predators away.

It is the sheep dogs who the predators fear, not the sheep. Live a peaceful life, but keep your skills sharp. Don't count on thugs and predators to simply not target you or your loved ones. Be ready for whatever may come your way.

Keep your skills like your knife – razor sharp and ready for use at a moment's notice. You never know when you will have to step up and pull your skills from their hidden sheath. Be peaceful, but be ready.

I live a peaceful life and keep my martial arts skills sharp.

January 10

Our obligation to our own family or clan is greater than our obligation to the faceless multitude.

M. F. Bradford

A warrior has a duty to provide for, and protect, his or her family. Warriors take their duty more serious than the average person. Their duty is an obligation that they are honor bound to fulfill. Not fulfilling their duty would be dishonorable.

In the same way, a warrior should also protect those around him, when it is in his or her power to do so. This said, when the warrior has to choose between what is best for his family or what is best for some stranger, he is duty-bound to put his family first. You foremost duty is always to your family.

While we should help those in need, those who deserve our help, we *must* take care of our family. Your duty to your family must always come first. If you can't take care of your own family, what makes you think that you can help or protect others?

This brings up many other considerations. If you are careless in the defense of someone else, and you get permanently injured or even killed, you are putting your family at risk. Considering this, you have a duty to be well-prepared and to keep your skills sharp. Doing otherwise, and being a warrior, is putting your family's welfare at risk.

In all things, always consider your highest duty. The warrior's duties are hierarchical; he must always understand what his highest duty is. Never neglect your duty to your family.

I always honor my duty to my family.

January 11

Be slow of tongue and quick of eye.
Cervantes

In simple terms, this quote from Cervantes boils down to keep your mouth shut and pay attention, although Cervantes put it a little more elegantly than that. The majority of people that I observe today, love to hear themselves talk. They never really listen to the people around them or pay any attention to what they are saying. Their mind is always focused on the next witty thing that they can say to make themselves sound intelligent or humorous.

Rarely do these types of people learn anything from the people around them because they simply do not pay attention to the conversation. They don't engage their mind or put any thought into what is being said. As a consequence, they also tend to put their foot in their mouth on a frequent basis, saying things which either do not make sense or which are inappropriate, just to have something to say.

This should not describe the warrior. The warrior should use his words sparingly. He should spend more time listening and observing, than babbling away. Using your words cautiously and thinking about what you are saying before you actually say it, are two traits which the warrior needs to develop.

These are traits of the wise man and the man of substance, and should be traits of the true warrior. Always be wary about what you say and how you say it. Being careless with your speech can cause you many unnecessary problems. Be slow of tongue, quick of eye, and quick of mind.

I am slow to speak, but quick to watch, listen and think.

I prefer peace, but if trouble must come, let it come
in my time, so that my children may live in peace.

Thomas Paine

If trouble must come, let it come in my time, so that my children may live in peace. This is the thought of every parent worth his or her salt. And it is definitely the thought of every true warrior. Any parent with honor wants his or her children to have a better life than they did.

Warriors are ready for trouble to come. That doesn't mean that they want trouble to come, but that they are prepared to handle it, should it come. That is why warriors train; they must be ready to handle trouble whenever it comes around.

Never shy away from taking trouble on and setting things right. Too many people have been too self-centered for too long! It is time for people to stand up for what is right. Stand up for what you believe and stop thinking that someone else will take care of the trouble for you.

I have news for you – no one is going to save you. You are 100% responsible for your own life. Don't depend on the government, the police, or anyone else to be there when the wolf is at your door; they won't be. You have to learn to be self-sufficient.

The self-sufficient warrior never expects others to take care of his problems for him. He takes responsibility for his own life. This is why he trains and stays prepared for whatever may come his way. It is time to toughen up and start meeting your troubles and challenges head on! Be ready for whatever may come. Never bank on someone else coming to save the day for you.

I always remain ready to handle whatever comes my way.

January 13

Courage doesn't always roar. Sometimes courage is the
quiet voice at the end of the day saying,
"I will try again tomorrow."
Mary Ann Radmacher

We have a mental image of courage as being bravely standing up to others in the face of some type of danger. But that is not the only kind of courage. It takes courage to continue to try, despite failure after failure.

It takes courage to continue to live, when it seems like everything in your life is hopeless. It takes courage for the cancer patient to refuse to give in to hopelessness and despair. It takes courage to continue to search for love, when all that you experience is rejection.

Courage doesn't always roar, nor is it always celebrated by others who congratulate you on your bravery. Courage is a very personal trait. Many people have been extremely courageous without anyone else ever knowing that they were actually in some kind of battle.

You don't have to be a lean, mean, fighting machine to incorporate courage into your life. Courage is more often shown in small, personal ways that others never see. There are no accolades, no pats on the back, and no celebrity status for these kinds of victories.

Nevertheless, the courageous person lifts himself up and continues the struggle, refusing to give up until he has emerged from the darkness victoriously, and the quiet voice at the end of the day is his only accolade, saying, "Well done warrior, well done!"

No matter how bad things seem, I will never give up; I will never quit!

January 14

The fire of anger only burns the angry.
Chinese Proverb

There is a time and place for controlled, righteous anger. Anger is like a very hot fire – it can be very useful, but if not handled correctly, it can also be very dangerous.

Uncontrolled, lingering anger is much like having an uncontrolled fire in your home, it only hurts you, and those closest to you, not the person that you are angry with. Unlike the uncontrolled fire, your uncontrolled anger will eat away at you from the inside, preying on your mind and your spirit.

When you allow your anger to run rampant, lingering for weeks, months, or even years, you are allowing it to get the best of you. You are allowing your enemies to hurt you, even after their malicious actions have long passed.

Think about it. If your enemy no longer thinks about you at all, but your inner peace is constantly agitated because of your refusal to let go of your anger, your enemy is continuously getting the best of you, without even trying. He has been successful by getting into your heart and mind, and continuously torturing you.

Don't allow your enemies to continue to get the best of you. Control your anger and let it go. Instead of allowing anger to take root in your mind, deal with your enemies rationally and win. If there is nothing you can do, let it go; if you can set things right, do so. But don't allow anger to control your thoughts and your actions. The angry warrior is never a rational warrior.

I stay in control of my anger at all times.

14

January 15

Never send a sheep to kill a wolf.

Not everyone has the training or the ability to take down the thugs and predators that lurk in the dark places in this world. Everyone can learn how to keep themselves safe, but not everyone will be able to go toe-to-toe with an experienced street fighter.

You should know your abilities and understand your skills *before* you have to make a choice about using them. If you are not prepared to kill the wolf, don't walk into the wolf's den. And don't *think* that you are prepared to kill the wolf, *know* that you are prepared to kill the wolf. If you don't know whether or not you are prepared, you're not.

Sheep cannot kill the wolf, no matter how much they desire to. They may *want* to be able to. They may *wish* they could. They may have the heart to do so. They may even talk themselves into thinking that they can. But when it comes down to it, when there is a fight between the sheep and the wolf, the sheep will lose.

You must understand that the wolf is an expert predator. He kills for a living. He has trained to kill sheep his whole life and he is good at it. He does not *think* that he can kill a sheep; he *knows* that he can kill the sheep.

You must understand the wolf and have the same skills that the wolf has – the skill to maim or kill. Your skills must be superior. You must have the resolve to do what has to be done, and then you must have the will to do it! When it comes down to a kill-or-be-killed situation, you must be willing to kill in order to survive. Are you sure that you have the skill set to go face to face with an experienced predator? If the answer is no, then you have work to do!

I always train and keep my skills sharp.

January 16

Project Strength to Avoid Conflict.

Predators look for the weakest target. They look for victims, not challenges. If you project strength, real strength, not some false bravado, then there is a very good chance that they will pass you by and look for easier prey.

You should not try to bluff your way past these predators. Remember, these guys fight for their living; they aren't school boys boasting about who is tougher.

Experienced predators can see through your bluff from a mile away. Sooner or later, those who try to bluff their way through life get their bluff called; and when that happens, you lose. Bluffing is a dangerous game, especially when you are dealing with a life-or-death situation.

Instead of trying to project something you don't have, actually develop that strength. Don't try to find shortcuts to developing this kind of strength. It will only come from training and experience.

Those who say they know how to fight, but who have never actually been in a real fight, are working only with theory. If you want to learn how to fight, really fight, not spar, then you must train with someone who has that experience. People can't teach you what they don't know.

You must project strength through strength. This can only come through serious training. Once you have developed strength and martial arts prowess, you automatically exude an aura of strength. People, especially predators, can sense that you are not a victim and that you are not someone to mess with. Project strength, but at the same time, be able to back it up if you have to.

I project strength and make sure that I can back it up.

January 17

Wise men do not argue with idiots.

Japanese Proverb

In the same way that one would not expect a first grade student to understand physics or chemistry, you should not expect idiots to comprehend the way of the warrior. They have no more capacity to understand the complexities of honor or the benefits of virtue than a dog has to program your DVD player.

These concepts are totally foreign to them. They just don't understand the warrior lifestyle, and therefore should not be expected to carry on an intelligent conversation on the subject. Oh, they will talk about the subject at length. They will talk as if they are the experts, not only on the subject of the warrior, but on virtually any other subject that may be brought up in the conversation.

But, as the old saying goes, a fool talks because he has to say something; a wise man because he has something to say. There is a big difference between the two. Just as you could never explain to a summer insect the concept of snow, you will never be able to win an argument with someone who does not think rationally.

It is wiser to just avoid the argument to start with and let them think what they will. Why should you care what they think? Their opinion, no matter how ridiculous, doesn't affect you. Don't waste your time arguing with these people. In fact, it is even wiser to not socialize with idiots. Call me "idiot intolerant," I have been called that before, but I had rather spend my time with men of character and honor. Your time on this earth is short, use it wisely. Don't argue with idiots!

I absolutely refuse to argue with idiots!

January 18

Deprived of all else, one remains undisgraced
if still endowed with strength of character.
Tiruvalluvar

Many things can be taken away from you in this life. You can lose your loved ones. Your home can be lost. Money, possessions, titles, health, can all be taken away with hardly any advance notice. And, although it is unimaginable in our country, you could also lose your freedom. In fact, there is very little in your life that can't be taken away from you in one form or another. One of the few things that can't be taken away is your character.

No one can take away your character, your honor, or your integrity. You have total control over these things. Whatever else you may lose, Tiruvalluvar tells us that you will remain undisgraced if you hold on to your character. This doesn't mean that you can't lose your character, integrity or honor. You can certainly lose your integrity and honor, and your character can be tarnished. You must be careful and work to make sure that this doesn't happen.

Notice that I said no one can take these things away from you, but they can be lost. You make this decision yourself. You are the deciding factor as far as whether or not you maintain your character, honor and integrity. As a warrior, you have to ensure that your character is always intact. Don't lower your expectations, where your character is concerned, for anyone or anything. Make the hard decisions according to your unyielding code of honor, which sets you apart from other men. Maintain your character, honor and integrity at all cost. This is your duty. This is the lifestyle of the warrior.

I always maintain my character, honor and integrity.

January 19

Those who know the least obey the best.
Farquhar

Warriors of the past have always valued improving their mind. Reading and studying were a part of their routine because they valued knowledge. Just like your counterparts of old, you should also value knowledge.

Those without knowledge, as Farquhar states, are easy to control and to take advantage of by those who have knowledge. When knowledge is looked at from this vantage point, you can consider studying and acquiring knowledge on various things, as being part of your self-defense.

Self-defense involves much more than defending yourself physically against some thug, especially in today's society. There are so many ways that people can hurt you today. A physical assault, although the main focus of self-defense for the warrior, is but one way that you can be attacked. Your enemies, who are less physical and more educated, will more likely assault you through other means, usually having to do with their knowledge and twisted character.

For this reason, it is vital that you also arm yourself with a well-balanced knowledge of the world. Know your rights and the law so others cannot use your ignorance as a weapon against you. This is important even in a physical confrontation. You must know the law concerning how much force you can legally use, in order to defend yourself against legal prosecution, even though you are in the right. If you lack knowledge, you are putting yourself at risk. Those without knowledge have a hole in their defense.

I increase my knowledge every day.

January 20

There is much to be considered
before the sword is drawn.

Baltasar Gracian

Fighting is serious business. Even when you win a physical conflict, there is a very real chance that you will not walk away from it unscarred. I have won many fights, but have ended up with the short end of the stick in the long run in a couple of them. Breaking a bone in your hand can take well over a year to heal. Sure, you may have won the fight, but the other guy's black eye and busted nose will be healed much quicker than your broken hand. This is only one of the many things that you must consider when it comes to fighting.

The bottom line is that you should never fight unless you absolutely have no other options. The warrior realizes this. He is not out to prove himself to others or to test his martial arts skills in the streets. Warriors know how fragile the human body is and how easily it can be damaged, especially by a skilled fighter. Fighting can cause more problems than you can imagine. It is not the carefree brawl which is depicted in so many movies and television shows.

Every fight carries with it the very real possibility of death, even if no one is consciously attempting to mortally injure the other person. Many people have died in fights which consisted of only one punch. People get hit, fall, and hit their head on something, and that's that. As Gracian states, there is definitely much to be considered before things get physical, and these things have to be considered ahead of time. You have to know what you are willing to fight for and how far you are willing to go before you find yourself in that spot.

I only fight when I absolutely have to.

When you react, you let others control you.
When you respond, you are in control.
Bohdi Sanders

At first, this quote appears to be nothing more than word play, but the fine line between reacting and responding is very important. When you react to what another person says or does, you are allowing the other person to direct your actions. Many people will figure out your "buttons" and push them at will in order to get you to "react" just as they want you to. When this happens, they are in control of how you think and act. You don't want this. Never give another person that kind of power over you.

Whenever someone is pushing your buttons, it should be a clue to you that you are starting to get emotional. Take a breath and think rationally. Most of the time, when someone is trying to get you to react, they are doing so for some agenda, usually unknown to you. So what do you do when someone is pushing your buttons?

You slow down and think. Think about why they are doing what they are doing. Think about what their objective is, what is behind their actions. Then you choose your response rationally and wisely. Don't take the bait.

This puts you in charge instead of the other person, which is exactly where the warrior should be – in charge of his own thoughts and actions. Never take the bait that is designed to get a reaction out of you; calmly and carefully respond and you will take the wind out of their sails. This is another example of winning without fighting.

I stay in control of myself and respond instead of react.

January 22

When you think you're safe is precisely when you're most vulnerable.
Seven Samurai

The warrior should never let his or her guard down. When you think you're safe, you have a tendency to let your guard down and relax. This is the exact opportunity that your enemy is looking for. Always stay alert and aware of your surroundings.

This doesn't mean that you should never relax and have fun. It simply means that you need to stay aware and ready. Have fun, but never to the point of being unable to protect yourself or unaware of your surroundings.

You are most vulnerable when you think that you have nothing to fear from your enemy. But you should always expect the unexpected from your enemies; and always be ready to respond. Never give your enemies an opening.

Think of all the movies that you have seen where the hero gets into an epic fight with the villain at the end of the movie. After a long, hard fight, the hero takes the evil villain down, but stops short of taking him out.

The next thing you know, the villain has caught the hero off guard and gets one last chance to kill him. Of course, the hero wins in the end, but real life is not like the movies. If you think the fight is finished and carelessly give your enemy one more shot to finish you off, it may be the last mistake you ever make. Be aware until the end!

I continue to fight until I am sure that my enemy is defeated.

January 23

Announcing, "I'm offended," is basically telling the world that you can't control your own emotions, so everyone else should do it for you.

You choose whether or not to be offended by what someone says or does. It is totally up to you. Nobody can offend you if you don't let them. Nobody has any power over your mind or emotions – only you. You are in the driver's seat; you are in control.

Maybe it is time to quit looking for chances to be offended and start seizing the power that you have over your own thoughts and emotions. Quit giving that control to other people, most of whom are complete strangers that you will probably never meet again. These people should absolutely not be able to offend you.

If you look for chances to be offended, you will find them at every turn. If you walk around with a chip on your shoulder, you will find that many people are more than willing to knock it off for you.

Start observing things with a rational mind instead of an emotional mind. Start choosing what you will and will not allow to affect you. You have the power – take it back and quit allowing every moron with a mouth or a keyboard to offend you.

Start taking control of your own mind, and you will find it easier take control of your own life. When you quit allowing other people to rob you of your inner peace, you will find that you can deal with any situation rationally. If someone needs to have something explained to them in a forceful manner, do so. But don't allow them to actually get to you. Refuse to be offended; just simply respond as needed.

Nothing offends me! I am the captain of my own mind.

January 24

When I am silent, I have thunder hidden inside me.

Rumi

Not every dangerous person is loud and threatening. In fact, as a rule, those who are the loudest and most obnoxious are usually not the ones that you have to worry about. They are merely blowhards that want everyone to think that they are tough, all bark and no bite so to speak.

These people are like the barking little dog, protected by a fence, which constantly barks at the large, silent dog walking down the sidewalk. The little dog barks every day, but quickly has a change of heart (and bark) when it finds that the front gate has been left open and the big, silent dog steps inside.

On the other hand, the silent introvert, who has no interest in being the center of attention, many times has thunder hidden inside. Introverts are not shy and meek, as many seem to think. They sit quietly, listening and thinking because that is who they are. They are calm, quiet, and thoughtful people, but none of that means that they can't handle themselves.

While the blowhard is running his mouth, the introvert is listening and preparing for what may happen. This is just the way he is, but it has many advantages. Those around him do not know what he is thinking, or what his next move may be. While the blowhard announces to the world what he is "going to do," the introvert doesn't announce his plans; he simply acts when he is ready to act. Never take the quiet person for granted. It is a mistake to take his silence as weakness; it is a mistake to think that he can't fight. It is a mistake to disregard the silent person's intelligence, attention, or skills.

I don't judge anyone based only on his appearance.

January 25

Be polite, be courteous, show professionalism,
and have a plan to kill everyone in the room.
General James Mattis

Many people misunderstand the concept behind this quote. To some, it sounds like something that a psychotic killer might say. But if you fall into that category, you are missing the point.

If your martial art training is really what it should be, you already have a plan to kill anyone that might be in the room with you. If you are really well-trained in the dojo, then you will understand anatomy and the vulnerable points of the body. You will know how to kill or seriously injure someone. You will know how to use common, everyday things as weapons.

This doesn't mean that you are going around thinking about killing everyone, but you will have that capability. And you will, at times, see someone who you just get the feeling might be dangerous, and almost automatically, you will visualize how to deal with him should he truly become a threat.

This also doesn't mean that you are hoping that something will happen so you can prove to everyone how dangerous you are. That is immature thinking. True warriors don't hope for trouble, rather they prefer to live a nice, peaceful life. But they are ready for trouble.

I would say, be polite, be courteous, but be certain that you know how to take down anyone in the room, should that become a necessity. If you are not sure, then you are not ready. Thinking positively and believing in yourself is a great practice, but it is no substitute for knowing that you are prepared.

I am always courteous and ready for action.

The society that separates its scholars from its warriors
will have its thinking done by cowards
and its fighting done by fools.

Thucudides

Our society seems to have done just this, at least where our leaders are concerned. We no longer have warrior leaders who lead with honor, integrity, courage, and backbone. We get a pre-selected group of candidates to vote for, all picked by men of riches and influence with their own agendas, and almost none are selected because of their character, courage, or ability to lead and do what is right for the people that they propose to lead.

These men are not only in charge of our country, but of making decisions concerning war, the security of our country, and the oversight of our military. Therefore, we have moved closer to what Thucydides stated – our thinking is done by cowards, and those same cowards make decisions about where and when our fighting men fight.

This is not the way it should be. We should be led by courageous warriors, warriors who understand and live the warrior lifestyle – men and women who live their lives by codes of honor and will not bend their principles for political gain.

Oh how amazing it would be to have leaders that we could actually admire, leaders who we could hold up as role models for our children, instead of cowardly liars who grovel for our votes. I wonder if I will ever see such a thing in my lifetime. I sincerely doubt it and that makes me sad for future generations.

I will strive to be both a scholar and a warrior.

January 27

True humility is not thinking less of yourself;
it is thinking of yourself less.
C. S. Lewis

Many people are confused about the trait of being humble. They think that being humble means to basically put yourself down, refuse to accept compliments, and to basically think less of themselves than they should. That is not true humility; it is poor self-esteem.

True humility is not thinking less of yourself, but rather not thinking that you are the best of the best all the time. As Mr. Lewis stated, it is thinking of yourself less, as in less often.

When you put your focus on others, on what you are doing, on the task at hand and doing your best, you are not focused on how great you are. You are focused on living life to the fullest and helping others.

The opposite of humility is arrogance. Arrogance is being conceited and thinking that you are better than everyone else. It is putting too much importance on *you*, being too prideful.

Thinking of yourself less, does not mean that you think *less* of yourself. You can, and should, think highly of yourself. Have confidence in yourself and your abilities. But don't allow your self-confidence to turn into arrogance and vanity.

Don't spend every waking moment thinking about yourself, how you look, what people think about you, etc. Think highly of yourself, but keep things in perspective. Be truly humble, not self-deprecating. Think highly of yourself, but don't think solely of yourself.

I am truly humble and maintain my self-esteem.

Blood makes you related; loyalty makes you family.

Who says you can't choose your family? You choose everything in your life. The people, who are loyal to me no matter what, are my family. These are the people who will come to my aid when my back is against the wall; these are my warrior brothers and sisters.

There are those who are related to you by blood, who couldn't give a tinker's damn about what is really happening in your life. They may show up on holidays for family dinners, but they wouldn't put their life on the line for you. They are related to you, but have no loyalty to you whatsoever.

It is not blood that makes you family, but rather love and loyalty. True family puts the family first. They are loyal without fail. If someone comes against you, he comes against everyone in your family. It is a one for all, all for one type relationship that not many people really find in this lifetime. The people who are completely loyal to you, will never turn their back on you or leave you to face the wolf alone.

If someone attacks my family, they attack me. In fact, I will respond much more fiercely when someone attacks my family, than if they attack me personally. You may get a pass when you attack me, but nobody messes with my family. That is complete loyalty; this is family.

The next time someone quips that you can't choose your family, respond with a smile knowing that you absolutely can choose your family. You choose them from those men and women who are completely loyal to you and will stand by you no matter what. You choose them by their honor, integrity, character, and their loyalty.

I choose to associate with men and women of character.

January 29

The greatest enemies, and the ones
we must mainly combat, are within.

Cervantes

Everyone has enemies, even the most jovial, well-liked person has people who would love to see him crash and burn. You have enemies, even if you don't realize it, but most of your enemies are no threat.

Most of them don't care enough, or are not malevolent enough, to truly cause you any problems. In fact, you may never have to deal with your enemies at all, at least not your external enemies, but there are enemies which we all have to deal with on a regular basis, and, as Cervantes stated, they come from within.

These enemies are the ones that the warrior must conquer in his quest to live the warrior lifestyle. Just like external enemies, these internal enemies are different for each person. Some may take the form of laziness or fear, while others may take the form of anger or bad temper. Everyone has their own individual enemies to deal with during their journey on the path of the warrior. The important thing is that you do not let your enemies defeat you and prevent you from obtaining your goals.

You know what your own personal enemy is and it is your responsibility to figure out how to defeat this enemy. There are no small, insignificant enemies. Each one has the capacity to do some damage and to cause you unnecessary problems. Don't let your internal enemies slide – crush them and render them powerless. This is an important part of being a true warrior.

I work to defeat my internal enemies every day.

January 30

Fear is not real. It is a product of thoughts you create.
Do not misunderstand me. Danger is very real.
But fear is a choice.
After Earth

Where does fear come from? It is not a physical thing, but it can produce physical reactions. It is not a spiritual thing; your spirit knows no fear. Fear is totally a construct of your mind and your thoughts. It is not a tangible thing, but rather a mental manifestation, that when dwelt on, has real affects on your body, your mind, and your life.

If fear is a product of your thoughts, and it is, and you have total control over what thoughts you dwell on, then allowing fear to control you is a choice. Instead of choosing to banish thoughts of fear and doubt, you choose to dwell on them, thus giving them power.

Are there things that you should be afraid of? I know my answer to that is going to be controversial, but the answer is a resounding NO! Fear is a weakening, worthless emotion. It is something that should be banished from your life.

There are, of course, many things in life that you should recognize as dangerous. This doesn't mean that you have to fear them, only that you need to understand the danger associated with certain things or situations.

Acknowledge the danger, and then make rational decisions about what to do concerning the specific danger. Fear does not help you with this; it only distorts your thoughts, weakens the spirit, and clouds the mind. Danger is real, but fear is a choice, a bad choice. Think rationally!

I choose to control and overcome all of my fears.

January 31

There are nine hundred and ninety-nine
patrons of virtue to one virtuous man.

Henry David Thoreau

There are a lot of people who will talk the talk, but not walk the walk. Many people will refer to their honor, but at the same time will lie, cheat and steal if money is involved. Sure, they will have their reasons and will justify their actions, but you can't take *real* honor on and off like your jacket. Either you are a man of honor or you are not a man of honor. You can't have it both ways.

Don't be one of those people who talk about honor and character, but in the end really can't live up to what they profess. Living a life of honor is not always an easy path to walk. Men of honor put their honor before their comfort or their convenience. People, who are talkers but not doers, put their comfort and convenience first and squeeze honor in when it is convenient for them to do so.

The warrior should be a man of honor and virtue. He should walk the walk, and leave the talk to others. When Thoreau strongly disagreed with the government, he refused to pay his taxes. Because of his stand, he was threatened with jail, but still he refused to go against his conscious and pay his taxes.

He stated that it was against his conscious to support a government whose policies he considered immoral. As a result, he was arrested and did spend time in jail. Thoreau lived by his principles, no matter what the consequences were. This should be the warrior's attitude toward his code of ethics – uncompromising resolve.

I live by my principles at all times.

February 1

Don't let who you were talk you out of who you're becoming.

Quality people are constantly striving to be better today than they were yesterday. But you can't make positive changes if you are constantly allowing who you were to rob you of who you can be. Dwelling in the past will only hold you back from what the future has for you.

The past is in the past; it cannot be changed. Your job is not to erase the past or try to paint it in a different light, but rather to learn from the past and make yourself a better person today. Refuse to allow your past to hold you back in the present! You can't change who you were, but you can always decide who you will be today, and every day for the rest of your life.

Take control of your life today. Be the person that you want to be, and leave the past in the past. You have the power to change your life, but it will only work for you if you are willing to walk away from the past. You can't step forward with both of your feet stuck in the past. You have to simply walk away from the past and rarely look back.

Too many people allow their past to hold them back, as if they are in this strange kind of prison which they carry with them everywhere they go. It is almost as if they are thinking that they just have to deal with it, but that they will do better the next time around.

There is no next time. This is not a dress rehearsal; this is your life. You get one shot at it. It is time to leave whatever is in your past and move on with your life. Every day is a new chance to start with a clean slate; be wise enough to take advantage of that opportunity.

I leave the past behind and I am becoming who I want to be.

February 2

Have the courage to say no. Have the courage to
face the truth. Do the right thing because it is right.
W. Clement Stone

Sometimes it takes more courage to say no than it does to say yes. When someone asks you if you are going to go here or there, or if you are going to do one thing or another, the first thing that enters many people's mind is, "No, I am not going to do that." But they do not want to hurt the other person's feelings, so they simply lie.

If you know you are not going to go to someone's party, but you say, "Yeah, I will try to be there," that is a blatant lie. You are leading them on and giving them hope, when you already know for a fact that you are not going. Not only is that a lie, but you are leaving them hanging when they probably need to know.

It is more honorable to just be truthful. If you have something else planned, say so. If you are just plain tired and don't feel up to going, just say, "No, I am not going to be able to make it this time." Of course, turn down their invitation with class and tact, but be honest. After all, it is the truth. Have the courage to face the truth and to speak the truth.

It is these small tests of courage and honor that prepare you for the larger tests. If you can't muster the courage to give your friend an honest answer when it comes to small things like this, do you really think that you are going to automatically have the courage to stand up when it comes to larger things with much bigger consequences? Just do the right thing, at the right time, and then do it right.

I always do the right thing, at the right time, and in the right way.

February 3

The difference between who you are, and who you want to be, is what you do.

If you are not happy with the person that you are right now, make some changes. What are you waiting on? Are you simply writing this life off because you have screwed it up too much, and are just planning on doing it better next time? There is no "next time." This is not a dress rehearsal. This is it!

If you want to be a better person or a better martial artist, do it. If you want to live according to the warrior lifestyle, do it! Your thoughts and actions are what will ultimately change your life, or keep you exactly where you are.

It is time to take control of your life and be the person that you want to be, instead of allowing the world to dictate who you will be and how you will live your life. Step up and take back your control!

Thinking about doing it is worthless if you don't actually act on your thoughts. Thinking about something without acting on it, is nothing more than daydreaming; and daydreaming, while it may be pleasant, never accomplishes your objectives.

In order to achieve your goals, you must act. Wishing for something is easy. Planning the steps to achieve your goals is just one step past wishing. If you truly want to accomplish what you want in life, you must take those wishes and those plans and turn them into action. Don't settle for less than what you can be; you must get up and take what you want in this life. Make it happen!

I never settle for less than my best.

February 4

If you find yourself in a fair fight, your tactics suck!

Either a fight is a serious threat to you, or someone you are protecting, and you have no other choice other than stepping up and defending yourself, or it is not really a real fight. And, if it is a real fight, then you had better use anything and everything to make sure that you walk away from it with as little injury to your body as possible. Fighting fair does not enter into this equation.

Fighting fair is a romantic notion used only by those who have no idea what a real fight is. When your life is in danger, you use whatever means possible to protect yourself, whether that is gouging the eyes, biting, hitting someone with a brick, or using a more traditional weapon. If it helps get you home safely, use it!

If the fight is not threatening to your life or your physical welfare, then you should not be in it to start with. It doesn't matter what was said, how he insulted you, or how much you would like to rearrange his face; if you do not have to fight, walk away.

But, if you are forced to fight, never let the bogus idea of fighting fair enter your mind. You fight to win, period! If this means feeding the other guy a brick for dinner, then bon appétit.

There is no dishonor is using whatever you must use to defeat a vicious predator. When a predator attacks you, it is not a game. He isn't there to see how well you spar or to test your martial arts skills. He is there to kill or maim you, period. In a life-or-death situation, there is no such thing as a fair fight!

I use what I must to defeat my enemy and return home safely.

February 5

Don't ever mistake my silence for ignorance, my calmness for acceptance, or my kindness for weakness.

It is a mistake to believe that the silent person is ignorant. The silent person is almost always the one that you should listen to most. Instead of spending time babbling about unimportant things, he listens and learns. He spends time in thought instead of meaningless conversations about nothing. Ignorant is the last adjective that I would use to describe him.

Likewise, the person who can stay calm in all situations is a person of quiet confidence. Do not read anything into his calm demeanor, except for the fact that he probably has his act together. The warrior, who is confident in himself, has no reason to lose his cool. He maintains his composure in spite of the storm around him. You may even find that the more critical the situation, the more calm and rational the warrior becomes because he is even more focused than normal.

Many people also tend to look at the kind-hearted man as weak or wimpy. This is another common misconception. Kindness is not a weakness; it is a strength. A warrior's benevolence does not signify weakness; rather it signifies the warrior's good heart. You can have a good heart without being weak. In fact, I would suggest that it takes courage and self-confidence to be kind in every situation.

The person, who can maintain a calm silence in troubled times, and at the same time, can continue to be kind to everyone in his path, while others lose both their composure and their benevolence, is a person of honor and integrity. He has mastered the art of inner peace. Those who truly understand this will hold such a person in great regard.

I maintain a calm mind in troubled times.

February 6

Expect anything from anyone.
The Devil was once an angel.

Drake Graham

You really do not know what another person will do or what he is capable of. You may think that you know him, you may believe that you can trust him, but in the end, you really don't know. The only way to accurately judge how someone will react or respond is to know their underlying character.

Is he a person of character, honor and integrity? Does he really take his principles seriously? Are you completely sure that you understand what his principles are?

These are all questions that you need to answer before you put too much trust in someone. And even then, realize that many people change with the circumstances. Someone who proclaims to live his life by honor and integrity in good times, may throw those standards out the window when hard times hit. You must learn to expect anything from anyone, hope that they are honorable and honest, and be prepared in case they are not.

Of course, the true warrior will always live by his principles. But, how sure are you about who is a true warrior and who is not? The best you can do is evaluate someone according to their actions, after knowing them over a period of time. Never trust someone to the point that they can hurt you, if you can avoid it. Remember, expect the best, but always keep in mind that history has proven that you should expect anything from anyone. Trust, but verify!

I expect the best but prepare for the worst.

February 7

Complaining about a problem without proposing a solution, is called whining.
Theodore Roosevelt

Many warriors have allowed the state of the country, the state of their relationships, their finances, etc., to cause them to forget this basic truth by Teddy Roosevelt. It is an easy trap to fall into. I have to admit, I have been guilty of this myself from time to time.

The heart of the matter is, if you can do something about the problem, stop whining, propose a solution, and take action. If you can't do anything about the problem, stop whining and continue to work on perfecting your own life. Notice that neither choice includes complaining or whining incessantly about the problem.

It is looking more and more like we have raised a generation of wimps and whiners who do not have the backbone to stand up for what is right and take action. Rather, they cling to the safety of their own little hiding places or "safe zones" and complain about everything that is going on in the world from behind a computer screen or from their overused couch. It is time to put up or shut up. Take action or sit quietly on the sidelines.

True warriors do not whine. We need to remind ourselves of this from time to time. Cowboy up and have the courage to take action where action is needed. And where you can't offer any productive solutions, go about your own business without throwing more gas on the fire. Refuse to whine about anything!

I refuse to whine and complain. I am a problem solver!

February 8

It is not only what we do, but what we do not do, for which we are accountable.

Moliere

Some people think that if they simply do nothing and don't get involved, they are free from any blame. Well, legally, in most circumstances, that might be correct; but is it right? At least for the true warrior, the philosophy of just ignoring a wrong and being free from blame, doesn't cut it.

If you see an elderly lady being harassed on the street by two street punks, and you do nothing about it and just walk on by, you are less of a warrior than the squirrel that just ran across my yard. No real warrior would allow something like that to happen if it were in his or her means to put a stop to it.

If you could stop it, but chose to ignore it, then by what definition are you a warrior? Warriors help those in need. Warriors help those who are weak and can't help themselves. If you leave a defenseless lady to the mercy of two punks on the street, you aren't a warrior, in fact, I wouldn't even call you a decent human being. You must stand up when circumstances require you to, not turn your head and walk away.

Just remember, you are solely responsible for your actions *and* your lack of action. You don't get a free pass for doing wrong simply because you didn't "do" anything. Not taking action, when action should be taken, is doing wrong. And, for the true warrior, that is unacceptable. Make sure all your actions are right, and at the same time, make sure you do what should be done.

I make sure that all of my actions are right!

February 9

*Do not allow anger to rob you of your
rational mind or your inner peace.*

We have to keep a tight reign over our emotions, especially our negative emotions like anger, envy, hate, etc. Before you know it, negative emotions, especially anger, can take control of your mind and body, if you aren't careful.

Some people think that anger makes them stronger. They feel almost undefeatable when the cocktail of adrenalin and other hormones start pumping throughout their body, but they aren't. Giving in to this feeling not only robs you of your rational thought process, but can get you into hot water very quickly.

Remain calm in every situation. You can remain calm, think rationally, and still function at a high level. This is the way of the warrior. Have confidence in yourself and your abilities. Don't feel that you have to get angry and lose control in a physical confrontation. Maintain control and let your training take over – go into mushin.

Does this mean that you will never get angry? Of course not. Anger is a valid human emotion. What this means is that you will control your anger; your anger will not control you. You will calmly acknowledge your anger, and then respond with the correct response for the situation.

Do you see the difference? One is losing control and allowing anger to direct your actions, while the other is feeling your anger, but staying in control and directing your actions. If you do this, anger will rarely rob you of your inner peace or your calm resolve.

I maintain my inner peace at all times.

February 10

We do not rise to the level of our expectations.
We fall to the level of our training.

Archilochus

This great quote is especially important for martial artists and warriors. As we get older, it is very easy to start to lean on the skills that we have acquired in the past, and start to let our workouts slide a bit. Jobs, family, friends, lethargy, and injuries can all start to cut into our training time, if we let them. And, if you do not stay on top of things, your skills will start to regress.

The challenge, for martial artists and warriors, is to see our skills realistically. When we stop working out as much, or as hard, we regress, period. But, as that happens, your mind still thinks that you have the same skills that you used to have, and that those skills will be there when you need them. This is deceptive thinking.

For our skills to be there when we need them, we have to maintain them. Martial arts skills aren't something that you achieve and then you have them for life; they are more along the lines of "use them or lose them."

Thus, you will not rise to your expectations, but will fall to the level of your training. See your skills honestly and maintain them as you would a fine knife. If you don't keep that knife sharp, when you get ready to use it, it will not perform at the level that you want it to.

Maintain a high level of training, and bring the level of your training up to the level of your expectations. When it comes to your training, you can't rest on your laurels.

I maintain a high level of training and keep my skills sharp.

February 11

If you don't stand for your principles when they are being tested, they aren't truly your principles. They are just your wish list.
Bohdi Sanders

Every person will have their dedication to their principles tested several times over their lifetime. In the world we live in, it is a given. You must be prepared to have your principles tested and to stand for what you believe. If you abandon your principles when your back's against the wall, what good are they?

Just like your martial arts skills, you have to continually practice and reinforce your principles. Know what you stand for and why. Have a deep understanding of your own code of standards, which will guide you throughout your life.

If you don't build up your strength and confidence in your principles, just like the man or woman who does not continually practice their martial arts skills, when you need them most, you will falter.

Take the time to think about what principles are important for you to live by and then practice living those principles daily. Study them, visualize different scenarios where your principles are tested (and where you come out victorious), and reinforce your commitment to your code of honor daily.

Never allow any situation to cause you to lower your standards. Live like a warrior who knows what he stands for and what he will not stand for. Always stay faithful to your principles!

I stay true to my principles; I live my principles!

February 12

You must unlearn what you have learned.

Yoda

How can you be open to learning the truth when you are unwilling to let go of false ideas that you have been taught? There are many things in your life that you hold to as the truth because they were taught to you by those in authority, or those who you trust, but they are not really true. These falsehoods have been ingrained deep into your psyche through years of repetition, and they place limits on what you can do and who you can become. It is these false "truths" that are the hardest to unlearn and that are the most damaging to you.

You may have heard over and over again, how you cannot do this or that. You may have been told that you are too small, too slow, or not smart enough. You may have been taught wrong beliefs, by well-intentioned people who completely love you, but just didn't know any better. These people were not trying to hurt you, rather they were trying to protect you, but that doesn't change the fact that they taught you wrong.

You must be open to learning the truth. Never be afraid to explore new knowledge, new philosophies, and new things. Don't be afraid! Obtaining knowledge is a good thing. But first, you must unlearn those things which are not true.

You cannot add more tea to a cup which is already full. You must empty your cup of milk before you can fill it with tea. Mixing the two will not produce the outcome you are looking for. Only by unlearning that which holds you back, can you learn that which will help you move forward in your journey.

I keep an open mind and learn from everyone I meet.

February 13

The true warrior fights not because he hates the one in front of him, but because he loves those behind him.

Many see the warrior as a brute who loves to fight and hates his enemies so much that he is willing to do anything to destroy them, but this is not really accurate. The true warrior doesn't fight because he hates the one he is fighting; he fights because he loves what he is protecting. There is a big difference.

Have you ever wondered how the warrior can meditate, be holistic, walk in love, and yet train to injure or kill another person? This is the key to the answer to that question.

The warrior knows better than to harbor hate in his heart. Hate is a negative energy that weakens your heart and mind, clouds your thoughts, and has bad affects on the body as a whole, such as causing diseases and even cancer, according to some studies.

None of these are things which the warrior wants to cultivate. The warrior needs to have a strong heart and mind, clear, rational thoughts, and a strong body. He (or she) stays away from things that go against his goals as a warrior. He stays away from hate, long-term anger, malice, and negative energy of any kind.

Wise warriors use love as their motivation – the love of life, the love for those around him, and love for his family and his principles. These things strengthen the warrior instead of weakening him, and ready him to do whatever he must to keep those he loves safe. Sometimes these differences seem like nothing more than semantics, but things aren't always what they seem.

I will always protect those that I love!

February 14

I do what is mine to do;

the rest does not disturb me.

Marcus Aurelius

You only have control over one thing – yourself. You control your thoughts, your attitude, and your actions, and this is exactly where your focus should be. Do the best that you can where these things are involved and don't be disturbed by the actions, attitudes, or behavior of others. You are not responsible for what other people do; you are only responsible for what you do. Too many people want to take ownership for the acts of others, but each person is ultimately responsible for his own actions.

Do your best to be the best person that you can be and let the chips fall where they may. Once you have done your duty to the best of your ability, don't be upset if the outcome does not come out exactly as you had hoped. Simply know in your heart that you did the best that you could, given the circumstances. You acted in the moment to the best of your ability and made the best decisions that you could. What more is there?

This is the way of the warrior. If a man does what is his to do, and does it to the best of his capability, he has fulfilled his duty. Moment by moment, day by day, this is all that any man can do. Being upset or stressed out about things over which you have no control is a waste of time. Only think about such things when you can do something to change the situation. If the situation cannot be changed, what good does it do to ponder it? Be rational and concentrate on what you can do – then do it.

I think rationally and do my duty the best that I can.

February 15

Nobody is born a warrior, in exactly the same
way that nobody is born an average man.
We make ourselves into one or the other.

Carlos Castaneda

Carlos Castaneda stated, "To be a warrior is not a simple matter of wishing to be one. It is rather an endless struggle that will go on to the very last moment of our lives." This is stated perfectly.

There is much more to being a warrior than simply wishing to be one or calling yourself a warrior. Nobody is born a warrior, or anything else for that matter. You have been given the free will to live your life as you see fit. In order to become a warrior, you must work at it. It is a matter of molding yourself into what you want to become, and it is an endless process that last your whole life.

You develop the warrior spirit deep inside of you. It is a deeply ingrained part of your soul that becomes so integrated in you, that it is something that continues to push you to maintain your skills and your mental awareness. You continue to strive to improve yourself and your preparedness. You continue to strive for excellence in everything that you do.

What you become in this life is totally up to you. You can become anything that you desire, but becoming a warrior is a struggle. The warrior lifestyle is not easy. It pushes your limits. It is a way of being and a way of living that requires work and dedication, unlike merely being an average person. The road is not easy, but the rewards are well worth it.

I work to perfect my warrior spirit every day.

February 16

If you can't handle the flames,
don't wake the dragon!

Bohdi Sanders

In today's society, many people are rude, obnoxious, and pushy. They like to act tough, look tough, and talk tough. They seem to think that freedom means treating other people any way they want, with no thought of being respectful or considerate. These people have a very high opinion of themselves, that is, until they run across the wrong person.

Sooner or later, people like this will run across the wrong person – the sleeping dragon whose claws can rip them apart like wet paper and whose flames will leave nothing behind but a pile of ashes.

These dragons are not easily riled, but once they are awakened, the claws come out and the flames put the fear of God into the thoughtless person who dared to push his luck too far. Only the fool pushes the dragon to this point.

Those who walk their path with respect and thoughtfulness rarely ever wake a dragon, for dragons live with respect and mindfulness. They respect those who honor and value the traits of respectfulness, courtesy, and honor. They hold character and integrity in high esteem.

But those who do not, are sure to run across a dragon sooner or later. And when that day comes, a change of heart, a change of attitude, and quite possibly, a change of pants are soon to follow. The warrior is the dragon. If you can't handle the flames, don't wake the dragon!

I don't fear dragons; I AM THE DRAGON!

February 17

Where you recognize evil, speak out against it and give no truces to your enemies.

The Havamal

Never be afraid to stand up for what is right against what is wrong or evil. To see evil, ignore it and go your own way, is to be a coward. This is especially true if you see someone doing something to hurt one of your friends or family.

I see the enemy of my friend, or my family, as my enemy. In my opinion, that is what a true friend does. And I will give my enemies no truces, no mercy. They will either back down or be destroyed!

The way that I look at these issues may seem harsh to many, but for me, they are my code. Too many people allow their enemies to slide by without any consequences. They allow rude, obnoxious people to treat others rudely, without any consequences. I can't, and won't, stand for that.

In my opinion, those who see evil, and do nothing to at least try to stop it, are a big part of the problem. Fifty years ago, men would not stand for the disrespectful garbage that people take for granted today. If some jerk would have used foul language in front of a lady back then, he would have gotten his ass kicked right there. And not one person would have thought the guy dishing out the beating was out of line.

Have the courage to speak out against evil, and give no truces to your enemies. Either destroy them or beat them into submission, but do not, under any circumstances, allow them to slide by.

I speak out against evil and give no truce to my enemies.

February 18

The things you think about determine the quality of your mind. Your soul takes on the color of your thoughts.

Marcus Aurelius

It is the intention behind your actions which determine if your actions are honorable or dishonorable; and your intention comes from your thoughts. An action which seems right to outside observers, but which originates from dishonorable intentions, is not an honorable action, even if there is nothing inherently wrong with the action itself. This can be a little hard for most people to grasp, but it is a very important point for warriors who take their honor seriously.

In order for an action to truly be good or right, the thought behind it must be right. In essence, things have to be right on the inside for them to truly be right on the outside. You can't do wrong right, but you can do right wrong. The intention behind your action makes all the difference in the world. People may judge you on the outcome, but your honor does not depend on the outcome, it depends on the intention behind your action.

If your mind is right and your intentions are honorable, you can rest easy knowing that you have acted honorably, no matter what happens. A conscience free from guilt leads to tranquility of the mind, and only a tranquil mind can see things as they truly are. This is one of the benefits of meditation. By quieting the mind through meditation, you are better able to think rationally and clear the fog that can sometimes cloud the mind. Not only should the warrior learn to meditate as part of his quest to learn to control his mind, but he should also meditate on what he wants to manifest in his life through his thought processes.

I maintain a tight rein on my thoughts at all times.

February 19

If I call you brother, it is because you have earned my respect.

I do not use the words "brother" or "friend" lightly. If I say that you are my brother or my friend, then you have earned it by your actions and your honor. I know the difference between an acquaintance and a true friend, and you should too.

Not everyone who is affable with you is your friend; not everyone who is your buddy is truly your brother. We have become so free with our vocabulary, in our modern society, that it has taken away the true meaning of many of our words.

Today, people's words can, and should, be taken with a grain of salt, at least most people's words. The warrior should be an exception to this rule. The warrior should take his words seriously. They should carry a specific meaning which is unmistakable.

When someone calls you a friend, it usually means no more than they know your name. But warriors take their words more seriously than the average guy. When a warrior calls you a "friend," that is really saying something. When you have a true warrior as a friend, you have a true friendship, one that is hard to break.

Really think about the meaning of your words before you speak; don't say things that you don't mean. Say what you mean, and mean what you say. When you do this, your words will have greater meaning and people will have more respect for what you say. If you call someone "brother," make sure there is meaning behind it; make sure that they have earned the designation.

I make sure that my words are meaningful and accurate.

February 20

It is better to sleep on things beforehand
than lie awake about them afterwards.

Baltasar Gracian

Do not rush important decisions. As Baltasar Gracian wrote, it is much better to take your time and make an intelligent, informed decision, than to make a quick decision and then lose sleep worrying about your decision for days to come. Most decisions that you have to make do not have to be made immediately. You should seek advice, do some research, meditate on the issue at hand, and then make your decision when you feel comfortable inside your spirit.

Take your time. When you try to rush the decision making process or spend too much time thinking about something, you will find that your mind will become clouded. Do your homework, talk to the appropriate people, meditate, and then do something different. Get your mind off of the topic for a while. The reason for this is that it allows you to clear your mind about the subject, and this allows you to listen to what your spirit has to tell you about what you should do. Always listen to your intuition or your spirit.

Another important thing to remember is that, once you have made your decision, do not continually second guess yourself. You took your time, you did your research, you spent time contemplating the different options, and you made the best decision that you could, now be at peace with your decision. Second-guessing your decision only adds stress and worry to your mind. This is especially true when your decision cannot be reversed. You made the best decision that you could, now stand by that decision with confidence.

I make decisions slowly and then stick by them.

February 21

Attack where he is unprepared.
Move when he does not expect you.

Sun Tzu

It is not always wise to rush in and face your enemy right away. Many of your enemies will set a trap for you; they bait you, hoping you will allow your anger to control your actions. They want you to take the bait because they have a hidden strategy that you know nothing about.

Don't be tricked into taking the bait. Remember, not everything is as it first seems. Your enemy will not be as honorable as you; he will be devious and unscrupulous. He will do everything in his power to not have to face you man to man.

Be smart about your response. You must out think your enemy, as well as be able to out fight him. Sometimes it is better to wait for the right time, a perfect time when he is both unprepared and does not expect you at all.

The element of surprise is a powerful tactic. If you catch your enemy unprepared, you can completely void his strategy. Refuse to play his game by his rules. Be unpredictable, be cunning, and be smart. Trump his strategy with your own.

Always remember, the most important thing in any war is walking away the winner. Be willing to seemingly lose a battle or two, to win in the end. Be courageous, but don't be rash. Never allow your emotions to be used against you. The cool and calm warrior will ultimately win over the emotional or unprepared opponent.

I always use strategy and defeat those who come against me.

February 22

The best defense against evil men is good men who are skilled at violence.

Evil predators do not think like the average person. Most people can't even grasp the way the predators' minds work or how they could possibly do the horrible things that these predators do. This simple fact gives the predators an advantage over most people.

Pacifists state that you must simply love these people because they are merely doing the best that they can do. To them, there is never any acceptable reason for violence. Well, I have news for people who think this way – predators are not doing the best that they can do, and they don't care. Predators only respect strength, not philosophy or love.

The best defense, and many times the only defense, against these predators, is good, brave men, who are skilled at violence. These are the men, and women, who will step up and do what must be done to stop these kinds of people. They are the warriors. They are those who have the courage to do what most others do not have the intestinal fortitude to stomach.

Being good at violence does not mean that you are some uncouth brute. It simply means that you have had the training to be both skilled at doing what it takes to stop these predators, and trained to understand when you must use those skills.

Violence is violence, period. There are some martial artists and martial arts writers who try to make a science out of violence. That is just silly. Violence is simply causing injury to someone to achieve your desired outcome. In the case of the warrior, it is used to protect himself and those he or she loves.

I train to be skilled at violence in order to protect good people.

February 23

It is better to be a warrior in a garden,

than a gardener in a war.

You may be wondering how it is that warriors teach the skills of violence, but talk about peace and tranquility. As strange as it may seem to some people, the two are not mutually exclusive. Think about it. The monks at the Shaolin Temple are peaceful people, but they teach the arts of self-defense.

All true warriors want peace. A life of peace is where you can pursue your goals, spend quality time with your loved ones, and live life to the fullest. But as history as proven time and time again, living a peaceful life is not always possible, so we must train in martial arts, even in times of peace.

George Washington stated that those who want peace should prepare for war, and this same train of thought has been taught for hundreds of years. While we should live in peace and love, we should also understand how to fight and defend ourselves.

Knowing how to fight is not in opposition to peace and love, but is actually a part of loving peace and our loved ones. If you love someone, you must be willing to defend them. In addition, being willing to defend someone is worthless, if you don't have the ability or training to do so.

Yes, teach your students the way of peace and love, but also teach them how to stand up against the evil in this world. Teach them to stand against those who hate peace and want to destroy our way of life, but also give them the tools to stand successfully.

I have both the skill and the will to stand against the evil in our world.

February 24

I would advise you not to trust either (men or women), more than is absolutely necessary.
Lord Chesterfield

This is very good advice that Lord Chesterfield gave to his son. Anytime you trust someone with anything more than trivial information, you are taking a chance that it will be used against you at some future time. Overall, people are just not trustworthy. Some will break your trust maliciously, others because of their lack of control or carelessness, but either way it is your fault for entrusting them with information which should have been kept secret. You should understand people and consider their nature before putting your trust in them.

It is best to keep your personal thoughts, actions and life private. You can be cordial and polite without sharing your personal thoughts. Your private life should remain private. Remember, if people like to share secrets with you, whether it is their own secrets or someone else's, they will also share your secrets with others. This is human nature. It is also human nature to enjoy sharing your thoughts, deeds, and ideas, but just because it is human nature and enjoyable, doesn't mean that it is wise.

The only way to ensure that your secrets are kept secret is to keep them to yourself. Be extremely careful about sharing personal information with anyone. Also, be very careful about trusting what others tell you. As a whole, it is a dangerous proposition to put your trust in others. Never trust someone too much or too soon.

I am always careful about who I trust.

You all wanted to deem my flaws as unworthy.
Now you will see that even angels fall, but a
warrior will never crawl beneath your feet.

Lorna Evol

When you are walking the path of the warrior, you will find that people will come against you in many ways. Some will try to get you to lower your standards. Others will be jealous of you and will maliciously wait for you to make a mistake so they can reveal it to the world in some misguided attempt to bring you down.

People don't like those of us who live our life at a higher level. When they look at warriors who live their lives with discipline, honor and character, it reminds them of how much they have lowered their own standards or how they have dropped the ball in their own lives. This makes them feel inferior or bad about themselves, but instead of using this to motivate themselves to live better, they simply attack those of us who do live by a code.

Everyone has flaws; no one is perfect. Don't let these kinds of people get to you. You are living the kind of life that makes them jealous, that reveals to them the fact that they are not living as they should.

Keep walking your path anyway! Never cower down to their pressure or their personal attacks. They may come against you, but in the end, it is you who will walk away victoriously, as they slither away, still envious of your way of life, your character, and your unshakable honor.

I bow to no man. I am a warrior and I walk with courage and honor.

February 26

Sometimes giving someone a second chance is like giving them another bullet for their gun because they missed you the first time.

There is a big difference between forgiving someone for wronging you, and giving them the opportunity to put a knife in your back a second time. When you forgive someone, you are ultimately doing it for yourself; you are releasing yourself from the hold that this person has had over your mind. Think of it as getting rid of dead weight that was dragging you down.

But, forgiving someone does not mean that all is forgotten and that he or she is back in your good standing. Forgive, but don't forget. Forgetting what this person has done, and what kind of person he or she is, is simply not wise. You learned a valuable lesson about this person; never forget the lesson you learned from this incident.

You can learn from everything that happens in your life. But, if you forgive *and forget*, then you are both losing the lesson that you have learned from what happened, and forgetting valuable information about the person who did you wrong. Knowing people's character is a very important part of knowing how to deal with people. Never wipe someone's slate clean thinking that he is not the person who he has proven himself to be by his own actions.

Forgiving is simply refusing to hold onto the pain of what happened; it doesn't necessarily mean giving that person a second chance to be in your life. Sometimes giving someone a second chance is like giving them another bullet for their gun because they missed you the first time – not smart! Forgive and move on; don't forget and repeat!

I forgive and move on, but I never forget and repeat my mistakes.

February 27

As long as it is realized and accepted that warriors must comprehend right and wrong, and strive to do right and avoid wrong, then the way of the warrior is alive.

Taira Shigesuke

I have been teaching for years that the way of the warrior involves more than simply being able to fight, or going to war; it involves something much deeper – living with honor, character and integrity. It involves knowing right from wrong, and choosing what's right.

If you go back and look at the great warriors from history, most of them cared greatly about their honor and about being people of character and integrity. Many guys now say that honor and integrity have nothing to do with being a warrior.

These guys get upset with me because, according to them, being a warrior means nothing more than "participating in war." The people, who claim that this is the only definition of a warrior, are the same people who seem to care very little about character, honor, or integrity.

I suspect that those guys who downplay the importance of honor, character, and integrity are doing so because they fall short in these areas, but they want to boast about being warriors anyway, so they claim that these traits are worthless to the warrior.

Nonetheless, I still stand by my claim that honor, character, and integrity are important to true warriors. All true warriors should strive to live the warrior lifestyle to the best of my ability and strive to live a life of honor and integrity.

I understand right and wrong, and I always do what's right.

February 28

Doing nothing is also an action;
not making a decision is making a decision.

Bohdi Sanders

If you are just sitting on the couch, vegging out, that in and of itself, is an action. Doing nothing is also an action; not making a decision is making a decision. Everything you do is an action, even if that action is the decision to not act.

By deciding not to get a workout, but instead, to take the afternoon off and sitting in front of the television, you are still acting. Watching television is an action. Taking a nap is an action. Everything that you do is some type of action. Whenever you decide not to do one thing, you are deciding to do something else. This is true even if what you decide to do is nothing. Doing nothing is in fact doing something.

Think about it. If you are just sitting in a chair doing nothing, you are sitting in a chair. That is what you are doing. The same thing applies to making decisions. If you decide not to decide, then your decision is to be passive and let life make the decision for you.

What the warrior should always be concerned with is whether his actions are right or wrong. Always use your sense of honor to determine the correct course of action, and remember, as Plutarch pointed out, "Not even the gods can undo what has been done."

You can't go back and change the past; all you can do is start living right, right now, this very moment. Starting now, strive to make your every action right, according to your own code of honor. Make sure that there is a good reason for everything that you do.

I make the right decisions and stick to them.

March 1

I don't love the bright sword for its sharpness, nor the
arrow for its swiftness, nor the warrior for his glory.
I only love what they defend.
J. R. R. Tolkien

Warriors don't work hard perfecting their martial arts skills because they love fighting. They don't hurt, bleed, and sweat in order to brag about their skills. True warriors don't train for glory or recognition. They train to protect those who cannot protect themselves – their family, the weak, the elderly, and those who deserve their protection.

The simple-minded pursue the warrior arts for immature, selfish reasons. They want recognition and people patting them on the back, telling them how great they are or how tough they are. They couldn't care less about protecting others, only about themselves. In reality, they are weak. They need the constant praise of others to validate themselves because inside, they don't know the way of the warrior.

The true warrior has found this path. He or she understands the difference between training to look tough and training to be tough. He knows how to be a weapon, a weapon that is not waved like a banner to get everyone's attention, but rather a weapon that is always quietly there, ensuring the protection of those around him.

He trains because he has understood the value of the warrior lifestyle and he has made a decision to live his life as a warrior. He trains because that is who he is; he needs no recognition, no accolades, and no praise. His spirit and mind are at peace with exactly who he is and what he does. He is a true warrior – a man or woman that lives the way of the warrior.

I defend all those who deserve my protection.

March 2

If you underestimate your enemy in battle,

odds are you won't live to see another.

Into the Badlands

Never underestimate any enemy. People are so jealous and petty in today's society that they will go to any length to hurt someone who they don't like or who they are jealous of. And the internet gives the coward just the ammunition that he needs to attack you anonymously, which is how cowards prefer to attack.

Many warriors underestimate their enemies because they know that they can take them down face-to-face. But they neglect the fact that many of their enemies are cowards and would never face them face-to-face. Self-defense covers everything, not just physical conflicts. You have to be ready for every kind of attack.

In today's world, many people prefer to attack you from the perceived safety of their computer keyboard. They will libel you or slander you. They will spread rumors about you or even hack into your computer to get to your personal or financial information. These kinds of attacks are more common than a physical attack in our modern society, so you have to be ready for them.

Make sure that you make yourself as safe as possible against every kind of attack, not just physical attacks. Be ready for the kind of attacks that inferior men will use against you. The attacks from second-rate cowards are much more common; so you should make sure you are prepared for them as well. Remember, self-defense must encompass every area of your life, not just physical attacks.

I never underestimate my enemies.

March 3

Love everyone.
But never sell your sword.
Paulo Coelho

Warriors are meant to walk in peace and love in a world which doesn't understand either of those concepts. But walking in peace and love does not mean that we were meant to be a door mat. Walk in love, but never lose your edge. Refuse to be treated badly.

When true warriors fight, they fight to defend what they love, not to destroy what they hate. Now, these two may overlap, and in fact, they often do overlap.

If you are attacked on the street, and you totally dismantle your attacker, that doesn't mean that you hate the guy, but that you respect your own life enough to defend it.

On the other hand, if some terrorists is about to open fire in a shopping mall, and you are there with your family, you are certainly both defending what you love and destroying what you hate. I personally despise terrorists and will take any chance that I get to destroy them and their agenda. At the same time, I will defend those I love against any attack.

Walk in love and peace, but always be ready to unsheathe your sword, should the circumstances demand that you do so. And make sure that you keep your sword sharp. If you need to use it and it is dull and rusty, it will do you little good. Never allow your martial arts skills to become rusty!

I walk in peace and love, but I always maintain my martial arts.

March 4

A good instructor teaches students how to fight;
a great instructor teaches students how to live.

Ricardo Almeida

Any good martial arts instructor can teach someone how to fight and how to defend himself, but a great instructor goes much further than that. A great instructor doesn't stop at teaching self-defense against physical attacks, he or she, teaches students how to live a life of honor and character, how to defend themselves against other kinds of attacks in life, and how to live life to the fullest.

I have had instructors which were pretty good martial artists, but when I saw how they actually lived their lives, I was no longer impressed by their martial knowledge. They were good instructors, but not good men. You have to be both to be a great instructor.

If you are teaching martial arts to a group of students, realize that they look up to you; they revere you. You have the opportunity to really make some meaningful changes in their lives. The question is, are you prepared to do so? Are you living a life of honor and integrity? You can't pass on to your students what you do not understand yourself.

Instructors, who neglect philosophical topics, overall self-defense, and/or the spiritual practices of the arts, are not offering their students a well-balanced program. If you are only teaching students to fight, but not how *not* to fight, you are doing them an injustice.

Endeavor to be a great instructor, not simply a good instructor. Your students have great respect for you; make sure you deserve it. Teach your students how to live, not just how to fight.

I earn my respect by my words and my actions.

March 5

I won't be wronged. I won't be insulted. I won't
be laid a hand on. I don't do these things to
other people and I require the same from them.
John Wayne in The Shootist

Every man of honor needs a code to live by, even if it is as simple as the one above. You need to know what you stand for and what you won't stand for in life. If you refuse to be wronged, insulted, or to have someone aggressively lay their hands on you, you need to be clear on how you will respond if these things happen to you.

There are some things worth fighting for and other things which are not worth injuring someone over. You must be clear about what is worth fighting for and what is not worth your time or effort. Not every offense is worth your response, much less your martial prowess.

While it is perfectly fine to not allow others to treat you like dirt, you must understand what is worth getting physical about and what is below you as a warrior. There is an old Chinese proverb that states, "Why blast a sparrow with a cannon?"

If you have honed your skills to a high level, then your martial arts skills are like a cannon compared to the fighting skills of the average guy on the street. Don't allow people to treat you badly, but at the same time, don't over-react to the situation.

Stand up for yourself and require that others treat you as they should, but don't lose your cool. There is more than one way to address a wrong. Make sure your actions are right, no matter how others act.

I refuse to allow the actions of others to destroy my inner peace.

March 6

A warrior is worthless unless he rises above others and stands strong in the midst of the storm.

Yamamoto Tsunetomo

What good is a warrior if he or she, doesn't have the discipline to rise above others or the trials in life? What good is he if he cowers down in the midst of the storm, whether it is a physical attack or an issue of honor? You must have the intestinal fortitude to stand strong in the midst of the storm. You must rise above your challenges; rise above the other people who allow the storm to break them.

When I refer to rising above others, I don't mean thinking you are better than others; I mean that you rise above others by the way that you live your life. When you truly live a life of honor and integrity, you purposely live a life that is superior to those who do not live by honor. And this should show in how you respond to life's challenges.

If you don't have the courage to live a life of honor, or to stand strong when the chips are down, what makes you any different than anybody else? How is that being a true warrior? Warrior up and stand strong in the midst of life's storms! Rise to the level of the superior man.

The only way that you can stand strong in the midst of the storm is to be prepared *before* the storm sets in. You must prepare yourself to meet life's trials. If you wait until the storm winds start to blow, then you will be unprepared to stand strong. Prepare in the good times for the bad times. Never rest on your laurels. Continue to prepare yourself daily for the inevitable storms that will blow into your life. If you are unprepared to meet the storm, you have no one to blame but yourself.

I am strong in the midst of the storm!

March 7

Many people give up just before they reach their goal.

Many people give up just before they reach their goal. They can't see any progress and everything looks bleak to them, so they throw in the towel. Little do they know that if they would have held on just a little bit longer, their objectives would have been reached and they would have been successful. But they gave up just before the storm clouds cleared.

I have seen this happen over and over again. Ronald Wayne is probably someone that you have never heard of, but I bet you have heard of his ex-partners, Steve Jobs and Steve Wozniak. Of course these gentlemen were the co-founders of Apple Computer.

Wayne gave up on his dream of creating personal computers that would be in everyone's home and sold his share of Apple for less than $800. Just a little more endurance and dedication to his dream, and he would be one of the world's richest men today, but he gave up on his dream before it had the time to manifest.

You can't see into the future. You don't know how your decisions will ultimately play out, but you can develop the endurance to hold on to your dreams during the hard times. Without perseverance and discipline, you will never accomplish anything worthwhile.

Never give up simply because times are hard. Only change directions when your objectives change or you need to modify your strategy for success. Discipline yourself to develop a never-say-die attitude. Refuse to give up unless your ultimate objectives change. You only live once; don't settle for less than what you want out of life.

I won't quit until my ultimate objective is reached.

March 8

You must be the change you
want to see in the world.

Gandhi

When you respond to something or someone, you remain in control, not just of your thoughts, emotions, and actions, but of the situation as well. The superior person responds and maintains control, whereas the inferior person reacts, loses control, and then is left cleaning up his or her mess at a later time.

When someone acts without thinking, it is like shooting for the bull's eye, but not slowing down and taking the time to aim before you shoot. You are just acting, but not mindfully focused on your objective. This is simply relying on luck to achieve your goal, and it is never wise to count on luck.

Responding, instead of reacting, does not come naturally. All men have the same basic thoughts and emotions. The difference is how we learn to control our thoughts and emotions, instead of allowing them to control us. Superior people refuse to allow their thoughts and emotions to control their actions.

They make a commitment to themselves to purify their thoughts, control their emotions, and make their actions deliberate, and this leads them to greater personal growth. They are dedicated to becoming the change that they want to see in the world. If you want to see more rational, thoughtful people in this world, then model those traits in your own life. Be independent of the actions of others and live your life as a superior man or woman.

I am the change I want to see in the world.

March 9

Always stand for what's right, even if you have to stand alone.

There comes a time in life when you start to realize that following your conscience and doing what you know is right, is the most important thing in life. We all have so many chances to cower down to all of the pressures to compromise on our honor and our integrity, but it is precisely at these times that we have to stand for what we believe. Anything less eats away at your warrior spirit.

Make a firm decision to stand for what's right, no matter what. Don't allow the pressures of life to get to you. Don't be influenced by how others live their lives, at least not those who don't live a life of honor.

You will find that if you will always stand for what's right, your self-confidence will increase. The more you stand for your values, the easier it will become to stand against the pressures of life. Soon, you will become a rock that cannot be moved, even in the greatest storms. Never back down! Always stand for what is right.

Many people profess to live their life this way, but they falter when their back is against the wall and they have to choose to stand against the majority. There is a big difference between professing that you will always stand for what is right, and actually standing for what is right no matter what.

You have to make a firm decision to always stand for what is right. It cannot be an option; it must be your way of life. When something is optional, it is dependent on the situation. When something is ingrained in your spirit, it is a part of who you are.

I stand for what's right, even if I have to stand alone.

March 10

A wise man fights to win, but he is twice a fool
who has no plan for possible defeat.

Louis L'amour

If a situation deteriorates to the point of becoming physical, you should do everything in your power to win the fight and keep yourself and those around you safe. This should go without saying, but you would be surprised at how many people are not prepared to do "whatever it takes." You have to spend time reflecting on what you are willing to do and what you are definitely not willing to do, and what circumstances would trigger certain responses. Are you willing to stick your fingers three inches deep into someone's eye, or completely destroy their knee in order to survive?

Where do you draw the line when it comes to fighting to win? Personally, if the situation has reached the point where someone is intent on killing or severely injuring me, or those I care about, there are no rules – anything goes. This is a personal decision, and a decision that you should make before you find yourself in this position. You should also be smart enough to have a backup plan in case things don't go your way.

You don't have a crystal ball; you can't see into the future. It is always better to be safe than sorry. Make sure that you have at least one backup plan, just in case your original plan goes awry. I would even go further and have a backup plan for your backup plan. You can never be too prepared. The better prepared you are, the better your chances of being successful. Being truly prepared means being ready for whatever you may encounter, even a failure in your original plans.

I fight to win and I always have a backup plan.

March 11

Honor is that which no man can give you and no man can take away. It's a gift a man gives to himself.

Rob Roy

Honor is an intense sense of right and wrong, and the adherence to the actions and principles that a man deems right. In the past, a man's honor was considered something that had to be defended, even to the death. Men fought duels to the death to defend what they declared to be an insult to their honor, or in today's terms, being disrespected.

Noblemen and warriors, both in the East and in the West, considered it part of their duty to defend their honor, especially if they felt that someone had disrespected them or challenged their honor in some way. And, these men took drastic measures to do so.

In many cases, these duels were not about honor at all, but more about someone's wounded pride. To fight to the death over some small insult or misunderstanding is not truly defending your honor, but rather defending your pride. The vast majority of these duels of honor were more about defending the man's reputation, not his honor.

Honor is not something that you have to defend by fighting other men, but you do have to fight for it nonetheless. You have to fight to keep your honor daily. Almost every day of your life you will have opportunities to turn your back on your honor by choosing actions that are dishonorable in one way or another.

The fight to maintain your honor is an internal battle, not an external one. Honor is not something that anyone else can take away from you, but it is something that you can lose. It is up to you whether or not you maintain your honor.

I live with honor at all times.

March 12

*The quality of a person's life is in direct
proportion to their commitment to excellence,
regardless of their chosen field of endeavor.*

Vince Lombardi

Excellence has to become the prevailing attitude in your life. It actually has to become a habit, and, as with everything else in life, you have to start from where you are. Start small and continue to build this attitude in your life.

You don't decide to start martial arts training one day, and enter the ring with expert fighters the next week. It takes time, it takes work and it takes consistent training. The same principle applies to anything you do in life. Nobody becomes an expert at anything overnight.

Although you can't change overnight, you can start changing immediately. The first thing you have to change is the way that you think. Your thoughts are the beginning of your actions; therefore it is vital that you get your mind straight first. If your mind is not right, you will never be able to become a man or woman of excellence.

How do you get your mind right? You learn to control your mind just like you learn to do anything else – you consistently work at it. You must cultivate thoughts of excellence, thoughts that bring you closer to your objectives.

At the same time, you must disallow thoughts that hinder your goals. Just refuse to allow them to dwell in your mind. If you will consistently control your mind, you will find that you gradually move closer and closer to excellence, to the perfection of character that we should all strive for.

I am committed to excellence in all that I do.

March 13

Make a least one definite move
daily towards your goal.

Bruce Lee

To achieve your goals, you must keep your attention on them daily. You must focus your energy on what you want in your life. Out of sight, out of mind, does not equal success. Discipline yourself to spend some time each day, working on achieving your goals. Boiling water soon cools down if you remove it from the source of heat. You must keep the fire burning!

If you want to reach your goals, keep your internal fire burning. Keep your desire and your motivation high. No one earns their black belt with lackluster motivation. You must fuel the fire! You have to find ways to motivate yourself. Whether your motivation comes from an internal source or an external source doesn't matter. All that matters, in the end, is that you keep yourself motivated enough to do what has to be done to reach your objective.

Find ways to motivate yourself. Without the proper motivation, you will never achieve anything. Think about it. If you are relaxing comfortably on your couch, but it is time for your workout, are you going to get up and go workout if you are not motivated to do so? Probably not!

Motivation is a must to achieve anything worthwhile in life. If you are unmotivated, you will choose the easiest option every time, and the easiest path is never the path of excellence. You have to work for what you want in life. Make sure that you know how to motivate yourself and keep yourself motivated.

I am my own motivation and I reach all of my goals.

March 14

Haters will see you walking on water
and say it is because you can't swim.

Anytime you have the courage to stand for something in your life, or the drive to be successful in some endeavor, you will have those small-minded, jealous people that will hate you and want to see you crash and burn. They take great pleasure in seeing you fail. Make sure they are disappointed!

Don't allow haters to affect you or to cause you to change what you are doing. Stand for what you believe! Haters are people who don't have enough drive or intelligence to improve their own lives, so they are simply content to try to bring other people down. They particularly hate successful people because successful people remind them of their own failures and shortcomings. Remember the old adage, misery loves company.

Live your life independently of what your haters and detractors think or say. Haters will see you walk on water and say it is because you can't swim. They can spin anything to look bad, but you have two things going for you. First, you know the truth, and also, you are too focused on improving your own life to worry about your haters' lies and gossip.

This kind of person cannot affect you unless you allow his attacks to sidetrack you. Refuse to allow their attacks to interfere with your success. Just ignore them and keep moving forward as if they were nothing more than a gnat. If they become more of a threat than a gnat, take them down with the truth and move on. Don't give them even a temporary home in your mind. Stay strong and move on!

I won't allow haters to waste my time or energy.

March 15

Success is going from failure to failure
without loss of enthusiasm.
Winston Churchill

Success requires endurance. In your martial arts journey, you will meet with failures, you will have to overcome injuries and pain, and you will be challenged. To be successful, you must endure. No one ever became a great martial artist by quitting or losing their enthusiasm.

You must find ways to keep yourself motivated. One of the best ways to remain motivated to train is to remember why you began to train in the first place. Remember those who have threatened you, those who hate you and would love the chance to destroy you, and those deadly predators that most people prefer to never think about. These people are out there, and they have no mercy for you!

If that isn't enough to motivate you, find something that is. Without enthusiasm and motivation, you will find justifications and excuses for not training. Keep those internal fires burning! You never know when your training will save your life, or the life of someone else.

Master Funakoshi stated that your training should be deadly serious. There is a reason for that. If you are not serious about your training, how do you possibly think you will be prepared to deal with the worst of the worst, or the toughest of the toughest? You won't!

Never lose your enthusiasm for keeping your warrior skills sharp and ready. If you don't have that enthusiasm, you will simply go through the motions, and that will not prepare you for a life-or-death situation.

I have enthusiasm for life. I am a warrior!

March 16

Repetition is the mother of all skills
Edgar Sulite

New students to the martial arts often complain about the repetition of the kicks, punches, and blocks. And many of them get bored and quit simply because they do not understand why we practice our techniques over and over again. Repetition is vital for any skill, not just martial arts. The more you do something, the better you get at it. It doesn't matter if it is a martial arts kick, painting, or cooking.

As you repeat an action, that action becomes ingrained in your mind, body and spirit. When it comes to a physical skill, such as your kicks or punches, you are training your muscles to remember the action. This is known as muscle memory. Essentially, we are burning that skill into our mind and our muscles. This is exactly what you want. Once you have practiced a skill to the point that you can do it without having to think about it, you have started to master the skill. This is what the Japanese call entering mushin.

A great example of mushin is driving a car. When you first start driving, you have to consciously think about each little action. After you become proficient at driving, you simply drive; you don't have to slow down and think about having to turn on the turn signal or where to put your hands. You just do it because you know it.

This is why we practice the same techniques over and over again in the dojo. We want to come to a place where if we actually have to use our martial arts, we can enter mushin and do what has to be done without having to stop and think about what to do. Don't practice until you get it right; practice until you can't get it wrong!

I practice my art until I can't get it wrong.

March 17

Loyalty means I am your friend whether you are right or wrong. But I will tell you if you are wrong and I will help you get it right.

The warrior takes loyalty and friendship seriously. To the true warrior, when he enters into a real friendship, he enters into a bond which is as strong, or stronger, than family. And after he enters into that bond, for which he has made a commitment, he feels duty bound to uphold his word and his commitment.

The actions of others do not negate the commitment that he has made to enter into the bond of friendship. He upholds his end of the bargain in spite of what kind of trouble the other person may get into. This does not mean that he will support everything that the other person does – he won't. But he will honor his commitment to his friendship.

If his friend is wrong, he will let him know and give him his honest opinion and offer to help him. This is not the same as giving his stamp of approval; it is merely the warrior maintaining his principles. This doesn't mean that there are not some things that the other person can do to void the friendship – there are. Things such as being disloyal to the warrior, backstabbing the warrior, attempting to hurt him in some way, etcetera, are proof that this person is not your friend, and such actions void the friendship across the board.

But, other than those type things, the warrior will remain loyal and true to his friends, through thick and thin. This is just a part of the warrior's principles, the code that he lives his life by. The true warrior is a loyal friend to the end.

I am the best friend that anyone will ever have.

March 18

Don't take my kindness for weakness;
the beast in me is sleeping, not dead.

Many people are intimidated by the loudmouth, obnoxious guy who appears rough and tough, but are not worried about the kind, silent guy who calmly minds his own business. This is a mistake.

While the rough and tough guys may be bad news, more often than not, the guys who talk tough can't back it up. They use their words to intimidate others, much like the poker player who holds worthless cards but who tries to bluff his way to winning the pot. He knows that if anyone ever calls his bluff, he will be in serious trouble.

On the other hand, the silent guy who is kind and well-mannered may be able to take you out at will. This kind of man is like the player who sits silently and looks like he is afraid to bet, but who is holding a royal straight flush. There is no reason for any bluster or tough talk; he is holding all the cards and he knows it. If anyone dares to come against him, he will walk away with all the chips.

Never underestimate someone. You never know what cards the other guy is holding, but you do know what's in your hand. The good news is that, unlike a poker game, you get to decide what cards you will hold in the game of life. You are able to prepare yourself as you will.

Make sure that your silence and kindness is not because of weakness. Make sure that you consistently hold a royal straight flush behind your quiet, kind smile. And always be ready to go all in if the situation calls for it. Make sure your beast is not dead, but merely sleeping and ready to be awakened when needed.

The beast in me is always ready to be awakened.

There are only two forces in the world, the sword
and the spirit. In the long run, the sword will
always be conquered by the spirit.
Napoleon Bonaparte

It is one thing to have the skills, the training, and will to defeat someone, but if you don't have that fire in your spirit, you won't be successful. Those with that fire in their spirit will rarely lose in the long run.

Oh, they may lose a battle here or there, but they refuse to quit. They refuse to give up; they refuse to declare defeat. They refuse to forget and always come back again and hit their enemy harder than they did the time before. And they keep coming back until they win, no matter how long it may take.

Those with this never-say-die spirit will always win in the end. They may lose every battle, but in the end, they will win the war. It is impossible to beat the warrior who refuses to declare defeat. He or she will always come back one last time, every time.

Too many people lose one battle and throw in the towel; they get hit hard and run for the hills. This is not the way of the warrior, but rather the way of the coward, the quitter, and the weak.

Warriors refuse to accept defeat; they refuse to be conquered. Even if it appears that they have been defeated, they are simply biding time until the day comes when they will strike back, and strike back hard. The warrior's spirit is never defeated and his sword stays sharp! Never declare defeat. Always get back up one more time, every time.

I refuse to accept defeat; I refuse to be conquered.

March 20

*Always make certain that you are
in a better position than your enemy.*
Soho Takuan

You should always know what your objective is and what you need to do to achieve it. Then make sure that you are in a position for success. This same wisdom applies to dealing with your enemies. Always make sure that you position yourself for success, whether your enemy is someone you work with or a predator in the streets.

If your enemy is a predator, make sure that you are in a better position in the streets, you must always be aware of your surroundings. Know where you are and how to get the hell out of Dodge if you need to. And, if you are accosted by some predator in the streets, you still have to position yourself for success, which is getting out of the situation unharmed.

Start with de-escalation techniques. It is always best to defeat the enemy without fighting, even if he is under the impression that he has won when you walk away. If this is not possible, and things do get physical, make sure you are aware of your surroundings. Know who else is there, be aware of the obstacles around you, know the best escape route and position yourself to win.

Do not get caught in a dead end alley, or some other position where you are cornered with no options. Then, of course, make sure you take advantage of your positioning during the confrontation, which should be very short and to the point, if you get my meaning. Always make certain that you are in a better position than your enemy.

My strategy always puts me in the best position for victory.

March 21

Civilize the mind, but make savage the body.

As a warrior, you have to be balanced. Civilize the mind, learn as much as you can about everything that you can. Meditate, develop benevolence and love for your fellowman, behave with manners and respect, and learn to control your emotions. Make time for your spiritual practices. All of these are a part of civilizing your mind. But that is only half of your job.

The warrior should also savage the body. This means animal training, not just going to your martial arts class on Tuesday and Thursday nights. Train hard, as if you life depends on your training. Who knows, one day it just might.

Train daily. There is always a way to get some training into every day, whether it is a physical workout, stretching, visualization, or just some mental training. Don't let any day go by without doing some kind of training.

Stretch and maintain your flexibility. Lift weights and develop your strength and build more muscle. Practice your martial arts skills, and don't just go through the motions, but rather, go all out – 100%! Condition your hands, arms, stomach, legs, etc. Cross train, do whatever it takes to make your body savagely hard and fit.

Training both the mind and the body is essential to being prepared to deal with whatever situation may cross your path. Your mind is always your best weapon.

But when you combine a prepared mind with a prepared body, essentially integrating your mind and body, you become a true force to be reckoned with. Only a fool would stand against such a prepared warrior!

I civilize my mind, but I make savage my body.

March 22

Control the situation in such a way
that nobody knows how you control it.
Vasiliev Vladimire

Controlling the situation without anyone knowing how you controlled it, is the true art of winning without fighting. The best victory is winning without fighting; and doing so in such a way that your enemy doesn't even realize that you defeated him and his plans, until after the fact, is even sweeter.

He may even walk away thinking that he put you in your place and got the best of you, but you have the satisfaction of knowing that you handled the situation exactly like you wanted to, and he never had a clue that he just got manhandled.

Being able to control a situation like this takes practice, courage, and a willingness to put your ego in the back seat. Most people allow their pride and their ego to get in the way of achieving this skill. I can assure you that the satisfaction that you will feel from this type of victory is greater than any you will feel from defending your pride.

Learn the art of controlling the situation and winning without fighting. Practice your de-escalation skills to perfection. Many times, winning without fighting means that you have to learn to swallow your pride and your ego, but it is worth it. Think about it. What is your ultimate objective in a potentially violent situation? To be victorious!

It doesn't matter how you achieve your victory. If you can walk away from a potentially explosive situation, victoriously without fighting, you have an even sweeter victory. Control your anger and walk away a winner.

I control what is in my power to control; I don't worry about the rest.

Don't blame your behavior on someone else.
You are 100% responsible for all of your actions.

Every single day, I hear people say that so-and-so *made* them mad, or that they would not have done this or that if so-and-so had not done something that they didn't like. This is simply a way of shifting responsibility away from yourself and on to others. Saying someone else *made* you do something is making yourself into a victim. Warriors are not victims!

Here's a news flash for some people – nobody *makes* you do anything; you, and only you, decide what you are going to do. You are completely responsible for what you do and for what you do not do. You are 100% responsible for every single action that you perform.

Don't try to justify your actions by blaming someone else. That is merely saying that you aren't strong enough to control your own emotions or actions. That is weak! Take responsibility for yourself. Take control of your life. Nobody else is responsible for what you do; that is *your* job!

You should decide to live a life of honor and integrity in spite of what anyone else does or does not do. Remember what Baltasar Gracian taught, "The man of principle never forgets what he is, because of what others are."

Never forget that you are a warrior, a man or woman of honor and integrity! You are not a victim. You are not a sheep. No one forces you to do anything; you decide your own destiny. You decide how you will respond to everything in your life. Quit shifting the blame to others! Warriors take responsibility for *all* of their actions; lesser men always blame others.

I take responsibility for my own actions.

March 24

Out of suffering have emerged the strongest souls;
the most massive characters are seared with scars.

Khalil Gibran

The warrior not only has to defeat his (or her) enemies, but he also has to overcome his suffering and his scars, physically, mentally, and emotionally, in order to continue his or her journey of the warrior lifestyle.

Every warrior has to deal with scars from his physical training and fights along the way. This is pretty much a given. But what goes unseen are the mental and emotional scars that have been seared into his soul as he travels his path.

We must learn to not only overcome the pain that comes with training, injuries, etcetera, but to also overcome the unseen suffering that comes along with being a warrior. The warrior cannot allow the invisible pain and suffering to defeat him or her. We have to overcome these things and emerge even stronger than we were before. We must declare victory over those scars that would bring down lesser souls.

Remember the words of Khalil Gibran, "Out of suffering have emerged the strongest souls; the most massive characters are seared with scars." Be one of the victorious. Be strong and refuse to allow anyone or anything to defeat you.

Rise above and become strong – physically, mentally, emotionally, and spiritually. If you have something in your life that is trying to hold you back, address it and conquer it. Don't wimp out and tell yourself that this is easier said than done. Whiners and wimps always moan about things being easier said than done. Just do it! This is the way of the warrior.

I can handle anything. I am a victorious warrior.

March 25

Don't do something permanently stupid just because you're temporarily upset.

As warriors, we have to be in control of our mind, emotions, and actions. We are 100% responsible for our actions, no matter what. Being upset, being angry, being totally irate, is no excuse, and certainly won't hold up in a court of law. We have to learn self-control; we have to discipline ourselves to live by our principles, no matter what.

Our prisons are filled to overflowing, and many of those who are caged like animals, are there simply because they did something permanently stupid while being temporarily upset. As soon as their anger subsided, they were sorry for their actions, but their remorse does not win them their freedom.

The actions, which may have only lasted for a couple of minutes or even seconds, are costing them years of their precious life. This is something very important for the warrior to remember. You must always think rationally, not emotionally. Never allow your emotions to control your actions. Allowing your emotions to take over is walking on the razor's edge.

Stay in control. Don't allow yourself the luxury of losing your temper, especially when it comes to physical confrontations. Self-defense includes defending yourself from the law. Even in self-defense situations, you must think fast and think ahead.

Many times, in today's society, the law is not on your side. It is up to you to make sure you are safe, in every way. Always be in control of your actions; never allow your emotions to take control. Be smart and think rationally.

I take control over my emotions; my emotions do not control me.

March 26

A wolf eats a sheep but now and then;

ten thousands are devoured by men.

An open foe may prove a curse,

but a pretend friend is worse.

John Gay

The sheep considers the wolf its enemy and men its friend, but how many more sheep are eaten by men than by wolves? The difference is that the sheep *knows* that the wolves are its enemy; it is too dumb to know that men, who under the pretense of taking care of it, have a hidden agenda and that they will soon be led to the slaughter house.

Personally, I had much rather know who my enemies are, than to have enemies who hide under the disguise of being my friend. Many enemies do this because they are either too weak or too cowardly to confront you face to face. They pretend to be your friend and secretly try to hurt you or wish you harm. They clandestinely wait in the shadows for the chance to ambush their unsuspecting "friend."

Make it a point to know who your friends truly are and who your real enemies are. Many times what you discover will surprise you. Don't put too much trust into someone until you know, without a shadow of a doubt, that you can trust them.

Never make the mistake of trusting someone with much before they have proven themselves to be trustworthy. Warriors can easily handle open foes, but it is the pretend friends who blindside us. Know who your true friends are and watch those who you are unsure about. Don't allow yourself to be blindsided.

I am aware of my environment and those in my world.

March 27

A lion does not have to prove it is a threat.
You already know what it can do.

The warrior does not need to prove that he is a warrior; he (or she) is content in simply knowing that he is a warrior. He doesn't have to go around bragging about how tough he is or what he can do. In fact, he had rather others didn't know about how tough he is or what he may be capable of. He likes to keep the element of surprise on his side.

Everyone already knows that a lion is a deadly creature; just as they know that warriors have the skills to be deadly should circumstances require them to be. There is no reason for you to go around telling people how deadly you can be. Doing this only invites thugs and morons to come find out for themselves.

In fact, when someone tells you how tough they are, that is usually a sure sign that they are not someone you have to worry about. They are probably not very tough or skilled. The man that you have to worry about is the one who is quiet until he is pushed too far. And by the time you figure out how tough he really is, it is too late for you!

Those who constantly tell everyone how tough they are, are usually very insecure. The warrior, who is secure in his abilities, has no reason to brag about what he can do. He already knows what he can do and really couldn't care less whether others know about his skills or not.

These are the quiet guys who sit calmly while things are moving towards the boiling point. They don't participate in ridiculous pushing and shoving or tough talk. These guys simply act when it is time to act. They aren't interested in proving anything to anyone. They know what they can do and couldn't care less whether you know they are dangerous or not.

I don't talk the talk; I walk the walk.

March 28

Victory is reserved for those
who are willing to pay its price.
Sun Tzu

Victory doesn't come by wishing for it. It doesn't come because you want it badly. Victory comes about because you pay the price, because you prepare for it, you work for it, and you earn it.

Today there is a social movement that wants everyone to feel like a winner, even when they don't earn victory and don't deserve victory. Martial arts tournaments give out "participation awards" as if you are owed some kind of recognition or award simply for getting out of bed and showing up. I have news for you – NOBODY OWES YOU ANYTHING!

Don't look for someone to stroke your ego or to give you something that you did not earn. Victory is earned. Not everyone who enters a competition is going to be the winner; there can be only one winner. Don't buy into this politically correct, feel good garbage.

Teaching people that they are a winner for simply showing up is merely lying to them. It is giving them a false sense of pride. And the kicker is that *they know it*! People who do this aren't fooling anyone; people know if they are the winner or not.

If you want victory, work for it, fight for it, and win it! Victory is truly reserved for those who are willing to pay the price. Remember, there are no second place trophies on the street. You win, get hurt, or die. Don't buy into this political correct garbage. To quote the highlander, "There can be only one!"

I am prepared and I am always victorious. I never lose!

March 29

*A man cannot be too careful in
the choice of his enemies.*
Oscar Wilde

At first, this quote may seem a little strange. After all, who would choose to be enemies with someone? Why would you be making a choice when it comes to your enemies? But, if you think about it, we frequently make choices when it comes to our enemies.

We choose to make enemies by our own words and actions. Sometimes we do so accidentally, sometimes carelessly, and other times we do so out of anger. Most of the time, we give our enemies a reason to be our enemy because of something we have said or done.

A sarcastic comment, a rude action, or causing someone to lose face, can all lead to bad feelings; and bad feelings can lead to anger, hate, envy, and jealousy.

Of course, there will be enemies who made a personal decision to come against you for whatever reason – jealousy and envy are two of the most common reasons that people decide to become your enemies. But as a rule, we can avoid making enemies by thinking before we speak or act.

It is wise not to make enemies when you do not have to. There are, however, times when honor will require that you make an enemy of someone, and at those times, don't hesitate to burn that bridge to the ground.

But don't burn a bridge when you don't have to. You never know when you may need to cross it again. If you will be mindful of your words and actions, you will have fewer enemies to deal with.

I am careful with my thoughts, my words and my actions.

March 30

If a battle cannot be won, do not fight it.

Sun Tzu

You have to pick your battles wisely. Not every conflict is worth turning into a major battle. There are certain battles which simply cannot be won no matter how much effort you put into them or what strategies you use.

They are simply losing causes and fighting such battles does little to help you accomplish your ultimate objectives. The wise man will not let his pride get in the way of obtaining his goals, and fighting a battle which cannot be won is a prime example of allowing your pride to cloud your thinking.

It is important to keep in mind that retreating from an individual battle does not mean that you are surrendering or declaring defeat in the war. A battle is no more than that – one battle. To continue with the battlefield/war analogy, a battle is simply one skirmish; your ultimate objective is to win the war. Many a pawn has to be sacrificed in a chess match in order to capture your opponent's king, which is ultimately all that matters in the overall scheme of things.

Always keep your ultimate objective in mind. Don't let your pride or anger interfere with your overall victory. I know that this is easier said than done at times, but it is a very important part of the game, and one that takes some self-discipline and practice to perfect.

Have an overall plan for victory. Be willing to sacrifice a battle here and there in order to win the war in the end, and don't expend energy fighting a battle which cannot be won at any cost. Be rational and deliberate.

I keep my ultimate objective foremost in my mind.

March 31

*It is madness for sheep
to talk peace with a wolf.*
Thomas Fuller

Peace can only be successfully discussed from a place of power. Sheep cannot talk peace with the wolf because the wolf has no motivation to make peace with the sheep. After all, what are the sheep going to do about it if the wolf rejects their offer? Nothing! That is not a very good bargaining chip, to say the least.

In order to persuade a predator not to attack you, you must be coming from a place of power. Anything less is simply begging for mercy. Be willing to walk in peace, even with those who hate you, but never beg for peace. You must also be willing to destroy your enemy if he refuses to live in peace with you and forces your hand.

Make sure that the wolf knows that the only alternative to peace is his destruction, not roasted leg of lamb. Make yourself a sheep and the wolf will slaughter you; make yourself a sheep dog and the wolf will avoid you. If you want peace, you must make yourself strong enough to demand peace with your enemies. This can only be done if you are strong enough to back up your ultimatum.

For the most part, it is unwise to try to bluff your enemy into peace. If he ever calls your bluff, you are in trouble. Your credibility will be destroyed and your only option will be to leave with your tail tucked between your legs. Always talk peace from a place of power. Make sure that your enemy understands that his only alternative to allowing you to live in peace is his ultimate destruction. Never negotiate from a position of weakness. Strength is power!

I consider what leverage I have in any negotiation.

April 1

Double the fear in your enemy's heart and you will halve the chance that he will ever put a sword in his hand.

Vlad Tepes

Mental warfare has been successfully used throughout the world to stave off attacks from enemies. When you strike fear into your enemy's heart, mind and spirit, you have all but won. After fear has a grip on his mind, even if he does attack you, he will be hindered by his fear and will be easier to defeat.

When you have an enemy that you know has malicious thoughts towards you, use fear as a part of your self-defense plan. This is a time-tested way to ward off your enemies, and is exactly what is meant by the saying, if you desire peace, always make it know that you are prepared for war.

Predators, and others with evil intent, do not want to walk into the fight of their lives; they want to prey on the weak, not the strong. Make it known that you are strong. Make it known that you are willing, and more than able, to destroy your enemy, and your enemy will think long and hard before attacking you. This tactic has been used throughout the ages.

Fear is a very useful tool, when used correctly. This tactic was used by pirates to convince their prey that they should not resist. The pirate flags were used to instill fear into the crew of the ship they were attacking. Everyone on the seas knew what the symbols on the pirate flags meant – death! And through the use of fear, pirates were able to plunder many ships without ever having to fight for their booty. Never take a chance when you don't have to.

I always use strategy to my advantage.

April 2

Every time you train, train with the motivation
and purpose that you will be the hardest
person someone ever tries to kill.

Tim Kennedy

Although the warrior may enjoy sparring with his friends or participating in martial arts tournaments, that is not his ultimate goal when it comes to his martial arts training. His ultimate goal, outside of developing his character, is self-defense. Warriors train to develop the skills that will save their life or the lives of their loved-ones.

Warriors want to build up their defenses to the point of being unassailable. When you train, you should train with this purpose in mind. Your training is not a hobby, it is not for exercise, and it is not for fun; it is to develop the skills that you may need to keep yourself, or those you love, alive.

Keep this in mind when you train and you will never have to worry about having a lackluster training session. It is only when we forget our ultimate goal that we find that we start to slack off. Picture the meanest, baddest guy you can imagine and keep this image in your mind when you train.

If you need motivation to train or to increase the intensity of your training, do a little research on some of the thugs in our prisons. Check out some of the toughest thugs that you can find; there are many photos on the internet. Then picture these guys attacking you on the street, not just one of them, but several. If that doesn't motivate you to take your training seriously, nothing will.

I train with motivation and purpose.

April 3

The ultimate aim of the martial arts is not having to use them.
Miyamoto Musashi

Most people train hard in their chosen field in order to use their skills and be really good at what they do. The warrior trains hard to develop his martial arts skills, but does so hoping that he will never really have to use them.

He knows that using his skills outside of the dojo or maybe a tournament or two, means that someone is going to get hurt, probably bad. True warriors are men and women of peace. They don't want to have to hurt anyone that they don't have to, but they are ready, willing, and able to do just that should a situation arise that requires them to do so.

They are not perfecting their martial arts skills in order to go out and use them; they are perfecting their skills in case they ever *have to use them*. His ultimate aim is the perfection of character, not the destruction of life; but his overall goal of perfecting his character, in no way means that he is unwilling to use his martial arts should he need them.

Many people have a hard time understanding this fact. They think that warriors train to kill people because they are brutes. This could not be further from the truth! True warriors are not brutes, but men and women who have a set of martial skills and who have trained for excellence in every area of their lives. The true warrior is a man or woman of character, honor, integrity, and control. He knows what he can do and has no desire to go out and prove his skills to the world.

I only use my martial arts for self-defense.

April 4

He who is not prepared now,
will not be prepared when needed.
Colonel Phil Torres

You can't wait until you need a skill to develop that skill. At that time, it will be too late, especially if the skill you need has to do with martial arts or self-defense. You have to prepare now in order to be prepared when your back is against the wall. Procrastination can mean death in certain situations.

If you wait until the rain sets in to patch the hole in your roof, then you are going to have water in your house. In order to be completely safe from the rain coming into your house, you must prepare for the rain before it comes, not during or after. After the rain sets in, no matter how quickly you move to solve the problem, you will have a mess to clean up.

Maintain control over your mind and your body. Don't allow yourself to give in to laziness or apathy. As the *Havamal* states, you can't feel a battle in your bones; you have to be prepared for it when you leave home (paraphrased). In short, you must be prepared to defend yourself whenever you leave your home because you never know what kind of challenges will come your way.

Never allow yourself to be caught unprepared. Now is the time to prepare; tomorrow is too late. Don't procrastinate when it comes to your self-defense preparations. It is never too soon to hone your skills because you never know when it may be too late. Prepare today for the battles of tomorrow! He who is not prepared now will not be prepared when needed, *unless* he takes action to prepare himself today.

I prepare today and I am victorious tomorrow.

April 5

*Today is victory over yourself of yesterday;
tomorrow is your victory over lesser men.*
Miyamoto Musashi

Before you will be ready to achieve victory over others, you must first achieve that victory over yourself. You must discipline yourself to become a better person. You must discipline yourself to train harder, work smarter, and think rationally. You must focus totally on your goal at hand. Become faster, stronger, more skilled, wiser, and more knowledgeable.

You must push yourself to become the best that you can be, and then you will be ready to confront lesser men, those men who do not have the discipline to truly improve their lives, who instead prey on weaker people. These men are due no respect, but you still must prepare to defeat them. Never underestimate your opponent!

Discipline yourself today, so that tomorrow you may defeat the wolf at your door. Never let a day go by where you do not improve yourself in some way, and make yourself better than you were the day before!

Make constant, never-ending improvement you goal in life. Those who constantly strive to improve themselves, find that they improve in every area of their lives, not just the one area that they mainly focus on improving.

When you seek excellence in your life, it shines through in every part of your life. Push yourself to be a better person each day – better skills, better character, a better spouse, a better parent, better in every way. Warriors seek perfection, even if they never achieve it.

I seek perfection and excellence in everything I do.

April 6

Surround yourself with those
on the same mission as you!

Not everyone around you wishes you the best or is cheering for your success. Some may not wish you harm or malice, but their negativity may still be holding you back. Others may simply be waiting in the shadows for the perfect time to bring you down.

Never feel obligated to continue to associate with someone once you know that they are holding you back or possibly want to find a way to stop you from obtaining your ultimate objectives. Some people will try to sidetrack your goals simply because they see you moving forward, while they are comfortable not striving for excellence. These people are afraid that you will leave them behind because their life is stagnant.

Others may simply want to stop you from achieving your goals because they are jealous of you or because they have something against you. Still others may actually think they are helping you by stopping you from making a mistake. The reasons are endless, but the result is always the same – they interfere with you achieving your goals.

Make sure that you surround yourself with like-minded people, people who are going to help you succeed, not hold you back. Associate mostly with those who are on the same mission as you and make them a part of your mastermind group.

Positive people who support your goals and are working towards the same goals in their own life, help motivate you and keep you on track. Remember, it only takes one weed to eventually destroy your whole garden.

I surround myself with men and women of honor.

April 7

There will come a time when you think everything is finished. That will be the beginning.

Louis L'Amour

To the novice martial artist, earning his or her black belt feels like the completion of a long-term goal. He or she feels like they have achieved their objective and that they have reached the pinnacle of martial arts success. They think that they are finished, not understanding that they have only reached the beginning of their martial arts journey.

Earning your black belt is merely getting to the point that you are really ready to start learning. It can be compared to getting your degree. Yes, you have a diploma, but your real education doesn't start until you get out in the real world, get a job, and actually learn your profession. The same goes for martial arts.

You have earned your black belt, which means you have mastered the basics. You have graduated with your first degree, but that is not the end. For those in the know, that is only the beginning. There is so much more to learn and to perfect.

It is like that with most things in life. Think about it. Learning how to safely operate a skill saw and use a nail gun does not make you an expert carpenter. Those are only the basic skills of a carpenter. It takes years of working with those tools to finally become an expert with them. If you are truly a warrior, you won't settle for simply knowing the basics skills you need to know.

The warrior lifestyle is a life-long endeavor; don't quit when you are just getting started. Be determined to endure to the end.

I stay the course and finish victorious.

April 8

Expect the best,
but prepare for the worst.

People should live life to the fullest and have a positive attitude. You only live once, so pack as much as possible into your life. Have fun, enjoy yourself, love others, be healthy, stay in shape, and live with passion. Be the best that you can be, but at the same time, make sure that you prepare for the worst.

Understand that not everyone will share your integrity or your sense of honor. Not everyone will share your respect for life. In spite of what some may teach, not everyone is doing the best that they can do. There are those out there who are simply bad to the core and who will prey on other people; ensure that you are prepared to deal with them.

Some people cannot comprehend how you can have a positive outlook on life, love others, love life, but train in an art that teaches you how to injure or kill another human being. These are the people who you hear saying things like, "There is never any reason for violence." Well, I have news for these people – there is absolutely a time and a place for violence.

Don't buy into this pacifist attitude. Wise people understand that they can be positive and loving, while at the same time train to keep their families and themselves safe. Always be prepared to die, but never chase death. Live your life to the fullest, but be aware and ready for trouble. Live like you are dying, but at the same time, train and prepare as though you will never die. Be the best that you can be, but prepare for the worst that others can be. None of these things are mutually exclusive. That is living the warrior lifestyle!

I expect the best, but I prepare for the worst.

April 9

What I do have are a particular set of skills, skills
I have developed over a very long career, skills
that make me a nightmare for people like you.

from the movie, Taken

Really proficient warriors have a very dangerous, very specific set of skills, which do make us very dangerous for people who give us no other option other than to use our skills. We know how to inflict pain on the body that most people have never even imagined. Many of our skills can do permanent damage. And, some of our skills will simply leave our enemy lifeless. Yes, this is very blunt, but it is also the reality of the situation; it is the reality of true warrior training.

And, because this is the reality of the skills that we train to perfect, we must discipline ourselves to never use those skills except as a last resort, and never take those skills lightly. The human body really is very fragile, especially to the person who knows where the weak spots are and how to use his skills to attack those body parts.

Jesus stated that from those who much is given, much is required. If you have been given these skills, much is required and expected of you. You must be thoughtful, both in training and on the streets, as to when and how to use your skills.

Much is required of the true warrior. Not the least of which is restraint when dealing with those who we least want to restrain ourselves with. Those are the people who try your patience, your discipline, and your ultimate skills of winning without fighting. Always think rationally and never be rash.

I perfect a dangerous set of skills.

April 10

We can fight the sword or we can fight the man swinging the sword. Which one breaks more easily?

Spartacus

As Spartacus stated, "We can fight the sword or we can fight the man swinging the sword. Which one breaks more easily? Break your enemy's sword, and he will soon purchase another one. Break his courage, and what merchant sells that keenest of blades?"

Always fight the man, not the weapon that he is holding. If you fight the weapon that he is holding, that leaves his other hand and two feet free to attack you. Be aware of the weapon, but fight the man.

That being said, you must also control the attacker's weapon. You can't simply ignore the fact that he is carrying a weapon which he intends to use against you. While you don't fight the knife, you do have to stop it from being used against you. Control the weapon, fight the man.

Even more so, fight the man's mind. If you destroy his courage and his will to fight, his weapon will be of little use. When you attack a man's mind in the right way, and at the right time, you may never even have to worry about his weapon.

Your greatest weapon against your enemies is to get inside their heads and plant the seeds of fear, doubt, and worry. Once planted, those seeds will do a lot of the work for you. Destroy the man's courage to attack you and his weapon will not be a threat. Destroy the man, and the weapon becomes a harmless, inanimate object, or another fine addition to your collection. Always fight the man, not the weapon.

I think rationally, even in the midst of the storm.

April 11

Be like water! Don't get set into one form;
adapt it, and build your own, and let it grow.

Bruce Lee

When it comes right down to it, martial arts are about one thing and one thing only – self-defense. If you are focused on self-defense, then you shouldn't worry about doing things exactly as other people do them, but rather you should adapt all the techniques that you learn and make them work for you, your body type, and your abilities.

Trying to make something work for you, which simply doesn't work for you, is silly. Is your purpose to mold yourself into a carbon copy of what everyone else is doing or to develop your own self-defense skills to the highest level possible? Are you trying to learn to defend yourself as well as possible or are you trying to impress your peers?

Everyone is different. Just as the same diet doesn't work for every single person, the same martial arts techniques will not work equally for every person. Some people rely more on speed, and others more on power. Adapt the techniques of your martial art to your own needs. Never try to use a technique for self-defense just because you were taught to do so. Only use what you know will work for you.

Once you figure out which techniques work for you and which ones don't, then you know which techniques to actually practice and perfect. If you are studying martial arts for self-defense, why would you consistently practice techniques which you know you would never use in a fight? Find out which techniques come naturally for you and feel right, and then perfect those, for those are the ones you will use.

I make every technique my own and they always work.

April 12

A tiger doesn't lose sleep over the opinions of sheep.

Everyone has an opinion, but not everyone's opinion matters. The tiger doesn't lose sleep over the opinions of sheep, as the sheep's opinions don't matter, at least not where the tiger is concerned. The tiger walks without fear in a ruthless jungle. He roams the jungle unconcerned about what the sheep think about him, knowing that the sheep's opinions on the life of a tiger are meaningless.

The same thought applies to the warrior. The warrior does not lose sleep over the uninformed opinions of those of lesser character. True warriors live by their own code of honor. Character and integrity are important to them. They stay informed and on top of things.

They know what is going on in the world and are aware of what needs to be done. They have a specific purpose in life, and are unconcerned about the opinions of those who are uninformed and ignorant, or those who have a problem with how they live their life.

The warrior, who is walking his own path, does not need the approval of others. He is unmoved by what others think of his path. He laughs at the criticism of the envious and the haters, and walks his path in defiance of his enemies who try to harm him or to smear his reputation. The opinions of the sheep mean less to him than his compost pile, for he knows who and what he is – a true warrior.

This is not a politically correct way to think. Most people think that everyone's opinions matter, but they are wrong. Only informed, intelligent opinions matter; all other opinions are just noise from fools who delight in hearing their own meaningless voices.

I don't lose sleep over other people's opinions.

April 13

My forefathers were warriors.

Their son is a warrior.

I am the maker of my own fortune.

Tecumseh

Like, Tecumseh, you are the maker of your own fortune. You, and only you, decide whether or not you will be a warrior and live the warrior lifestyle. You decide whether or not you will live your life based on a code of honor and integrity. Ultimately, no one but you controls the direction of your life.

Your life is 100% in your hands. The only question is whether or not you have what it takes to take the reins and design the kind of life that you want to live. And then, whether or not you have the discipline to follow through and live that life. Making the decision to live the warrior lifestyle is just the first step; you must have the discipline to consistently live a life of honor and integrity.

Contrary to what many think, being a warrior has nothing to do with what you do for a profession; it is about who you are inside. I have seen military men that are the definition of scum, and I have seen average, every day guys who are definition of men of honor, warriors through and through.

You make that decision. But it takes more than just dreaming of being a warrior; you have to walk the walk. You have to design your life and then live your design. You have to discipline yourself to live the life you choose. The traits of the warrior lifestyle must be internalized and become a part of you. Are you up for the challenge?

I am a warrior. I am the captain of my own destiny.

April 14

It's not the size of the dog in the fight;
it's the size of the fight in the dog.

Mark Twain

In most cases, it is the will to win that defeats the skill to win. There is just something about a warrior that refuses to lose, refuses to give up, and keeps coming back, no matter what. A person like that is very hard to beat.

Of course, if you have that will to win, that fighting spirit, that never-say-die attitude, *and* a good set of honed skills, then you are a force to be reckoned with in every situation. It is good to have that fighting spirit; but it is even better to have that internal fortitude, combined with the specific skills that you need for total victory. When you have the will and the skill, you become hard to beat.

Size can be intimidating and it is a factor that must be dealt with, but it is not always the determining factor in a fight. Sometimes, the bigger they are, the harder they fall. Strategy and determination win out over size every time, just ask Goliath. Never allow yourself to be intimidated by someone's size. In fact, don't let someone intimidate you, period.

All human bodies have the same weak points, no matter how tough they may look on the outside. There are specific points on each body that are easily attacked and destroyed. No matter how big someone is, you can attack their eyes, their throat, their groin, and their knees, just to name a few vulnerable spots. These targets are defenseless to the correct attack. Don't allow intimidation and fear to defeat you.

I have the will and skill to win. I am never intimidated!

April 15

You wear the belt; it does not wear you.

Many people seem to be overly impressed by a black belt; it is almost like they expect the belt itself to carry some magical powers or something. The first thing that most students that I have had, ask me is, "How long will it take for me to get my black belt?" It is as if they are there for that magical belt, and not the training itself.

Let's get one thing perfectly straight right now. A black belt is nothing more than a belt made of cotton and/or silk, and stitching, that's it. You can buy one for about $5 from some of the martial arts supply catalogs. It is not magical. It carries no super powers. Being awarded a black belt doesn't make you invincible. It is not the belt or the rank that matters, but the skills that you have developed while you worked toward earning that belt. The black belt is simply a symbol of what you have achieved, nothing more.

You wear the belt; it does not wear you. Wearing a black belt does not give you martial arts skills; it doesn't all of a sudden make you a fighter, a self-defense expert, or enlightened. All of those things are things which you develop through hard work, working through pain, injuries, blood, sweat, and tears. You wear the belt externally; those qualities come from the inside.

Make sure that you understand not only what your belt represents, but where your skill level actually is. There are black belts, and then there are *black belts*. Not every black belt is awarded equally or earned by the same standards. Believing that you can defend yourself against anyone and everyone, simply because you have been awarded a black belt, is a sure way to get yourself in big trouble. See your skill level honestly and know exactly what your black belt means.

I train for self-defense, not for belt rank.

April 16

An able man shows his spirit by gentle words
and resolute actions; he is neither hot nor timid.

Philip Dormer Stanhope

Let's say you are shopping at your local grocery store and it is filled with several elderly people, and some punk is walking down the aisle loudly spouting profanity, offending these elderly people. If you approach him in a polite way and show him the error of his ways, there is nothing wrong with that. But if you approach him, loudly rip him, with some four letter words of your own, and put him in his place, you have been just as discourteous to those in the store as he was.

You let his actions upset you and you lost your temper, when in fact, you could have accomplished the same goal without lowering yourself to his standard of behavior. You do not have to be rude or discourteous to get your point across. Warriors do not lower themselves to the standards of other people; they live independently, according to their own standards and code of honor. You can be forceful and resolute without being loud and rude. As Sir John Vanbrugh said, "Good manners and soft words have brought many a difficult thing to pass."

Just about now I can hear you thinking, "Yeah, but this jerk didn't deserve to be treated with respect. He deserved to be firmly put in his place!" And you would be completely right. The guy in my example certainly would not deserve to be treated in a courteous manner. He was acting like a jerk and deserved to be put in his place, but remember, there is always a best way to do everything. As Clint Eastwood said in *Unforgiven*, "Deserve's got nothing to do with it."

My words are calm and my actions are resolute.

April 17

Knowledge will give you power,
but character, respect.

Bruce Lee

Knowledge is the key to many things in this world. Knowledge is power, especially if you put what you know to use in your life, but all of the knowledge in the world won't get your true respect if you do not have the character to go with it.

If you want true respect, you have to first deserve it; you have to earn it by your actions, your character, your honor, and your integrity. This politically correct notion that "everyone deserves respect" is bogus. Everyone does not deserve respect. Everyone should be treated with respect, but not everyone deserves respect. There is a big difference between the two.

You can treat someone with respect without that person actually deserving your respect; that is merely being courteous and acting as a man or woman of honor. We should treat everyone with respect, until they have earned our disrespect, but we should only truly respect those who deserve our respect and who have earned our respect through their character and honor.

If you want others to respect you, you must be worthy of their respect. You can't *make* anyone actually respect you; you have no control over what others think. But you do have control over whether or not you actually *deserve* someone else's respect; and in the long run, that is what truly matters. Live your life with honor and integrity and you will find that you are respected, even by those who hate you.

I gain knowledge and power daily, and I earn my respect.

April 18

The truth is that strength lies in the interior of
the warrior; in his heart, his mind, and his spirit.

Miyamoto Musashi

Your real strength does not depend on your physical strength training program. It does not depend on your physical training at all; it depends on your mental and spiritual training, your internal training. As Musashi stated, the true source of your strength comes from inside, from the warrior spirit and a focused, disciplined mind.

Anyone can develop a degree of physical strength just by sticking with a weight training program. But real strength comes from the inside. It is the will to win, the mindset that you can do anything, and the never-say-die spirit. With the right internal strength, you can overcome your physical shortcomings.

Just think about Nick Vujicic. He was born with no arms or legs. Nick could have simply resigned himself to thinking that he could never do anything in life. He could have just felt sorry for himself and no one would have blamed him for it; but Nick refused to live like that.

Nick refused to feel sorry for himself, motivated himself, and made something of his life. Today he is one of the top motivational speakers. He participates in many different activities and is an inspiration to hundreds of thousands of people. Now that is internal strength!

The warrior should never neglect his or her internal training. Of course physical training is important, but your internal training is even more important, and will be used much more often. Develop your internal strength and there will be very little in this life that you can't handle.

I strengthen my heart, mind and spirit daily.

April 19

I choose this life. I know what I'm doing. And on any given day, I could stop doing it. Today, however, is not that day.

Batman

The true warrior chooses to live the warrior lifestyle; nobody makes him live his life this way. It is a personal choice. He could change his mind any time he wants to, walk away, and live his life just like the vast majority of people on this planet. But, to the true warrior, this is not a possibility.

The warrior lifestyle is more than simply a lifestyle choice; it is a way of living that is engrained deep in your soul. Warriors can't walk away from what they are. It is a part of who they are deep down in the core of their spirit.

Those who have decided to live the warrior lifestyle have made a life-long choice. They would live the same way even if nobody else on the face of the earth lived with character, honor and integrity. No amount of criticism, no amount of disapproval, and no amount of enemies, could ever cause him to abandon what is in his spirit. The warrior lifestyle is his life.

The true warrior is a warrior, period. It is engrained in his DNA. Living up to his own standards and principles is his choice; being a warrior is his destiny. You don't walk away from your destiny.

You may have bad days or even bad weeks, but you will find that you always return to the warrior lifestyle, as it is always with you, a part of you, driving you to be the warrior you are meant to be. On any day, you could throw in the towel, but today is not that day!

I choose to be a warrior; I choose excellence.

April 20

Practice not your art and it will soon depart.

German Proverb

It doesn't matter what your art is, if you don't continue to use it and work at it, you will find that your skills have faded. This is true of everything, but it is especially true where your flexibility is concerned. Flexibility is a must for the martial artist. Without flexibility many of your techniques are unusable. The older you get, the more important it is not to allow your daily stretching routine to slide.

It is foundational to your self-defense that you protect yourself, not only from your enemies, but also from self-inflicted injuries. If you injure yourself in your training, you certainly won't be prepared to protect yourself on the street, at least not until your injury has had time to heal. Inflexible muscles are easily pulled or torn during a hard martial arts workout, and injuries such as this take a long time to heal properly.

Therefore, time spent stretching and increasing your flexibility is vital to your self-defense. Everything matters! You can't afford to take any part of your defenses lightly. Stretch daily to develop and maintain flexibility. Don't just go through the motions half-way, but rather concentrate on your muscles as you stretch. See the muscles lengthening and becoming more flexible.

Flexibility is the foundation of your martial arts. If your foundation is not solid, everything that you build will be on shaky ground. Practice all aspects of your martial arts often. Don't take anything for granted. As far as this goes, neglect is not your ally. If you neglect your training for one day, it will neglect you for two. Train hard and consistently.

I practice hard and my skills grow daily.

April 21

When nothing can be done about the way things are,
the wise stop worrying about the situation.

Lao Tzu

In today's society, it seems that many people are addicted to worry. They worry about the weather, they worry about the economy, they worry about their health, and the list goes on and on. Does their worrying accomplish anything? Well, actually it does have an effect. Everything that you do carries with it some significance, no matter how small it may be. I guess the question should be, "Does their worrying accomplish anything constructive?" In this case the answer would be, no.

Your thoughts have power. Thoughts of worry, like all of your thoughts, affect your mind and your body, but they do nothing to change the situation that you are worrying about in the first place. Worry is a totally useless thought process. Don't worry about things. If you can do something to help the situation, do it. If you can't do anything about the way things are, then don't waste time worrying about it.

Spend your time in ways that produce positive and useful results. If you have a problem, don't worry about it, but rather think rationally about what you can do to fix the problem. Realize that *not worrying* about something does not mean that you just ignore it. Take steps to protect yourself. Do what you can and then move on. The wise man will continue to monitor the situation and stay aware of the current circumstances, without allowing his mind to be troubled by the things which are out of his control. Quit worrying!

I refuse to worry about anything!

April 22

In peace do not forget war.

Japanese Proverb

We live in a fairly peaceful society. Most of us may go our entire lives without having ever been in a real life-or-death conflict. As a rule, we don't feel threatened when we go out at night, even in the cities. And because we live in such a peaceful society, we can start to get complacent concerning the need to keep our martial arts skills sharp. But it is important to understand that just because things are peaceful today, doesn't mean that they will always be that way.

You never know when you may have to use your martial arts skills to defend yourself or your loved ones. It could be today or it could be 15 years from now, you just don't know. No one ever really expects to be a target of some thug when they leave home, but every day, someone somewhere is mugged. You have to be ready.

You must continue your training and keep your skills ready at all times. Don't get complacent about your training. It is easy to do, especially when you feel safe and there are so many other things which compete for your time. Always remember that any skill not used will regress. Your martial art skills are no different than any other skill – you use them or lose them.

The question is, do you want to leave your life up to fate or do you want to make sure that you are ready for whatever may come your way. For the warrior, there is no question; it is his duty to be prepared. He cannot afford the luxury of forgetting about the evil that is in the world, just because everything appears peaceful. He must be prepared for whatever he may encounter. Stay sharp!

In peace, I train hard for war.

April 23

Warriors are not what you think of as warriors.
The warrior is not someone who fights.

Sitting Bull

You may think that this is a very strange statement coming from a famous warrior, a warrior who fought in one of the most famous battles in our country's history, the Battle of Little Big Horn. What does Sitting Bull mean by his statement that the warrior is not someone who fights? It goes without saying that the warrior is someone who certainly has the ability to fight when the occasion calls for it. So what was this warrior trying to say to us?

Basically, what Sitting Bull is saying is that fighting is not the only component or the most important part of being a warrior. He goes on to explain himself, "The warrior, for us, is one who sacrifices himself for the good of others. His task is to take care of the elderly, the defenseless, those who cannot provide for themselves, and above all, the children, the future of humanity."

This is a very good description of the warrior lifestyle. You will find these same characteristics of a warrior throughout history. Of course you find a different definition of what a warrior is in the dictionary, but true warriorship goes much deeper than defining it as only someone experienced in warfare. It involves the character traits which Sitting Bull described. Helping others is a major aspect of the warrior lifestyle. It is part of your duty as a warrior. Street punks fight, but they are not warriors. Dogs and animals fight, but they are not warriors. Being able to fight is only a small part of the path of the warrior. The warrior lifestyle entails much more than fighting.

I am a skilled fighter and I protect and serve those in need.

April 24

We cannot become what we
want by remaining what we are.

Max DePree

Many people want to change their lives, but at the same time, they don't want to step out of their comfort zones to make any real changes happen. They kind of want to have their cake and eat it too, but life doesn't work that way. You can't become someone new if you aren't willing to leave your old habits and old ways of thinking behind.

People like this can see the advantage of changing their lives, but don't want to pay the price to obtain those changes. This is like seeing the advantage of getting a new car that runs well and is dependable, but not being willing to pay for the car. If you aren't willing to pay the price for it, you are not going to have it sitting in your driveway.

Nothing in this life is free. You have to be willing to pay the price for what you want. This goes for everything. Now, you may say that viewing a beautiful sunset if free. But you still pay a price to see it. You have to get off of your couch, go outside, and spend time viewing it. The cost may not be great, but you still have to trade something for the pleasure of seeing this sight.

If you want to make changes in your life, you have to being willing to pay the price, whatever it may be. Different things have different prices, but none of them come for free. One thing is sure – you can't expect to get different results by doing the same thing that you have always done. If you want to become someone different, you have to be willing to step up and change your thoughts, actions, and habits. You have to make it happen!

Every day, in every way, I am becoming stronger and more skilled.

April 25

Muddy water, let stand, becomes clear.
Lao Tzu

Stress, worry, anxiety, and fear can cloud your mind. When these emotions are allowed to take control of your mind, it is hard to see things clearly or make good decisions. Your mind can't focus and will begin to become "muddy" if you will.

It is hard to think rationally when your mind is bombarded with these emotions. Just as a crystal clear lake can become muddy when the sediment at the bottom is disturbed, your mind will become "muddy" when it is disturbed.

So what do you do to clear your mind when it has become cloudy from these emotions? Do the same thing as the lake does to become clear again – nothing. The lake simply waits for the muddy particles to settle back where they belong, and once again the lake becomes crystal clear. You should do the same thing. Quit thinking about the issue at hand. Just put that subject on the shelf for a while. Do something else like meditate, work in the garden, or work out.

It really doesn't matter what you do, as long as you get your mind off of the problem that is causing these emotions to cloud your thinking. Just get away from it and allow the "mud" to settle. When you come back, your mind, like the lake, will have cleared up and you will be able to see things differently.

Once again, you will be able to think rationally and intelligently, the way the warrior should think. The key here is to be patient. Just remember, you can't *make* the mud settle back to the bottom of the lake by pushing it back down; it has to settle on its own, at its own pace.

I maintain a calm mind and think clearly and rationally.

April 26

It is better to be a tiger for one day
than a sheep for a thousand years.

Tibetan Maxim

This is an interesting maxim from Tibet. It is better to be a tiger for one day than a sheep for a thousand years. Most people today are sheep. This is not a derogatory statement, but rather a statement of fact. Sheep go through life pretty much oblivious to what is happening around them. They eat, drink, sleep, and follow their shepherd wherever he desires to lead them. A sheep is a peaceful animal which presents no threat to other animals; it just kind of goes through life on auto-pilot.

The tiger, on the other hand, roams the jungle with confidence and awareness. Tigers have no shepherds to protect them or guide them to food and water. A tiger is a self-sufficient animal capable of not only providing its own food, but of also defending itself against pretty much any threat. Tigers are proficient killing machines when they have to be. Their confidence shows in their unflinching gaze. They set their own law in the jungle.

The Tibetan maxim above tells us that it is better to live like a tiger, even if it is only for a short time, than it is to live many years as a sheep. The warrior has much more in common with the tiger than he does with the sheep. He is confident and independent. He is self-sufficient and fierce. Warriors roam the streets of the jungle knowing that they can handle most anything that comes their way. We are tigers, who are aware of our environment and ready for action. It is better to be a warrior for a year than a sheep for 100 years.

I refuse to be a sheep! I am a warrior!

April 27

*If you are forced into a position in which you must
either hurt or be hurt, be sure to make your
move before someone else does.*

Francesco Guicciardini

In the event of a physical threat or an attack, you cannot afford to wait to make your move. Many times it only takes one punch, one kick, or one slash with a knife to end an attack. If you wait until that punch, kick or slash has occurred, it is could be too late for you to come out of the encounter victoriously. This is where the skill of personal awareness is crucial for the warrior. You have to be able to foresee the attack or threat before it actually materializes.

There should be no "first attack" in karate or in the warrior lifestyle for that matter, but the "first attack" is not necessarily physical. The first attack happens when you realize that someone means you harm. Once you know that someone means you harm, it is time for you to act, whatever that action may be. Your action does not necessarily have to be physical, but you do have to take some kind of action.

Your move will depend on the situation. Whether or not you make the first move will depend on your awareness and willingness to take action when action is required. Don't take the chance that your enemy will not follow through on his threat or his "first attack." Don't wait until it is too late to make your move. When you sense that first attack, respond with the appropriate response, whatever that may be. Different attacks require different responses, but all attacks or threats require some response, and it is always best to make your move first.

I listen to my intuition and know what action to take.

April 28

It's okay to lose to opponent,

must not lose to fear.

Mr. Miyagi

The warrior must control his mind. If you don't control your mind, it can defeat you faster than any opponent that you face. The uncontrolled mind will allow fear and doubt to slither in, disrupting your focus and destroying your self-confidence. If you allow fear to get a foothold in your mind, you have severely hindered your chances of winning.

Don't allow your mind to defeat you. Be mindful of every thought that you have; control and eliminate the thoughts that weaken you – fear, anger, hate, and negative self-talk. Nurture the thoughts that build you up and strengthen you. Replace negative thoughts with mental pep talks and positive affirmations. This is the beginnings of learning to control your mind and your thoughts.

No one can stop random thoughts from popping into his or her mind, but being mindful of the thoughts that you allow to remain in your mind allows you to negate the negative thoughts when they do arise. Replace your negative thoughts with empowering thoughts that will strengthen you.

Control your mind and always think rationally. You must manage your mind just like you manage your body. You don't go around eating whatever you want and expect to have your body function at an optimal level. In the same way, you don't just allow negative thoughts to reside in your mind and expect to maintain a strong spirit. You have to train your mind just like you train your body. Never submit to your fears.

I control my mind and I overcome all fears.

April 29

If it is not right, do not do it;
if it is not true, do not say it.

Marcus Aurelius

In a day and age where most people do and say whatever they consider to be in their own interest, the warrior still lives his or her life by the old ways. If it is not right, he won't do it; if it is not true, he won't say it. The warrior is not moved by what is acceptable to others, but by what is acceptable according to his or her own standards, standards which are based on his keen sense of right and wrong.

In today's world, everyone seems to be struggling to find a way to be different, to stand out from the crowd and be unique. Well, if you want to be different, to be unique, to stand out from the crowd, all you have to do is be a man or woman of honor; you will stand out like a bodybuilder at a ballerina convention.

So few people live a life of honor in today's world that is seems as if honor is an endangered trait. The warrior lives a life of honor, regardless of how anyone else lives. Warriors are not concerned with how everyone else lives their life; he is only concerned with living his life as he should.

Make up your mind that you will do what's right, no matter what anyone else thinks about it. Decide, once and for all, that you will speak the truth, no matter how many people get angry about it because they had rather believe a lie than hear an uncomfortable truth. Make up your mind that you will live by your principles, principles based on right and wrong, no matter what; then live by them. Warrior up!

I always do what's right!

April 30

He who dares not offend,

cannot be honest.

Thomas Paine

Political correctness is a misguided attempt to never offend anyone, over anything. Those people, who try to walk the politically correct line, have a list of words they can't say and things they can't do. They basically stand for nothing at all, because standing firm on anything will undoubtedly offend someone, somewhere. In their minds, there is no absolute right or wrong, only personal perceptions and beliefs.

Warriors see things a little differently. A warrior's concerns are not about whether or not someone gets offended, but about his words or actions. The warrior stands firm concerning his beliefs, and allows others to do the same. He doesn't try to be abrasive or offensive, but if others are offended by his beliefs, or what he holds dear, so be it. He is not going to walk on glass in order to please the delicate sensitivities of those who can't handle the truth.

The warrior refuses to lower his standards because others have lower standards than he or she does. He lives by his own set of standards, independent of how others live or what others believe. He has the courage to speak the truth. He understands that those who are offended by the truth, choose to be offended; they are not strong enough to handle the truth.

Don't allow the weaknesses of others to cause you to think dishonestly. Don't allow those who are offended by the truth, to cause you to quit being honest and truthful. Don't lower your standards for those who refuse to raise their own. Live your life, you way!

I do what's right and let the chips fall where they may.

May 1

Justice is a kind of pact, not to hard or be harmed.
Epicurus

There is a big difference between a pacifist, who is totally anti-violence, and a true warrior who desires peace. A pacifist doesn't believe that violence is ever called for, no matter what the circumstances may be.

The warrior knows that there are times when violence is unfortunately required, and that there absolutely are times when violence is not only justified, but mandatory as a part of his duty. Does this make the warrior a violent person? Absolutely not!

The warrior puts his honor and duty first place, even if it means temporarily leaving his sanctuary of inner peace and tranquility to put his life on the line to protect others. The warrior is selfless when it comes to protecting his loved ones, those who can't defend themselves, and stopping the predators of this world.

The pacifist can get by chanting, "Give Peace a Chance," because the warrior is there to save his butt when the pacifist crosses paths with some predator that has different point of view about violence. If you consider yourself a pacifist, you should thank God for the true warriors that *know* there are times when violence is required and justified to battle the evil in this world.

These are the people who would never do harm to any innocent human being, but will absolutely not take any crap when it comes to protecting their loved ones, the weak, or the defenseless. The do no harm, but take no shit. There is a time for peace, and a time for violence. Know the difference!

I desire peace, but I am prepared for trouble.

May 2

Walk a mile to avoid a fight; but when one starts, don't back down an inch!

The true warrior doesn't like violence. He or she doesn't want to hurt anyone and will, in fact, do everything in his or her power to avoid fighting. The warrior understands anatomy and how easy it is to injure someone else, sometimes permanently or fatally. The warrior has no desire to permanently cripple or injure someone one.

In addition, he has no desire to waste his time dealing with our corrupt legal system which is just as likely to throw him in prison for defending himself, as it is to punish the predator that attacked him. For these reasons, and more, the warrior does everything in his power to avoid a fight.

But there are those out there who never give these things a single thought. These people still have a high school mentality, and many of them, less than a high school education. They are not bright enough to think about these things, much less to understand the philosophical side of the warrior.

They will fight for just about any reason and will fight like a wild animal. They are led by their rage, and because of this, they will hurt or kill someone before they even realize it. That is why we must train and train hard.

Always do your best to avoid a fight, but, if you have no other honorable choice, don't back down an inch. And, if you must fight, WIN! Don't allow your enemy multiple chances to hurt you. If the fight is brought to you, finish it. Make sure that you don't leave your enemy any desire or capability to attack you again. Walk a mile to avoid a fight, but if a fight starts, FINISH IT!

I avoid trouble, but when trouble comes, I AM READY!

May 3

The more you sweat in training,
the less you bleed in battle.
Navy Seal Maxim

Staying in top physical shape is important to the warrior. Many times physical encounters can end up being won by the man who is in the best shape. If the fight ends up going for more than just a few seconds, you had better have good aerobic capacity. It won't matter how skilled your techniques are if you are so out of breath that you can't stand up straight after a 60 second encounter.

Physical fitness is even more important if the fight ends up going to the ground and becoming a grappling contest. This doesn't even take into account the fact that you may have to face multiple attackers. Even professional boxers can become winded after a hard three minute round of one-on-one boxing, and these guys train hard and long. It is imperative that you not only train for good form and useful techniques, but that you also train for endurance. Endurance training will help ensure that you have enough staying power to not lose a contest because of poor aerobic capacity.

You should be cross training. Don't just focus on one area of training. Think balance. Think of your overall goals. What is the overall purpose of your training? What do you want to get out of your training routine? Remember, no matter what you are doing, it is important for you to know why you are doing it. For the warrior, the answer is that you are training hard, so you will bleed less. You are training hard to keep yourself and your loved ones safe in the event that some predator ever targets you or them.

I train hard today and I am victorious tomorrow.

May 4

Do not let your power be seen;
be blank and actionless.

Han Fei Tzu

Don't reveal too much about yourself. Being completely open only benefits others and can actually be used against you. Be a bit of a mystery. People have more respect for someone who they really can't quite figure out. As the old saying goes, familiarity breeds contempt. Once someone knows you well enough, a certain amount of respect or admiration is lost. Be friendly and outgoing, but at the same time maintain a sense of privacy and mystery.

While it is important to preserve that sense of mystery, it is equally important not to appear to be secretive or standoffish around others. Maintain your privacy without appearing overly private. Appearing distrustful and secretive will put others off and cause them to feel and act the same way towards you. The trick is to be able to keep certain parts of your life hidden without allowing others to know that you are being secretive. This takes practice and skill, but it is definitely worth the effort.

Don't let anyone see the full extent of your power or talents. Always keep something in reserve. As I have already said, you don't want to disclose too much information about yourself. Jesus said, "A prophet is not without honor, save in his own country, and in his own house." The reason for this is that familiarity does breed contempt. There is much to be said for preserving some mystery and not displaying all of your power or intelligence. Don't disclose all of your sources. Keep others dependent on you to some extent.

I protect the weak and defenseless.

124

May 5

Make your enemy think that your
normal force is extraordinary, and
your extraordinary is your normal.
Sun Tzu

This is a great quote to meditate on and let the implications sink into your spirit. Part of warfare, whether you are talking about military tactics or the art of self-defense is attacking the mind of your enemy, and this is exactly what Sun Tzu is telling you to do here. This is psychological warfare at its best. If your opponent thinks that your normal force is extraordinary, he wonders, in the back of his mind, just how devastating you will be if you kick it up a notch.

This not only causes him to fear your abilities, but it also causes him to doubt his ability to actually defeat you. Once he starts to doubt himself, or his skills, your enemy is on his way to being defeated. Thomas Cleary translated several ancient samurai writings in his book, *Training the Samurai Mind*, and he tells us that the key to the warrior's heart is maintaining courage. If you get into your enemy's head and start to chip away at his courage, you have an advantage over him.

It is extremely hard for your enemy to maintain his courage when he truly believes that he cannot defeat you. Use psychological warfare to your advantage. Seed your enemy's mind with doubt and fear. Cause him to doubt his own skills, while at the same time seeing you as a stalwart of steel. Make him think that your normal force is extraordinary, and that your best is simply undefeatable. Allow his own doubt to defeat him. Make him think that if he comes against you, it will be the worst mistake that he ever makes.

My strategy defeats the enemy.

May 6

Someone out there is training.

Law Enforcement Maxim

There are many days when you will not feel like training. The opportunities to do something else in place of your training are endless. It's all too easy to think to yourself, "I just don't feel like it today," or "It won't hurt to take today off." The problem is that one day turns into one week, and one week turns into one month, and one month turns into two, etc. We are creatures of habit. Once you start getting into the habit of not training, it is easy to continue on that path.

You have to find ways to continue to keep yourself motivated. One way to stay motivated is to contemplate the fact that somewhere out there, somebody else is training, and training hard and seriously. This guy is not taking the day, week, month, or summer off. He is honing his martial arts skills to perfection.

He is pumping weights and his strength and muscle mass are increasing weekly. He is working on perfecting his martial skills, and not for self-defense, but for less than honorable purposes. You see, he is not training to be a warrior; he is training to perfect his skills as a predator. This guy is a thug; he is the type person that you are training to be able to protect yourself and your family from.

If he continues to train hard, while at the same time you continue to take time off and take your training a bit less serious, the gap between his skills and your skills will widen. This is a dangerous situation for the warrior to be in, because in the event that your paths cross, and your duty requires you to confront this guy, you will lose. Someone out there is training, are you? Stay prepared!

I am always training!

May 7

Protecting yourself is self-defense.
Protecting others is warriorship.
Bohdi Sanders

Many people consider themselves to be warriors just because they have spent time training in a dojo and have learned how to fight. They feel that they can protect themselves against almost any attacker. Having developed their skills to the max, they walk around with the self-confidence of a lion, just waiting for some poor soul to make the mistake of harassing them in a bar or on the street. They feel without a shadow of a doubt that they can protect themselves, but does this really make them a warrior?

Protecting yourself is self-defense by the very definition of the term. Being a warrior means much more than being able to protect yourself. It means developing your character and your spirit. It means being willing and able to protect others as well as yourself. Warriors feel a sense of duty to protect those around them where the ordinary man only feels the need to protect himself and get out of Dodge. There is a big difference in the two.

The warrior is willing to put his well-being on the line for those he loves or for those under his protection. Many times, he puts their well being ahead of his own. He could easily defend himself and leave the danger behind, but he chooses the path of chivalry and warriorship. He knows there is a difference between self-defense and warriorship, and he also knows that the lifestyle that he has chosen demands that he put his warrior ideals over simple self-interest. Protecting yourself is self-defense; protecting others is warriorship.

I perfect the skills of self-defense and warriorship.

May 8

Power of the mind is infinite
while brawn is limited.

Koichi Tohei

Even the biggest, most ripped bodybuilders have their limits as to how much muscle mass they can add to their body. No matter how much you work out or train, there is only so much you can do to perfect yourself physically. This is just the way it is. Although "no limits" is a popular slogan at many gyms, everyone's body has certain limits. The mind, on the other hand, has no limits.

The power of the mind is far beyond anything that anyone has yet to experience. It is said that even the most brilliant men only use approximately 10% of their mind. These are the most intelligent individuals on the planet, and they only use 10% of their minds! This obviously leaves ample room for the development of the mind. When you look at intelligence in this manner, it is plain to see that the power of the human mind is truly infinite.

This is important to the warrior. The warrior has to train his mind, as well as his body. Mental training is just as important as physical training. The best martial arts skills in the world will do you no good if your mind panics during a crucial encounter. Your mind should be the first weapon used in any encounter, and the sharpest weapon in your arsenal.

Don't get so caught up in your physical training that you neglect your mental training. Everything that you do has a mental component to it. Neglecting to train your mind, as well as your body, is unbalanced training. Think balance. Train your mind and your body.

I train my mind to be sharp, strong, and alert.

May 9

*One must transcend techniques so
that the art becomes an artless art,
growing out of the unconscious.*

Daisetsu Suzuki

Today it seems that many so-called martial artists get "bored" with their training because they find that they have to do the same kicks, punches, katas, etcetera, over and over again. The attention span of people today is much shorter than in times past. Our lifestyle today has changed to the point that our news comes in short 10-20 second spurts. Even our educational systems have changed to accommodate the short attention span of today's students.

This is not how the warrior should train. It takes thousands of repetitions to perfect your techniques. You must pay attention to every detail of your kicks, punches, throws, stances, and movements. In order to internalize the elements of each technique, you must practice them over and over. There are no short cuts. You must perform them time and time again for them to become a part of you. When your back is against the wall, your techniques must be an integral part of your unconsciousness in order for them to be effective.

You will not have time to stop and think about what to do or how to do it; it has to come naturally and automatically. When you get to this point, you will find that your techniques flow without any conscious thought on your part. Your mind will transcend your technique. You will be in mushin. Mushin is a mental state where your body goes on auto-pilot. You simply respond as you should. This state can only come from practice and experience. Transcend the mind; enter mushin.

I internalize my art. It is a part of me.

May 10

A warrior's heart is like a sword;

it must be cleaned daily.

Billy Shearer

Perfecting your character takes a lot of effort. It is not a goal that you accomplish and then you can relax because you have "made it." Developing your character is an ongoing process which never ends. There will always be something or someone who will try to throw a monkey wrench into your peaceful existence. Controlling your thoughts and your emotions takes work, but the more that you practice these skills, the easier they will become.

The art of self-control is like every other endeavor; you will have good days and bad days in your quest to perfect this skill. Nobody is perfect, especially when it comes to controlling thoughts and emotions. There will be days when you fall short of your goal. I can assure you that you will have days in which you allow your anger or impatience to get the best of you, just as you will have days when your back kick does not click for whatever reason, but it is important that you don't quit.

When you find that you are having a bad day with your physical training, you don't say this is not working and never go back to the dojo. The same goes for your mental training. When you have a bad day, go home and relax, meditate, and cleanse your heart and mind. Get things back in balance and know that every day you start with a clean slate. Once you actually get your heart clean, it is much easier to keep it clean. If you find the same things continue to throw you off balance time after time, go to the source and remove the root of your of your problem. Think about this.

I take time each day to cleanse my heart and mind.

May 11

One must make the warrior

walk his everyday walk.

Miyamoto Musashi

Being a warrior is a huge responsibility. Walking the path of the warrior is not something that you can decide to do for a couple of months then take a few days off and come back to it later. To be a true warrior, you have to commit to this lifestyle. The warrior is a warrior, period. He doesn't pretend to be a warrior, he doesn't try to be a warrior, he doesn't want to be a warrior; he *is* a warrior. Therefore, the warrior walk must be his everyday walk, there is no other way.

This does not mean that a warrior has to be in training every minute of every day. In today's world this is impossible for most people. What this does mean is that every day the warrior is living up to the ideals that a warrior should live by, whether he is at work, on vacation, or just relaxing at home. The warrior makes these ideals a permanent part of his character, daily. He lives by his code of honor.

His code of honor dictates his every action. It is his moral compass which points, not north, but towards what is right and just. No two warrior codes are completely alike. The Native Americans say that each man must find his own path, and the same thing applies to the warrior.

Each warrior has to determine his own code of honor, but one thing is certain, there is no such thing as the "weekend warrior." The term, "weekend warrior," basically means, "wanna-be warrior." You live this lifestyle 24/7. It is not something that you can set aside until you need it, like your coat. Make the warrior path your only path.

I walk the path of the warrior every day.

May 12

Do not be tricked into thinking that there are
no crocodiles just because the water is still.
Malaysian Proverb

The majority of people today live a fairly peaceful life. Most of us do not have to defend our lives weekly, monthly, or even yearly. With the exception of law enforcement officers and military men and women, most of us do not have to deal with dangerous criminals or life threatening situations on a daily basis.

As a matter of fact, the vast majority of people today will live their entire life without ever encountering a kill-or-be-killed situation. This being the case, you may ask why you should train to be a warrior when the odds are that you will never have to use the skills that you are working so hard to perfect.

The answer is found in the Malaysian proverb above. If you have ever watched one of the wildlife shows on television, you have probably seen how crocodiles attack. An unsuspecting animal, going about his business, stops at a peaceful waterhole for a drink, and out of nowhere the crocodile explodes from the water and ambushes the unsuspecting animal, taking his life.

Don't become complacent with your life or your training. Just because your life seems to be normal and peaceful, doesn't mean that the bad guys aren't out there. Don't make the mistake of believing that "those kinds of things never happen to me." The very minute you let your guard down, is the opportunity that the crocodile has been waiting for all day. Consider the fact that no one who has ever been murdered actually thought that, "This kind of thing *will* happen to me."

I stay alert to possible dangers.

May 13

He is victorious who knows
when and when not to fight.

Sun Tzu

In Sun Tzu's famous book, *The Art of War*, he makes it clear that it is not always time to fight. You must pick your battles with special care. Granted, sometimes you are faced with a situation that leaves you no other options except for defending yourself on the spot, but these circumstances are few and far between.

You have to listen to your spirit and allow your inner voice to guide you. There are no hard and fast rules about when to fight and when not to fight, but it is always wise to only resort to physical action when all other honorable options have been exhausted.

When all other options have been tried and have failed, you still have to know when and when not to strike. Timing can be the difference in victory and defeat. Again, you have to listen to your spirit in order to know when to strike. Opportunities are rare and you must take advantage of them quickly when they arise. When you know in your spirit that it is time to act, don't delay.

If it doesn't feel right inside, it is not right. Remember, sometimes it is necessary to retreat and regroup before you engage. Use common sense in every situation.

Don't allow your emotions to dictate your actions. Let your spirit and your intellect show you when and when not to fight. Your spirit will not steer you wrong if you learn to listen to it closely. Start thinking rationally, not emotionally.

I perfect my de-escalation skills and I win without fighting.

May 14

Don't trouble a quiet snake.
Greek Proverb

Never go looking for trouble. Do your best to live a peaceful life. You will run across a lot of bad guys in your journey through life, but that doesn't mean that you have to confront all of them. It is best to keep your distance from them.

Don't associate with them. You can pretty much tell which guys are out looking for trouble instead of looking to have a good time. Avoid them! This is not being a coward or a wimp; it is being smart.

Some guys are just plain dangerous, like a poisonous snake. Sure, if you see a poisonous snake lying coiled on a rock while you are out hiking, you could probably kill it with a stick. But why bother, when it is much easier and safer to avoid it.

If you don't confront the snake, there is no chance that you will suffer a deadly bite, and you can both go about your own business. You never know how deadly or how aggressive that snake really is, and it is best not to find out if you don't have to.

The same principle applies to ruffians and street punks. If you are aware, you can pick them out of the crowd. Don't encounter them if you don't have to. Let them go their way and you go your way. It is not necessary to find out how dangerous they may be.

Those who play with snakes, even if they are professional herpetologists, many times end up with life-threatening bites. Most times a quiet snake will go his own way, in peace, if it is not challenged. Don't tempt fate; don't trouble a quiet snake. Never go looking for trouble, but always be ready for trouble.

I don't go looking for trouble and trouble rarely finds me.

May 15

In cases of defense tis best to weigh
the enemy more mighty than he seems.
William Shakespeare

Never underestimate your enemy. You really never know just how dangerous or how vicious someone else actually is, and it is always a mistake to see an enemy as no "real" threat. With the weapons available in today's society, there is no enemy that should be taken for granted. Every enemy should be seen as a threat, even if that enemy seems weak and vulnerable.

Your enemy has multiple ways of attacking you in today's world, and the enemies that you may consider weak, will not "play fair." They know inside that they cannot stand up to you man to man. These people are cowardly and underhanded. They do not have the courage to work out their problem with you face-to-face; it is much more likely that they will attack you behind your back.

Expect the unexpected. Expect your enemy to be dishonorable and to fight dirty. If you do not underestimate your enemy, you will not allow yourself to become lax in your defense. Don't give your enemies an opening because of your overconfidence.

Overconfidence can be a deadly mistake. Even if you consider your enemy to be weak, watch him like he is mighty. In all honesty, you never really know for sure what someone else is capable of, or the extent of his skills. Many martial arts masters do not look like much of a physical threat, but looks can be deceptive. Don't underestimate any enemy. It is much better to be safe than sorry. Think about this.

I train to defeat the biggest and baddest.

May 16

If an art is concealed, it succeeds.

Ovid

Many of the masters tell us not to reveal too much about our abilities. It is smarter if you keep your personal information, your skills, and your knowledge hidden. Don't reveal everything about yourself. Avoid the temptation to "brag" about how talented you are, how you won the last tournament, what a great roundhouse kick you have, etc.

You really don't want everyone to know your strengths and weaknesses. This gives your enemies information to use against you and tells them how to prepare to counter your skills if they ever have to encounter you physically. Never give your enemy knowledge or information that you don't have to. Silence is the best policy when it comes to your enemies.

Now I'm not saying that you can never have conversations about your martial arts, but you should be careful about whom you include in those conversations. Even if you are talking with your close friends, don't reveal everything. You should always keep in mind that today's friends could become tomorrow's enemies, and if they do they will not hesitate to use whatever information that they have filed away against you.

Be smart and play your cards close to your vest. Be even smarter still, and do so without revealing that this is what you are doing. No friend or acquaintance likes to feel as though you don't completely trust him. Consider your actions carefully in order to conceal what needs to be concealed, and at the same time develop relationships with others. The trick is to think before you speak.

I refuse to brag or boast. I keep my skills hidden.

May 17

When irate, clear-minded men never
show it then and there. Holding it in,
they watch for an opportune moment.
Tiruvalluvar

Stay in control of your emotions. Just because you get angry about something, even very angry, that doesn't mean that you need to let everyone know about it. You cannot allow your emotions to control your actions. You have to control both your emotions and your actions. It is a common ploy in battle to try and make someone angry in order to cause him to make a mistake or trap him into doing or saying something stupid. The wise warrior will realize this, control his anger, and make a careful decision about when, or if, to let that anger show, as well as the proper way to express his anger at that time.

Anger can and will confuse your mind if you let it. Instead of focusing on the anger, focus on the situation and what is actually happening. Stay clear-minded and calm, and make a conscious decision concerning the situation and how you should deal with it. There is a time to let your anger out; just make sure that *you*, not your temper, decide when that time will be.

Many people will try to push your buttons purely for entertainment purposes. See their obnoxious attempts to cause you to stumble as nothing more than one more challenge for you on your path to warriorship. Don't let them win. Act as if their rudeness has no effect on you at all. Practice your wit and self-control. When you look at this type of ploy as just part of the game, your anger will be easier to control.

I refuse to lose my temper. I am always in control.

May 18

The man of true valor lies between the
extremes of cowardice and of rashness.
Miguel de Cervantes

The warrior is neither a coward nor a fool. He is a man of character who evaluates each situation and then takes the appropriate action. If, after careful thought, he decides to engage in battle, it is because he has made a mental decision that he has no other choice. He has weighed his options and made a firm decision that he will then follow through, to the end. His action comes from a place of mental clarity. It is not a rash action, but a calm, rational decision.

Moreover, if he decides that it is not wise to engage in battle at this time, he makes his exit with as much honor as possible. This is not an act of cowardice. His action is not based on fear. It is an act rooted in inner wisdom. He listens to his spirit and follows his inner voice. Although deep inside he would like to engage in this battle and put things right, he realizes that now is not the time and waits for a more opportune moment.

At other times, he simply takes pity on the other person, walks away, and forgets about it, knowing what he could have done had he chosen to take action. Although to others this may seem like an act of cowardice, it is actually an act of honor. The warrior refuses to harm another person if there is any other way out of the predicament. Walking away from an encounter without fighting, no matter how others may perceive it, is a valid and honorable way to end an encounter. Only get physical when all other options have been exhausted.

I chose my actions; they do not choose me.

May 19

Never walk away from home ahead of your axe and sword.
You can't feel a battle in your bones or foresee a fight.
The Havamal

You really never know when you will have to defend yourself, especially when you are away from home. The Viking book of wisdom, *The Havamal*, tells us that you should never leave your axe and sword behind when you leave the security of your home.

This means that you shouldn't leave home without being prepared to defend yourself. No one can foretell if they will be attacked or mugged when they are out and about. You have to be ready.

The way things seem to go, most people aren't attacked on the street when they are feeling pumped up and ready for anything that may happen. It seems that most attacks happen when people are least expecting something to happen or when they are sick and tired and don't feel like dealing with problems. You just never know. This is why you have to be aware and be prepared at all times, not just when you feel powerful and ready for some punk to cross your path.

Always be aware. Don't let your guard down. Don't get in such a hurry running around trying to complete your "to do" list that you become oblivious to everything around you.

It is easy to allow your mind to become preoccupied when you are busy or when you have a ton of things to get done. Being aware and observant can save you much more time in the long run than all the rushing from place to place. A few minutes of your time is a small price to pay for your safety and security.

I am always prepared!

May 20

In seeking to save another,
beware of drowning yourself.

Sir Francis Osborne

As a warrior, it is your duty to protect those weaker than you and to help those who you have the power to help. Wherever you go, whatever you do, those around you should be safer because you are there.

You have been given special training that should enable you to step into the role of "protector" at a moment's notice. You have taken the lifestyle of the warrior seriously and therefore you should take this sacred duty seriously. But there is a difference in protecting others, and being rash and placing yourself in danger.

It is your duty to serve and protect others. It is not your duty to sacrifice your life. Your life is as important as anyone else's life. Your duty is to do what you can to save the drowning person, not to switch places with him.

If you have a family to protect and to provide for, you have a higher duty to them than to others. You must make sure that you are safe in order to fulfill your filial duty. Therefore you must do your duty, but do it wisely and rationally.

Although the warrior must be willing to risk his life at times, it is never to be done rashly. Situations do exist in which every warrior must be willing to risk his life, but these times are rare. Don't think that it is a great honor to lose your life for a cause. Think of fulfilling your duty. How can you serve and protect your family and friends if you are no longer around? Think rationally. Be smart.

I am always careful and aware.

May 21

One who is good at battle does not get angry.

Lao Tzu

You don't have to get angry in order to get your adrenaline pumping in a confrontation. In fact, if you find yourself in a physical confrontation, getting angry will actually hinder your performance. Anger causes your mind to become confused and to think less clearly. It causes your actions to be controlled by your emotions rather than your rational mind. Letting your emotions control your actions is always a dangerous proposition.

Instead of getting angry in these situations, you should go into mushin. Mushin literally means "mind, no mind." This simply means that you are acting without consciously thinking about what you are doing. You are allowing your subconscious mind to take control, not your anger. This is why you perform the same techniques and the same fight scenarios over and over again in the dojo. This anchors the techniques into your subconscious mind so that you can perform them without thinking, when you need them.

Mushin is much like driving a car. When you first started driving, you had to concentrate on every part of the driving process. You had to consciously think to yourself to turn on the turn signal and to start slowing down, but after several years of driving, simple things like turning your turn signal on, or slowing down when you come to a turn, come naturally. You don't have to consciously think to yourself, "Now I need to start slowing down." You just do it naturally, without thinking about it. This is the mind in mushin. You can perform actions without your mind actually telling you what to do because you have performed them so many times that they are now automatic.

I control my anger; it does not control me.

May 22

Abandoning the ego is
the secret of right living.

Taisen Deshimaru

The warrior can't afford to allow his ego to get in the way of his goals and his responsibilities. There are a lot of people in the martial arts who are driven solely by their egos. These people are not true warriors. Their pride drives most of their actions.

The warrior never fights for issues which are based on ego. Ego is one's exaggerated sense of his own self-importance. It is a feeling of superiority when compared to other people. Ego has nothing to do with honor; the ego has to do with pride. Allowing pride to dictate your actions is hardly ever wise.

Warriors should not allow feelings of self-importance, superiority, or pride to control their emotions. It is your duty, as a warrior, to help the weak and the needy, not to look down on them and to feel that you are above them. Abandon feelings of self-importance and concentrate on your character and your duty as a warrior. No one respects an egotistical person, no matter how much character or integrity he has. Nobody likes to feel inferior. This is important to remember.

True, the warrior should be superior to others in many ways: character, integrity, honor, skills, etc., but you must control the feeling that you actually *are* superior. Don't think about how you compare to others as far as these traits go. Simply do the best that you can do to perfect your own character and to live right, and leave others to be responsible for their own character. Abandon your ego and develop your character.

I train for skills, not for my ego.

May 23

Remember how lucky you are to live in a time of
peace and plenty, but prepare for worse times.
Code of the Samurai

Most of us live a peaceful life. In our society today, unless you are in the military or work in law enforcement, you most likely live in peace and plenty. Even those in our country who are on the bottom of the economic pecking order live a life of plenty when compared to people in many third world countries. We live in a time of peace and abundance in the United States today, but there is no guarantee that things will always remain as they are today. You never know what will happen tomorrow; you must be prepared.

The *Code of the Samurai* points this out to us. The samurai saw both times of peace and prosperity and times of war which ravished their country. They knew from experience that things can change, and change quickly. Times of peace and plenty can turn into times of chaos and anarchy in the blink of an eye. It is wise to be prepared for the possibility of a time when things will not be so peaceful and when prosperity turns to scarcity.

You lose nothing by preparing for bad times during the good times. When things are good and you are surrounded by blessings, it is time to think of defending yourself against the change of tide. Be disciplined enough to save some of your wealth for a rainy day. Keep yourself physically fit and your martial arts skills sharp. Be wise enough to realize that nothing lasts forever, good or bad. Enjoy the good times while they last, but at the same time prepare for the bad times just in case your fortune changes.

I prepare for war that I may live in peace.

May 24

Try not! Do, or do not.
There is no try.
Yoda

Okay, you may think it is kind of strange that I would include a quote from a fictional character in *BUSHIDO*, but this quote actually contains a lot of wisdom for the warrior. When someone asks you if you are going to do something and you respond with, "I'll try" that is nothing more a than flimsy way to put the other person off. The warrior is not afraid of commitment. He knows whether or not he is willing to complete a task or not. Don't say you will try. Either say that you will do it or say that you won't do it.

As our little green friend stated, there is no try, you either do it or you don't do it. Don't be afraid to make firm decisions. If someone asks you to do something, and you know that you are not planning on doing it, don't say "I'll try" in an attempt to put them off. Be honest enough to say, "I would like to, but I just don't have the time now, so I can't commit to it." You will find that most people will appreciate your honesty.

Saying, "I'll try to do it," is just a way to avoid commitment. This should especially be avoided on the path of the warrior. You don't try to live a life of honor and integrity; you live a life of honor and integrity. You don't try to make time for your training; you make time for your training. You don't try to be prepared to defend your family and friends; you do defend your family and friends. You don't try to live the lifestyle of the warrior; you live the lifestyle of the warrior. Make a decision and then follow through with it. Try not! Do, or do not.

I don't try; I do. I refuse to fail.

May 25

By keeping your weapons in order,
your enemy will be subjugated.

Nagarjuna

Nagarjuna tells us that if we keep our weapons in order, our enemies will be controlled. As a modern warrior, you do not walk around carrying weapons, unless you have a specific job that requires that you do so, such as a police officer or a soldier, or you have a concealed weapons license.

The main weapons of today's warrior are his martial arts skill and his wit. You must keep your weapons in order. This means that you must continue to train, and train seriously. Your weapons will do you no good if they aren't ready for you to use when you need them. When the time comes that you need your weapons, they must be ready.

If your weapons are not kept up, they will deteriorate. You must maintain your weapons and make sure that they are in good working order when and if you ever need to use them. You cannot just obtain a good weapon, learn to use it, put it on a shelf for 10 years and expect to reach for it and use it like an expert when you need it.

Keep your weapons in order. It is a continual process to keep your martial arts skills sharp. Don't get lazy. Don't leave your weapons on the shelf to deteriorate and become useless. You may have once been a great marksman, but if you haven't touched your pistol in 15 years, your marksmanship will not be as sharp as it once was. The same principle applies to your martial arts, as it does with everything else in your life – use it or lose it.

I keep my weapons in order. They are always ready.

May 26

Let us not look back in anger,
nor forward in fear, but
around us in awareness.

James Thurber

Both anger and fear cloud your judgment and prevent you from making good decisions. These are two emotions that the warrior must learn to conquer and control. You must not let these emotions affect your thought process. Besides these two negative emotions, there are two other things that can negatively affect the mind of the warrior as well: dwelling on the past or the future. The warrior should not waste his energy with either of these.

You cannot live in the past or in the future; you can only live in the present. Being angry about something that happened in the past, or worrying about something that may happen in the future, is a waste of your time and energy. These are both things that you can do nothing about. What you can do is be aware of what needs to be done in this present moment. This moment is where your power lies. Live in the moment. Focus on where you are and deal with circumstances as they are at this present moment.

Dwelling on the past and dreading the future both have a strong connection to anger and fear. Many times thoughts of the past are accompanied by anger. This anger can be directed towards what someone else has done or it can have to do with something that you have done. Either way it is not constructive, just as fearing what may happen in the future is not constructive. Discipline yourself to live in the present moment with peace and awareness.

I am free of anger and fear.

May 27

Style does not matter,
what works is what is important.
Mitsusuke Harada

When it comes to defending yourself on the street, style doesn't matter. You use anything and everything that you can in order to assure, first that you are safe, then that the threat is completely neutralized. There is no such thing as "fair" or "unfair" when you find yourself in a life-or-death situation. This is a hard concept for some people to grasp.

You hear some guys saying things such as, "I would never throw sand in someone's eyes during a fight, that's not fair." or "That guy hit Jack with a brick, that's fighting dirty!" Actually, fighting dirty only applies to sporting events, not to actual self-defense. There is no such thing as fighting honorable; there is only victory or defeat.

If someone is about to attack you with the intent of doing some major damage to your person, and there is a brick lying by your foot, you are being foolish not to pick up the brick and use it. I can't emphasize this enough. In an actual fight, you use everything available to ensure your safety and the safety of those around you!

This has nothing to do with being dishonorable or taking cheap shots. Considering that the warrior will not engage in a fight unless all other options have failed, the fight must be a necessity. You have already acted honorably by trying everything in your power to avoid a physical confrontation. Once this point is reached, the only "rules" are to protect yourself and to destroy your enemy – by any means necessary.

I use whatever works.

May 28

The warrior is not led by others; but
by remaining true to his convictions.

F. J. Chu

As a warrior, it is up to you to decide what you stand for and what your standards will be. You cannot be led or misled by the winds of public opinion. Don't be like some politician who doesn't really have any true convictions, but rather waits until he sees how the public feels, and then sides with the majority. Throughout history, the sages have told us that the majority of people are not people of integrity and honor; you should never be influenced by people who do not live their life with honor.

Be independent of the opinions of others. Don't be easily influenced by what they say or what they believe. You have to take the time to meditate on what you know is right and wrong. Know what your code of ethics is and do not allow the arguments of others to cause you to doubt what you know is right. You must remain true to your convictions, even if everyone else disagrees with you. This takes courage and confidence in your beliefs.

This is part of the warrior lifestyle. You have to know what you believe and why you believe it. You have to know why you are living this lifestyle and what sets you, as a warrior, apart from everyone else. Your convictions are a major part of what makes you different. If you allow others to sway your convictions, what makes you any different than them? It takes courage to live up to your convictions, and courage is one of the character traits which sets the warrior apart from lesser men. Have courage and stay true to your convictions.

I stay true to my convictions.

May 29

Never get angry except on purpose.

Japanese Maxim

No one can *make* you angry. You choose your own emotions. You choose how you will react to each and every situation. Whenever you allow someone or some situation to anger you, without purposely making the decision that it is now time to be angry, you have allowed that person or thing to have power over you. You have given your own power away by not controlling when you will get angry and how you will display your anger.

A warrior must stay in complete control of his emotions. Don't give control of your emotions over to anyone or anything outside yourself. This is part of your training as a warrior; you must learn to control your mind and your emotions. If you allow someone else to control you by manipulating your emotional state, you are giving your power over to them.

A warrior who is not in control of his emotions is a loose cannon. He is a danger to himself and to others. If he allows outside influences to cause him to lose his temper, it is only a matter of time before this character flaw will cause him heartbreak and pain. Trouble always follows the man who doesn't have self-control.

This is not to say that the warrior should never get angry. There is a time and place for the righteous anger of the warrior. The point here is that the warrior himself must purposely decide when it is time to be angry, and exactly how that anger should be expressed. This is a conscious decision that the warrior makes, not an unconscious, immediate reaction. Stay in total control of your mind and emotions.

I only get angry on purpose. I am in control, not my anger.

May 30

When the victory is yours,
tighten your helmet cords.

Japanese Proverb

We have all seen the movies where the hero has "defeated" the villain at the end of the movie, and just when we think the movie is over, the villain who we thought was defeated, attacks the hero one last time. This happens because the hero *thought* the victory was his and that the fight was over.

As he lets down his guard and walks away, he finds out the hard way that he has declared victory too soon, and that he had not finished the job. Usually, the hero comes out of this victoriously in the end, but real life is not like the movies.

Don't quit before the job is finished. When you can see that the victory is yours, do not relax until the battle is over – completely. Too many times, people have victory in their hands only to let it slip away because they stop a little too soon. The fire is not out until the last glowing embers have been completely cooled and buried. The battle is not finished until it is over and the enemy is wholly and entirely defeated.

Declaring victory before the battle is 100% finished is a sign of underestimating your enemy. Any time you underestimate your enemy's ability to hurt you, you are taking a great risk. Never underestimate your enemy – any enemy! Make sure the battle is over before you declare victory. Don't let your victory slip away because of your overconfidence.

I continue to fight until my enemy is completely defeated.

May 31

There are people in every era who, however
adverse the environment, are not corrupted,
and do not become degenerate.

Masaaki Hatsumi

Today we hear many people blaming the crime rate on poverty. We are told, "It is not the fault of the individual that he committed the crime; it has to do with the extreme poverty that he has had to endure." Well, if this were true, everyone who has had to live in that adverse environment would be committing crimes. But, as we know, everyone who lives in an environment wrought by poverty does not commit crimes. Crime has more to do with individual standards than poverty.

The honor of a true warrior is not situational. By this I mean that you cannot decide to disregard your honor because of your environment. You either have honor or you do not have honor. A man of honor will not set his honor aside when the going gets tough. His honor is not corrupted because the times are rough now. Honor is a permanent part of his being and he will not allow it to become tarnished, no matter how difficult the times have become.

True honor does not degenerate, no matter how adverse the environment. Honor is independent of outside influences. The warrior is the only person who can tarnish his own honor. He is in total control where his honor is concerned. Blaming dishonorable actions on one's personal environment is nothing more than a flimsy excuse which doesn't hold up to those who truly understand the way of the warrior. You are the only person who is responsible for your actions; don't try to justify your behavior by blaming something or someone else.

I am completely responsible for my actions.

June 1

Discipline, not desire,
determines your destiny.
Bud Malmstrom

You can want something very badly, but that doesn't mean that you will achieve it. It takes more than desire to achieve your goals; it takes desire and discipline. Desire by itself is little more than wishing, and wishing for something will get you nowhere. Sitting around and daydreaming about becoming a black belt will not earn you either the skills of a practicing black belt or the rank of black belt. You have to take action to get what you want.

This is where discipline comes into play. You have to have discipline to achieve your goals. Without discipline, your actions will be sporadic and inconsistent. It takes discipline to live the lifestyle of the warrior. It takes discipline to achieve any goal that is worth achieving, and the goals that you achieve or fail to achieve, determine your destiny. Desiring something without disciplining yourself to attain it is like wanting money but refusing to go to work.

You have to work for what you want in this life. If you want a black belt, you have to have the discipline to work for that black belt several days a week, almost every week for several years. You have to put in the effort. This takes discipline.

If you want to walk the path of the warrior, you have to discipline yourself to develop the character traits of the warrior. You have to discipline yourself to live by a stricter code of honor than the average man on the street. It takes discipline, not simply desire.

I discipline myself to achieve what I desire.

June 2

I have seen the best karate.
All that really matters is what
kind of human being you are.

Masami Tsuruoka

This quote is very interesting. At first you may think, "This guy is probably someone who couldn't hack the martial arts training, so he has decided that all that really matters is what kind of human being you are." But this is not the case. Masami Tsuruoka is actually a martial arts master. He has taught hundreds of students and has dedicated his life to the martial arts.

Masami Tsuruoka is not alone in his philosophy of the martial arts. Many of the older martial arts masters have made similar statements. He is not saying that it is not important to train in martial arts, but rather that character training is the most important part of your training, especially if you are interested in living the warrior lifestyle. What matters in everyday life is what kind of human being you are.

You will have many more opportunities to use your character training than you will to use your martial arts training. In fact, you will find that you use your character training on a daily basis. Think about how many decisions you make each day. What determines which choices you make? If you are on the path of the warrior, the answer is your honor, character and integrity. What kind of human being are you? What kind of human being will you be tomorrow? This is really what the warrior lifestyle is all about – perfecting your character and becoming the person that you should be.

I train my character to be a superior human being.

June 3

The path of the warrior is lifelong, and
mastery is often simply staying on the path.
Richard Strozzi Heckler

The warrior lifestyle is a journey, not a destination. It is a lifelong approach to living your life, day by day, by the standards and code of ethics that you have set for yourself. To stay on this path you have to follow certain directions, just as you would follow a road map or signs to make sure that you remain on the right highway. You can't just aimlessly go through life with no direction.

Character training is the road map to the path of the warrior. You must study the qualities that make up the character of the warrior. Meditate on these character traits until they become a part of your spirit; until they become who you truly are deep inside. No one is born with all of the character traits which make the warrior an extraordinary man. These traits have to be developed through study, training, meditation, and learning from your mistakes.

Yes, the warrior makes mistakes. No one is perfect. The difference in the ordinary man and the warrior is when the warrior makes a mistake he learns from his error and makes the necessary changes that will help him make better decisions next time. He is constantly trying to improve his character. His mistakes do not mean defeat unless he allows them to cause him to give up the path of the warrior.

Mastery will come if you simply stay on the path and continue to learn and improve your character every day. Don't get frustrated with the apparent lack of progress in your journey. Remember, this is a journey, not a destination.

I stay on the path of the warrior and I come closer to mastery daily.

June 4

Never imagine that you are safe after
you deal a blow to your opponent.
Yagyu Tajimanokami Menenori

The warrior knows that fighting is a serious business and should never be entered into lightly. You should always do everything in your power to avoid a physical encounter. It is much better to avoid danger or to defeat your enemy without actually having to result to violence if at all possible. Never use your martial arts expertise unless you have no other recourse.

This said, when you do have to resort to violence, to defend yourself or someone else, don't play around. Don't assume that if you punch a threatening street thug in the nose, he has learned his lesson and will then straighten up, shake hands, and change his attitude. He won't!

In the movie *The Karate Kid*, Daniel, the character played by Ralph Machio, has an encounter on the beach, at the beginning of the movie, with another kid. This kid punched Daniel in the stomach, then Daniel punched him in the face and said, "Okay, now we are even," as he offered to shake his hand. The other kid proceeded to thoroughly thrash Daniel.

The point here is that if the situation is important enough to resort to using your martial arts skills, it is serious enough to do some major damage before you consider the matter settled. If it is not serious enough to dish out a hard core pounding, then you are in the wrong if you decide to use your martial arts training in this instance. Insight and discernment have to be your guide.

When I have to fight, I win!

June 5

The wise live among people, but are
indifferent to their praise or blame.

Chuang Tzu

People are fickle. They will sing your praises one day, and they will turn on you like a pack of wolves the next day. Throughout history, people have shown this same erratic behavior, and sages have always taught us, just as Chuang Tzu taught, to be indifferent to the praise or blame of the masses. Let their praise and blame roll off of your back just as rain beads up and rolls off of a newly waxed car.

This advice sounds easy enough to do. After all, it doesn't take much effort to ignore what other people say, right? Well, this is another piece of wisdom that is easier said than done. It is very enjoyable and ego-boosting to have people praising your work and patting you on the back. It is a very pleasurable experience for people to tell you how great you are or how smart you are.

Likewise, it is a very uncomfortable feeling to have people attacking you and blaming you for this or that. It can be very stressful to have people harass you verbally. Being indifferent to the public's opinions, either positive or negative, is something which has to be learned and perfected. It doesn't come naturally.

Just remember that the same people who cheer for you today, would cheer just as loudly if you were about to be hanged. Don't seek the approval of the public. Seek the approval of men of wisdom and honor. These are men whose opinions actually have substance. Above all, seek to live according to your own principles.

I am above praise or blame.

June 6

Hide your purpose.
Baltasar Gracian

Baltasar Gracian is one of my favorite authors. His writing contains an abundance of worldly wisdom. Here he tells you to "hide your purpose." Don't confuse this with being dishonest. He is not talking about lying here, but rather he is writing about not disclosing too much information. It is much easier for your enemies to prepare to disrupt your plans, your tactics, and your strategies if you make clear to them what you are thinking.

Many people constantly talk and disclose personal information which they should keep private. Your speech can cause many problems for you, especially when you are not careful concerning what you are saying and who you are speaking to. Your enemies will always welcome conversation with you if they know that you are careless with your speech. Disclosing personal information is rarely to your advantage.

It is much wiser to keep your personal information to yourself. Don't reveal your purpose to just anyone. You never know who they will talk to later, your friend has a friend, and your friend's friend has a friend. Think before you speak.

Think about why you feel the need to discuss your plans or your strategies with someone else. If it is to obtain wisdom from a wise friend, that is one thing; if it is because you feel the need to make conversation, that is another thing altogether. Be careful about who you share your purpose with, and always think about all the possible consequences.

I hide my purpose and my plans succeed.

June 7

Courtesy should be apparent
in all our actions and words
and in all aspects of daily life.

Masutatsu Oyama

Courtesy is a character trait which all warriors should practice. Too many "warriors" seem to only be concerned with manners and courtesy when they are in the dojo or around what they consider to be important people. Courtesy should not be a characteristic that we display only on special occasions. It should be a normal part of the warrior's daily life.

Masutatsu Oyama tells us that it should permeate all aspects of our daily life, from our actions to our words. Courtesy should be so much a part of your life that if someone were asked to describe you, one of the first things that they would say would be that you are extremely courteous and kind. Winston Churchill went as far as to say, "When you have to kill a man, it costs nothing to be polite."

Be courteous and polite to everyone regardless of how they act. These traits should be common practice for the warrior. Of course, there will be times when you may have to temporarily bend this rule to get your point across, but this should definitely be the exception to the rule for someone on the warrior path. Be nice.

Be nice until it is time to not be nice. The thing that the warrior has to realize is that even when it is time to "not to be nice," he must still maintain his own standards. Using manners is part of who you are, and you don't change who you are because of the circumstances.

I am always courteous.

June 8

When the enemy presents an opportunity,
speedily take advantage of it.

Sun Tzu

Everyone makes mistakes. It doesn't matter who you are or what you are doing, you will make a mistake at some point. This is a key point to remember when it comes to any physical encounter. At some point in any encounter, your attacker will make a mistake. You just have to be patient and ready to take advantage of the mistake when it happens.

Don't panic and rush into action. Be patient. Remember, the first rule of self-defense is to make sure that you are safe, not to beat your opponent. Keep yourself safe until the opening presents itself, and then you launch your attack. Don't delay. The window of opportunity will only be open for a split second. If you delay you will miss your chance, and there may not be another opening.

Speed is of utmost importance. If you don't act fast when you get an opening, you allow your attacker to recover from his mistake and regroup. Don't let him off the hook. When he screws up, make it a costly mistake; make it a mistake that is impossible to recover from because you had the insight to capitalize on his error.

Sun Tzu also tells us that opportunities multiply as they are seized. Basically, once the attacker starts to make mistakes, if you take advantage of his mistakes, he will start to fall apart. When this happens, destroy him as he continues to slip up. This is the art of self-defense. There is no such thing as "fighting dirty" when you are in a real fight. Think about this.

I fight to win. I never waste an opportunity.

June 9

Think, feel, and act like a warrior.
Set yourself apart from the rest of
society by your personal excellence.
Forrest E. Morgan

Forrest E. Morgan tells us in his book, *Living The Martial Way*, that the warrior is a different kind of person than the ordinary man. He takes his life, his honor, and his duty seriously. He has a real purpose in life. If you want to be a true warrior, you have to think, feel and act differently. You have to go beyond the ordinary. As Forrest Morgan tells us, you have to set yourself apart from the rest of society by your personal excellence in everything that you do.

This is a tall order. It takes discipline and perseverance to live your life this way. Not everyone is able to live the life of a warrior. This lifestyle is a commitment to personal distinction. The warrior knows who he is and what his values are. He sets his own standards and then he lives up to those standards. He is a man of character and strives daily to be worthy of being called a warrior. He lives by a code of excellence.

Living by higher standards than the rest of society is a choice, but for the warrior it is his duty. The warrior has an obligation to himself to strive for excellence in every part of his life. He makes the choice to take life more seriously than his counterparts, knowing deep inside that the reward for living a life of excellence is much greater than any perceived sacrifice. Think, feel, and act like a warrior, and you will become a warrior.

I set myself apart by my personal excellence.

June 10

Strength is defeated by strategy.
Philippine Proverb

Don't always depend solely on your physical skills to protect yourself and those around you. No matter how skilled you are, there is always somebody out there who is stronger, faster and more ruthless. You have to be smart. By all means use the skills you have acquired to protect yourself, but don't forget to also use your head. It is not wise to meet a bigger, stronger, and more skilled enemy head-on.

Use your intelligence and wisdom in order to defeat your enemy. There is no such thing as a fair fight when you are referring to a "real" fight. In a real fight, you use whatever it takes to protect yourself and those you have to defend. One of your weapons is your mind. This should be the first weapon that you employ in any encounter. Keep your mind sharp, just as you keep your other weapons sharp.

Practice the art of not losing control and controlling your emotions. Learn breathing techniques which allow you to stay calm, even in intense situations. No matter how dire the situation is, it only makes matters worse when you lose control and allow fear and stress to control your mind and emotions. Whatever the circumstances you may find yourself in, always keep your mind calm and controlled. Your skills matter little if you panic and fall apart under stress.

Think rationally and develop a strategy to deal with each situation; don't blindly try to wing it and hope for the best. You rarely hit what you want to without aiming at your target. Strength is defeated by strategy only if you execute your strategy. Decide on a wise strategy and then execute your plan to perfection.

My strategy defeats their strength. I always win.

June 11

In order to progress in life, one has to
improve every day in an endless process.
The Hagakure

There is a term in the Japanese language called kaizen. Kaizen, loosely translated, means constant, never-ending improvement. The warrior must strive daily to improve his life and to live up to the standards that he sets for himself. As Gichin Funakoshi stated in his book, *Karate-Do Kyohan*, "The ultimate aim of the art of karate lies not in victory or defeat, but in the perfection of the character of its participants."

This should also be the ultimate aim of the warrior, to perfect his character. Of course the perfection of character is only one of many goals that the warrior tries to improve on in his daily life, but each of the other goals ultimately lead to this perfection of character that Master Funakoshi spoke of in his teachings. The perfection of your character is the ultimate culmination of all your training.

The warrior has many areas of training that he has to focus on daily. It is his duty to keep his martial arts skills sharp and to train his mind through visualization and meditation. No matter what area he is working on, the warrior strives to improve his skills daily. There is no slacking off. There is no laziness.

You cannot rest on your laurels and expect to maintain a high level of readiness. There is no such thing as stopping your training and just maintaining your skill level where it is. Your skills are either improving or degenerating. Make constant, never-ending improvement your goal in life.

I improve every day in every way.

June 12

Life is a succession of here and now, here and now,

unceasing concentration in the here and now.

Taisen Deshimaru

You can do nothing about your past actions. What is done is done and cannot be undone. All you can do is be the best that you can be right now in the present moment. You can't change what will happen in the next moment by worrying about what might happen. Worrying and being fearful of the future is only wasting your time in the present. Take care of this moment now, and take care of the next moment when it arrives.

The here and now is all that you really have. There is no such thing as yesterday and tomorrow; they really do not exist. You may have your memories of yesterday, and your hopes for tomorrow, but in reality, the only time that you can actually *live* your life is the here and now. Live your life in the here and now. You really have no choice; the only choice that you have is *how* you will live in the here and now.

This is where the warrior has a decision to make. Will you waste your time brooding over how someone has done you wrong or wishing that you had done something differently, or will you move on? Will you spend your time daydreaming about things that you hope for or will you take action and make those dreams come true?

The answer for the warrior has to be that he will use his time wisely. The warrior is rational and knows that his time on this earth is short, and that he cannot afford to waste it. Always strive to be present and conscious, and live in the Now.

I live in the Now. The past has no control over me.

June 13

Be strong when you are weak, brave when you are scared, and humbled when you are victorious.

Warriors don't have the luxury of just not dealing with unpleasant situations; they must be strong when they are weak, brave when they are scared, and should be humble when they are victorious. Too many people depend on them for the warrior to let them down. They must find the courage to push through any roadblocks.

When you are feeling weak, reach deep down inside and find the strength that you need to persevere. You may not even know that you have any strength left, but you do. Never give up; there is always a little more strength left if you will only refuse to quit. Find your second wind and vow to endure until you have completed your objective.

When you are feeling scared, be brave. Find the courage to face your fears. Never allow fear to dictate your actions. Always act from a place of courage and wisdom. If you have prepared yourself for death, which every man should do, then you can always find courage in the face of fear. Never cower down to your fears. All fears can be overcome by facing them and thinking rationally.

And when you are victorious, be humble about it. People love to see the champions go down. Whether this comes from jealousy or resentment, they love to see the strong fall. By being humble, you can remove much of this common resentment that others harbor against those who are successful. You have enough enemies without making new ones by being cocky. Win with class and be humble about your victories.

I am strong, brave, and humble. I am victorious.

June 14

Avoiding danger is not cowardice.
Philippine Proverb

If you see a group of thugs standing on a street corner and you decide to cross the street and take a different route to your location, you are not being a coward. You are actually doing exactly what you should do. You are using your head, being aware of your surroundings, and taking the necessary steps in order to keep yourself safe. This is not an act of a coward, but an act of a modern warrior.

Sure, you may be able to handle any trouble that may occur if you walk past these thugs, but would that be the smartest strategy? Isn't it a better strategy to avoid danger instead of tempting danger? Not only is this the smarter strategy, but it is also the easiest way to achieve victory over this group in the event that they have less than honorable intentions.

Think about it. You have defeated their plans without them even knowing what happened. This is the best strategy, especially if you have other people with you that you should be protecting. Never take a risk that you don't have to take when it comes to your self-defense strategy.

The warrior doesn't feel the need to prove himself by putting himself in questionable situations. Every violent encounter contains the chance of injury, no matter how skilled you may be. Use your most effective weapon daily – your mind. Be smart and be aware of your surroundings. See danger before you actually encounter it and take steps to protect yourself ahead of time. Avoiding the trap is easier than getting out of the trap.

I am aware and avoid danger. I notice everything around me.

June 15

It is no honor for an

eagle to vanquish a dove.

Italian Proverb

As a warrior, you have had special training and know how to defend yourself and others. Not only do you know how to defend yourself, but you know how to render some devastating damage to the human body. With this training comes the responsibility of using that knowledge and those skills conscientiously.

The warrior would not consider it an honor if he defeated a small child in a fight. There is also no honor in using your martial arts skills at the drop of a hat. There is no honor in thrashing some drunk at a bar who has just made some derogatory comments to you.

Of course you *could* make him pay severely for his disrespect, but would that be honorable or necessary? Remember, it is an honorable act to walk away from an insult knowing that you have in your power the ability to destroy this person if you so decide, but instead you have decided to be merciful. Cowards act out of fear; this is not an act of fear, but an act of honor.

Honor requires that the warrior only use his martial arts skills when there is no other option, and then to only use that force which he needs to control the situation.

It would not be an honorable act for a warrior to completely annihilate a smaller man which he could easily control without actually injuring him. Not only does this have to do with the warrior's sense of honor, but it is also an important legal consideration. Use common sense and listen to your sense of honor.

I know when to fight and when to walk away.

June 16

Man is only as strong as his
convictions and beliefs.

Kensho Furuya

Your convictions and beliefs are a major part of who you are as a warrior. They determine your commitment to the warrior lifestyle, to your training, to your friends and family, and to your overall self-improvement. Without strong convictions concerning right and wrong, a warrior has no compass for his life. His convictions are the driving force behind his code of ethics.

Without a strong belief in the importance of honor and integrity, you will find that these traits become less important to you, and consequently, they will become situational. Situational ethics is not fitting for the warrior.

Honor and integrity should never be compromised. It takes a lot of courage to maintain your honor and integrity in the face of those who neither understand nor respect these qualities, and who will verbally attack you concerning your beliefs.

Without courage, you will stumble, and courage requires strong convictions. The warrior lifestyle is not the easiest path to travel. You have to believe in the value of living your life according to the strict standards that are required for this lifestyle. You will not be successful if you don't know *why* you have chosen the path of the warrior. You have to have a strong belief in what you are doing and know *why* you are doing it. Without conviction, you have a major chink in your armor.

I never compromise my honor or integrity.

June 17

Don't follow the advice of others; rather,
learn to listen to the voice within yourself.

Dogen

This quote by Dogen, the famous 13th century Zen master, is a little misleading at first. When you first read it, it seems as though Dogen is telling us not to follow the advice of others. What he is actually telling us is not to *blindly* follow the advice of others, but rather to listen to the advice of others, while at the same time listening to your inner spirit. It is wise to listen to the advice and opinions of others, but always think for yourself. Don't act on the advice of others until you feel deeply in your spirit, that their advice is right.

This is what is meant by listening to the voice within. Always trust your internal voice, whether you call it your "small quiet voice," or your intuition, it will not lead you astray if you will learn to listen to what it is trying to tell you. How do you know what it is trying to tell you? You listen. You have to spend some quiet time alone, just you and your spirit. For many this is challenging. We are so used to the constant bombardment of external stimuli going on today that silence can actually feel awkward.

Listening is a skill that has to be developed just like your roundhouse kick or your side kick. Can you remember when you first began martial arts, how awkward some of the kicks and techniques were? Nothing that is completely new is comfortable at first. You have to practice new skills and techniques until you become comfortable with them and they become second nature. The same is true of listening to your intuition or your spirit.

I listen to my intuition and it guides me in all my ways.

June 18

Noblemen discipline themselves to
be dignified at all times...Sharpen
your mind and show your dignity.

Matsura Seizen

The warrior should be dignified at all times. This is not to say that you have to walk around somber at all times, never smiling or joking with your friends. You can joke around with your friends and have a good time, while at the same time remaining dignified. There is a big difference between having a good time with your friends and making yourself the buffoon.

We all know the buffoon that I am referring to here. He is the one in the group that always plays the clown and tries to get the laughs. Inevitably, he says inappropriate things, insults people, drinks too much, curses, and in the end, loses the respect of his friends. He makes everyone laugh and continues to be a part of the "group," but deep inside, the other members of the group do not really respect him. He is not dignified and not really respected when push comes to shove.

This should not be the description of the warrior. The warrior should be a man of dignity. He should command respect from his peers, as well as his enemies. Whatever environment he finds himself in, he maintains a sense of who he is and what his values are. He remains dignified, even when he is at ease and relaxed. This is just a natural part of the process of becoming a warrior. The more your standards become ingrained in your spirit, the more natural it becomes for you to show your dignity, no matter what the situation.

I discipline myself to be dignified and noble at all times.

June 19

Cultivate the root.
Confucius

No matter what the warrior is studying or trying to understand, he should always strive to cultivate the root. Confucius taught that if you cultivate the root, the leaves and the branches will take care of themselves. This means that if you want to truly become proficient in any art or any profession, you first have to learn the basics of that art or that profession. You can't have a strong tree without first having strong roots.

Too many people today want to skip this vital step in the process of the martial arts. They want to learn the flashy kicks or the "secret" moves, but they are not very interested in learning the basics. They find the basics kind of boring and tedious. The novice martial artist wants to learn to do what they see in the movies and on television, not practice stances or basic kicking and punching techniques. It seems that they want to grow branches and leaves with no roots. They want to run before they can walk. This is the desire for instant gratification, but you can't build a strong house without a good, solid foundation. Never neglect your foundational building blocks!

This is not the way of nature and it is not the way of the warrior. You have to learn to stand before you learn to walk, and you have to learn to walk before you learn to run. This is just the natural progression of things. Learning a martial art should follow the same natural progression as everything else in nature. You must cultivate the root first; don't skip this essential part of your training. Without strong, deep roots, it takes very little adversity to kill a plant or to expose a martial artist's weaknesses.

I have strong roots and the storm does not affect me.

June 20

*Even when you have to kill a man,
it costs nothing to be polite.*
Winston Churchill

Being polite and respectful is not only a part of the martial arts, but is also a part of who the warrior is deep down inside. In any given dojo, you will see students bow when entering or exiting the training area. If you observe closely, you will notice that the majority of these "acts of respect" are done lackadaisically, with the student making a split second, half-hearted bow. One has to wonder if this is a real sign of respect or is it simply a mindless reflex.

Respect and honor comes from deep inside, it is not simply a physical action. If these students are not taking their time and thinking about why they are bowing before entering or exiting the dojo, why even bother? The warrior, as I have said before, takes things a little more seriously that the average person. Respect and politeness mean more to him than merely a learned routine that he mindlessly goes through at certain times. He gives thought to everything that he does.

This even applies to his enemies, as this quote by Churchill points out. You don't have to be rude or demeaning to your enemy, even if you are forced to get physical with him. Degrading someone else only speaks to your own character. It makes no difference whether they deserve to be treated with respect or not; that is the way you treat people because that is who you are as a warrior, not because they do or don't deserve it. There are many people out there who do not deserve your respect; and they may not deserve your courtesy, but act in a courteous manner anyway, because that is the way of the warrior.

I am polite and respectful, even when respect is not deserved.

June 21

In dangerous times wise men say nothing.

Aesop

Aesop was a wise man. Great wisdom can be obtained from his fables and astute tales. This quote is no different; in fact it is one that the warrior should take to heart. In dangerous times wise men say nothing. When you find yourself in a bad situation or in circumstances beyond your control, silence can be the best course of action. Let others vent, yell, accuse, and lose their cool, while you silently listen and rationally consider what has happened, what is being said, and what to do next.

It is during times of stress that others will let their guard down and speak without thinking, often expressing thoughts which should be kept secret. Resist the urge to do this and just be silent. Let others make the mistake of losing their temper and saying things which could hurt them or for which they will later have to swallow their pride and apologize. The wise man will see this as a trap and as a chance to practice self-control by controlling his emotions.

This is not the same thing as being silent because of the fear of what could happen if you speak. Acting out of a sense of fear, and acting out of a sense of rational wisdom are two different things. Once again, your intentions play a major part in everything that you do.

If your intent is to rationally control your emotions and act as a man of wisdom that is one thing, but if your intention is to be silent because you are afraid of doing what needs to be done, that is something entirely different. The first is an act of honor; the second is the act of cowardice. Never allow fear to rule your actions. Make sure things are right on the inside.

In dangerous times, I remain quiet and listen to my intuition.

June 22

Behavior influences consciousness.
Right behavior means right consciousness.
The actions of every instant, every day,
must be right...every gesture is important.
Taisen Deshimaru

Everything matters. Everything that you do has a consequence or result. Just as the smallest rock dropped into a still pool of water causes ripples, every action, every word, every thought, causes ripples in the universe. According to Taisen Deshimaru, even every gesture is important. You may not be able to see the results of some of the things that you do, but trust me they are there.

For this reason, it is important for you to strive daily to make your actions, words and thoughts right. You must work daily at perfecting your character. Nobody is perfect in this challenge, but if you continually monitor yourself, you will find that you are getting better and better at controlling your behavior and building your character. Know who you are and what you believe, and then live your code of ethics daily, to the best of your ability.

Behavior influences consciousness, but at the same time, consciousness influences your behavior. It is a never-ending circle. The more you act according to your code of ethics, the more those standards are embedded into your consciousness, and the more your standards are rooted in your consciousness, the easier it is to do the right thing. When you get to this point, doing the right thing becomes a habit; it becomes natural. This is the goal for the warrior.

I strive to make every word and every action right.

June 23

*Certain good qualities are like the senses:
people entirely lacking in them can
neither perceive nor comprehend them.*
La Rochefoucauld

True warriors tend to associate with other warriors or with men of integrity and character. They find that they have to associate with men of honor because they are the only people with whom they can really talk. Other people just do not seem to comprehend what they are talking about, nor do they understand the warrior's values and principles most of the time. As La Rochefoucauld taught, many of the qualities of the warrior are foreign to most people.

They do not understand or comprehend how anyone could think like the warrior thinks. The ideals of the warrior are seen as outdated and useless to many in our society, and they have no problem stating just that. They do so without giving any regard to diplomacy or understanding. They totally lack these qualities and therefore cannot even perceive of anyone who would make these ideals an important part of his life.

For this reason, the warrior finds it more rewarding and less confrontational to associate with men who, like himself, are men of wisdom and honor. While it may be a tall order, he does not look down on those who lack the qualities which are so important to the warrior lifestyle, but rather feels empathy for those who live a less principled life. All the same, the warrior refuses to give up his ideals in order to fit in with those who choose the lower road. Each man must make his own path and live with his own decisions.

I make my own path and take responsibility for my decisions.

June 24

Rage and resentment lead to rash action.
Sun Tzu

How many times have you heard someone say something to the effect of, "If I get mad, nothing can stop me?" Many people seem to have this attitude. The rush of adrenaline gives them the sense of unstoppable power and strength, but what they fail to realize is that their personal feelings of power and strength do not change their enemy's skills, strength or power. Likewise, it does not make their skills more powerful.

While it is true that a rush of adrenaline does bump you up a notch on the physical scale, it also comes at a price. As your body is raging, your mind is disengaged. This means that you are no longer acting from a rational place. You have allowed your rage and anger to take control in place of your rational thought process.

As Sun Tzu taught, this leads to rash actions which can many times cause you some major problems. The warrior should act from a place of rational consideration of each situation. He should respond rather than react. He should think rationally and act from a place of wisdom. This requires a calm mind.

While the warrior does need that rush of adrenaline, he has to learn to control it and use it. The warrior has to control his rage and anger, not let his rage and anger control him. This takes practice and self-control, and is developed through hours of realistic training and meditation. Don't give your power to anyone else or anything else. Maintain control at all times and remember that your mind is your best weapon, but only if you control your thoughts and think rationally.

I control my emotions. I never act rashly.

June 25

Pretend inferiority and encourage his arrogance.

Sun Tzu

When your enemy is overconfident or when he just plain thinks that he is better or smarter than you, encourage him to continue in his misguided thought. This gives you a huge advantage when dealing with him. Encourage his arrogance. Let him think that you are unintelligent and inferior to him. You may even want to go as far as feinting ignorance and naivety. Your goal is not to impress your enemy, but to defeat him. Victory is your objective and his arrogance will be his downfall.

There are many advantages to your enemy underestimating your intelligence and your abilities. To begin with, when someone underestimates your intelligence, he doesn't give you much respect. This means that he will not really consider you much of a challenge or a threat, and because he doesn't think that you present much of a challenge, he will not prepare to defend himself against your strategy as well as he should. This is a good thing for you. An unprepared enemy is an enemy well on his way to defeat.

The more unprepared your enemy is, the easier it will be to attack his strategy. An unguarded gate is easy to enter. If you have done your homework and prepared a sound strategy for victory, and your enemy has neglected to take you seriously, he will be in serious trouble. How many times have you seen a far superior sports team lose to a team which can barely put on their uniforms? This is because the superior team underestimated the other team and failed to prepare – their arrogance was their downfall.

I use all of my enemy's weaknesses against him.

June 26

*Cowards die many times before their deaths,
the valiant never taste of death but once.*
William Shakespeare

This famous quote from William Shakespeare is often used to justify unwise decisions. Don't use this wisdom to validate fighting when wisdom dictates that you should walk away. Walking away from a possible physical encounter does not indicate cowardice; it demonstrates wisdom. Many times it takes more courage to walk away from a fight, than it does to stay and slug it out. You must do what is right and not allow your ego to dictate your actions.

Always consider your ultimate objective when you find yourself in this kind of situation. Don't confuse pride with courage. While it is true that it takes a certain amount of courage to fight, whether you are fighting out of necessity or fighting out of pride, it takes more courage to walk away when people are jeering at you, than it does to stand and fight. The warrior can walk away with his pride still intact because he knows in his heart that he is able to defend himself.

This is totally different from the man who walks away out of fear. The man, who walks away out of fear, although his action may look the same on the outside, is actually acting out of cowardice. His fear dictates his action, not his sense of duty or wisdom. It is true that it is probably a wise move for him to make, especially if he can't defend himself, but it is a totally different action than that of the warrior. Many times it is hard to interpret the actions of others as courageous or cowardly. The important thing is that you yourself know in your heart whether or not your actions are courageous.

I am courageous at all times.

June 27

You must not show your weak points,
either in the martial arts or in everyday life.

Taisen Deshimaru

It seems in today's society that people really enjoy talking about their illnesses or their injuries. People seem to derive some joy out of other people feeling sorry for them because of their hard life. They constantly want to tell you about their new problem, ache or pain. Sharing personal information seems to come naturally to them, even if other people are disinterested.

This is not a wise policy for the warrior to follow. By giving others information concerning your weak points, you are actually giving them information that can be used against you at some time down the road. Your enemies can store away information which may seem insignificant and meaningless, only to use it against you at some other time. For example, you may mention in casual conversation that you have a bum knee from an old football injury; this is something that someone can easily use against you in a fight.

Even though you may be speaking with someone whom you would never suspect to be your enemy, or who would never present any threat to you, people talk and you never know what will be repeated. Your friend has a friend, and that friend has a friend. It is best to keep your weak points private. Why take a chance that something you say will be used against you at some point? What does it benefit you to share your personal weaknesses with others? It is safer to keep your weaknesses, mistakes, and faults private. Don't talk just to hear yourself speak or to be the center of attention.

I don't publicize my weak points. I keep my enemies in the dark.

June 28

The more quickly brought to anger,
the more quickly brought to death.
Chinese Maxim

The sages have always taught the dangers of allowing your anger to control your actions. They have taught throughout the ages, that you must control your anger. You must think rationally, not emotionally. Anger does not allow for rational thought. When your emotions are raging and your adrenaline is pumping, you do not think rationally. You have to control your anger in order to think properly. A angry mind is never a rational mind.

This principle has been proven throughout the ages. It has always been a successful tactic in battle, whether between armies or between individuals, to anger your opponent in order to cause him to make mental mistakes, mistakes that could cost him his life. Taunting, abrasive language, rude actions, etc. are all actions which your enemy will use against you in order to rile you and cause you to act rashly. Once you have allowed your anger to control your actions, he has accomplished his goal.

His goal is to upset you and draw you into his trap by disabling your ability to think rationally. As the maxim above states, the sooner this happens, the sooner you are finished. This is a sucker's game. See it for what it really is, and don't get suckered into that trap. Turn the tables on him. It is very frustrating for your enemy, who is trying his best to anger you, when you don't get angry. So much so that his tactic can actually backfire, and many times, he is the one who gets angry and loses control. See this game for the ruse that it is. Be smart.

I control my anger and my anger cannot be used against me.

179

June 29

The wise man adapts himself
to the circumstances.

Confucius

The warrior lives by a certain set of standards, a code of honor if you will. There are certain things that he will not do because those things go against his beliefs and the standards which he has set for himself. Many of his principles are not open to compromise; they are set in stone and he refuses to bend where they are concerned, but this does not mean that he is inflexible. Although the warrior is not willing to bend where his principles are concerned, he must be flexible in his strategy.

Warriors have to be able to adapt to the changing circumstances. The willow bends and adapts during the storm and is not broken, where the mighty oak does not bend and will break during the storm. The warrior must be able to change tactics as the situation changes. He will adapt his methods to that which the present circumstance requires. Not to do so would be foolish and costly.

This is not to say that the warrior should lower his standards or set aside his ethics as he sees fit. There is a difference between changing your strategy to fit the circumstances and changing your ethics to suit the situation. This is where time spent meditating on your code of ethics and honor comes into play. You must be clear about what you believe and why you hold those beliefs. Change your methods to accomplish your goal; don't compromise your ethics to serve your methods. This may seem like a subtle distinction, but it is an important one, especially for the warrior.

I adapt to every circumstance. Nothing can throw me off balance.

June 30

Honor is not black and white.

Forrest E. Morgan

Many people have a warped sense of honor. Some use their sense of honor to justify stupid decisions. For example, someone may think that he is "too honorable" to fight dirty. As I have said before, this is simply an unintelligent decision, but there are many people who view honor in terms of black or white. It is admirable that they at least have a sense of honor, even though their concept of honor is misguided and could cause them difficulty in certain situations.

Many people fail to even consider the significance of honor. To them, honor is a meaningless concept that went out of fashion with the knights of old. They couldn't care less about being honorable or whether their actions are right or wrong. They will tell you point blank that honor is a ridiculous concept. These are people with questionable ethics and not people with whom the warrior wants to associate. Many times it is easy to tell if someone is totally lacking in honor. Dishonor is more easily discerned than honor.

Honor is not a black and white set of rules which the warrior must abide by during his life. There is not one code of honor that is set in stone. As Samuel Coleridge wrote, "Our own heart, and not other men's opinion, form our true honor."

The warrior lives by a code of honor, but honor is much more complicated than many make it out to be. Honor is bound by intention, and no man is privy to another man's intention. Therefore, it is only the warrior himself who truly knows whether or not he is an honorable man.

My honor is intact. Other men's opinions don't matter.

July 1

The world is a dangerous place,
not because of those who do evil, but
because of those who look on and do nothing.

Albert Einstein

I think that this statement by Albert Einstein would be more accurate if he had stated that the world is a dangerous place *not only* because of those who do evil, *but also* because of those who look on and do nothing. There are some very dangerous, evil people in this world. That is just the way it is, and if anyone disputes that, they are living in a fantasy world. Some people are just plain bad and will kill you at the drop of a hat, and then order a Big Mac and smile.

As bad as that sounds, and it is pretty bad, Einstein considered those people less of a problem than the people who look on and do nothing. Can you see his point? If everyone took an active role in bringing the evil people to justice, swift and sure justice, the evil doers would become less and less prevalent. Even though there are a lot of evil men in this world, there are many more people who allow them to exist because of their apathy or fear. Those who allow evil, condone evil.

This world is a dangerous place both because of evil men and because of the apathy of others. This is why it is so important that the warrior be prepared to recognize and confront evil. If the warrior is not willing to stand up and do something about the evil in this world, who will? Can you rid this world of evil by protecting those around you? No. Can you make those around you safer, simply because you are there with them? Absolutely!

The world is safer because I am in it.

July 2

Don't protect people who don't deserve it.
Your job is to protect the good.
Observe one's true character.

Masaaki Hatsumi

I have stated many times that it is the warrior's duty to protect others. Serving and protecting others who do not have the ability or know-how to protect themselves is part of the warrior lifestyle, but does this mean that you are duty bound to protect everyone, all the time? According to Masaaki Hatsumi, the Ninjutsu grandmaster and founder of the Bujinkan Organization, the warrior should only protect those who deserve it.

This brings us to the question of who deserves your protection and who does not deserve your protection. How do you know? Masaaki Hatsumi goes on to explain that it is your job, as a warrior, to protect the good. Again, how do you know who is good and who is not? You observe people's true character. Yes, this may involve personal judgments concerning other people, but a wise warrior will make some judgments before placing his life on the line to help someone.

Would you consider it your duty to help a pimp who is being pounded on the street by some drug dealer for a personal disagreement between these two dishonorable men? I wouldn't. But this situation would be different if the drug dealer was pounding some innocent school boy. There is a big difference, and it requires your discernment to make the call. Serve and protect, but use good judgment. Protect the good and let the wicked live with the consequences of their actions. Be smart about when and how you get involved to help others.

I protect good people. Evil people stay away from me.

July 3

战
士

To be prepared beforehand for any
contingency is the greatest of virtues.
Sun Tzu

The Boy Scouts have it right – "Be Prepared." The warrior should focus his attention on being as prepared as possible for whatever may come his way. Of course it is basically impossible to be prepared for every possible thing that could happen, but you can train your mind to remain calm and to think rationally regardless of the situation at hand. Learning to keep a calm, rational mind in the midst of turmoil is one way of being prepared for the unexpected. If you are prone to panic in the midst of critical situations, you are not fully prepared.

Meditation is one way to train your mind to remain calm and tranquil. The more that you meditate, the more you will find that your mind is able to stay calm under pressure. Breathing techniques also help you to maintain your balance during times of stress. Those who work under high pressure situations find that autogenic breathing techniques enable them to maintain their composure when their back is against the wall.

Of course, it goes without saying that your martial arts training prepares you to meet physical confrontations with strength and confidence. You must continue to maintain you skills to be prepared for the unexpected trouble that you may encounter on the street. This doesn't apply only to your martial arts techniques, but to your meditation and your breathing techniques also. If you do not practice all of these things, they will not be available to you when you find that you need them. This is part of what it means to be prepared.

I stay prepared. Nothing catches me off guard.

July 4

战
士

The shepherd hunts the predators who attack his sheep.

On this July 4, while you are enjoying time with friends and family, and eating hotdogs and hamburgers, take a little time out of your day to remember the warriors who have lived before you. Remember those brave souls who put their lives on the line to win our freedom from an unjust monarch.

Remember the brave souls who continue to protect you and your family from terrorists and others who would take that freedom from you. Remember those who have given their lives so that you and your family may enjoy the leisure that you enjoy on this day. Many have given their lives to win the freedom that so many take for granted in today's society.

And remember that things can change when you least expect them to. In times of peace, the warrior keeps his sword close to his side. He maintains his skills, his health, and his principles, for he doesn't know what the future may hold. The one thing that you can always count on is that things change. You may not always be blessed to live in a time of peace.

Enjoy your holiday, but remember that there have been times when great warriors did not have the luxury of celebrating the 4th of July with their families. Be grateful for your freedom and your blessings, and be ever mindful that you yourself may one day have to step up to defend your freedom and your family against those who would rob you of that freedom. Never take freedom for granted! Happy 4th of July!

I am grateful for all the blessings in my life.

July 5

True Budo has an overwhelming emphasis on the development of moral character.

Glen Morris

Budo is the Japanese term for martial arts, and the martial arts should indeed have an overwhelming emphasis on developing one's moral character. The key word in this quote is "true." "True" budo has an emphasis on the development of moral character. But how many martial arts schools today really focus on the development of moral character? Can these schools which do not focus on the moral character of the student really be called true martial arts schools or are they simply teaching fighting techniques?

This is not only a distinction between the true martial arts schools and the schools which are only there to make money, but it is also the distinction between the true warrior and the man who is only trained to fight. The true warrior will not only be focused on his martial skills, but he will also be dedicated to the perfection of his character. Without this important ingredient, there is no warrior, only someone trained to be dangerous, just another possible menace to society.

Gichin Funakoshi stated that the ultimate goal of karate lies neither in victory or defeat, but rather in the perfection of the character of its participants. The ultimate objective for the warrior is the perfection of his character, everything else is simply tools which he uses to achieve his objective. This is the main trait that separates the true warrior from his counterparts. He is just as capable of rendering destruction as they are, but he is coming from a place of true honor and character, and therefore can be relied on to be a just man – a true warrior.

I seek perfection of character, every day in every way.

July 6

战士

A wise man, in great or small matters,
must act with due consideration.
Sakya Pandit

To the man of excellence, everything matters, even the small stuff. The warrior is a man of excellence and will take pains to do everything that he does to the best of his ability. It doesn't matter whether he is dealing with a life-or-death situation or making a new flower bed for his wife in his backyard, he will give his full attention to the task at hand. Small mistakes can turn into big headaches. The warrior knows this and thus acts with due consideration in every area of his life.

Think back throughout your life and consider how many times you have made quick, thoughtless decisions which have come back to haunt you at a later date. Wouldn't it have been much better to have taken the time to stop and think before you made those decisions? Many times we allow ourselves to hurry and make decisions without giving them much thought or consideration concerning the possible consequences, and many times this ends up saving us no time at all, but rather costing us time down the line.

Stop and think before you act. It doesn't matter if you are doing something that you consider important or whether you are doing something trivial – THINK. Always stay conscious of your actions and be in the moment. Not only is this smart, but it is also good practice for keeping your mind sharp and aware. Don't let yourself get into the habit of mindlessly going through the motions of life without thinking. Stay focused, whether dealing with small matters or a life-threatening situation. Always think before you act.

I consider every angle before I act.

July 7

Adversity is a mirror
that reveals one's true self.

Chinese Proverb

You never really know what you can do until you have had your limits tested through extreme adversity. No matter how much training you have had or how much time you have spent pondering certain situations, it is all speculation until you go through the experience of true hardship or danger. It is during these times that your true self comes to the surface and reveals who you really are. You can no longer bluff your way through, if indeed that is what you have been doing (hopefully it is not what you have been doing).

The bully can talk the talk, but often when someone stands up to him, we find that it has all been a bluff. He is not the tough guy that he portrayed himself to be. This never comes to light until someone calls his bluff and reveals his true nature. It is through adversity that we actually know who someone really is deep inside. During times of hardship people tend to give up their concern over their image and the true self appears.

Most people have a carefully protected façade built around them. This is the image that they present to the public, and many times it is quite different from who they truly are as a person. The warrior's true self and the everyday image that he portrays should be one and the same. He has no need to hide his true self because he lives his life as a man of honor and is prepared for the hardships and dangers which he may face during his lifetime. When he looks into the mirror of adversity, he simply sees the same image that he sees every day – the warrior.

I am a man (or woman) of character – a warrior.

July 8

All men make mistakes, but a good man yields when
he knows his course is wrong, and repairs the evil.
Sophocles

The warrior is many things. He is a man of honor, integrity and character. He is a man of courage and a hero if need be. He is a superior man in the sense of his lifestyle and character. But there is one thing that he is not – a perfect man. All men make mistakes, including the warrior. All of his decisions will not be correct, even though he will try his best to make them so. There will be times when he slips and makes mistakes that he will regret; this is simply part of being human.

What makes the true warrior different in this regard is the fact that when he does make mistakes and he knows he is on the wrong path, he is man enough to make the necessary changes to his course. He owns up to his mistakes, learns from them, meditates on what changes he needs to make, and then makes those changes. If his mistake has hurt someone or caused damage in any way, he does his best to make amends and right any wrongs which may have been caused by his mistake.

Personal responsibility is the hallmark of the true warrior. He alone knows that his true intentions were honorable, but still he knows that he is responsible for the results of his actions nonetheless. Knowing that his intentions were honorable, he is not ashamed to take this responsibility. He makes his own decisions and then deals with the results of those decisions as they present themselves. This is the way of the superior man – the way of the warrior.

I always make my mistakes right.

July 9

戦士

Brave hearts do not back down.
Euripides

Euripides tells us that brave hearts do not back down. However, this doesn't mean that brave hearts are stubborn or foolhardy. Brave hearts do not back down concerning their principles and important matters regarding their ideals. They show courage in the face of danger and hardship, but at the same time they think rationally and act with acute focus toward accomplishing their objectives. They do not let their pride or their emotions control their decisions. Rather they think rationally in every situation.

While it is true that brave hearts do not back down, this does not mean that there is never a time for the warrior to retreat and regroup. Your strategy must be flexible. Don't be hard-headed in your approach. As the circumstances of the moment change, so must your tactics and strategies change. When you see that the situation is not going your way and that your efforts need to be modified in order to achieve your goals, be willing to rethink your position and make the needed adjustments.

I have heard many men make comments such as, "They may kill me, but I will never back down." Well, that may be true, but does that accomplish your objective? Not unless your objective is to put up a good fight and be killed. Always focus on accomplishing your objectives, not on saving your pride. When thoughts such as the one above enter your mind, you know that you are now allowing pride and emotions to control your thinking instead of rational thought. Retreating and regrouping is not the same as backing down; do not confuse the two.

I always remember my ultimate objective.

July 10

戦士

Every single word is of great

importance to a samurai.

The Hagakura

The warrior should be careful with his words. His word is his honor. When you tell someone that you will do something, you have just given your word. As a warrior, you have entered into a verbal contract with this person. It would be dishonorable to break this contract by not following through on what you said you would do.

You owe this person. They are counting on you, as a man of your word, to do what you say you will. Your word should be your bond. It should be as good as any legal contract.

Another reason that you should be careful with your speech is that everything you say can and will be held against you, if at all possible, by your enemies. Your enemies are looking for ways to trip you up. They are looking for a weakness in your life, a place where they feel they can attack you. Many times we provide our enemies with the means to our own destruction through our own speech. Careless words can come back to hurt you in ways that you could never imagine.

The ancient sages knew the importance of being careful with your speech, even in ancient times when there was no internet, television, or press listening to their every word. They knew that your words could cause you much grief. Over and over the great sages warn of the importance of controlling your speech. If it was that important in ancient times, how much more important is it to watch what you say in today's society?

My word is my bond; my word is my honor.

July 11

To be prepared is half the victory.

Cervantes

No matter what you are doing, being prepared for the task is a must. Whether you are going hiking in the mountains or taking your wife or girlfriend out to dinner, you need to be prepared for the worst possible scenario. Just as you don't want to be caught in the mountains in some unexpected, emergency situation without the proper gear and supplies, you also don't want to be unprepared for the unexpected surprises when you are on the streets. Being caught off guard and unprepared in either case can be very dangerous.

It is easy to be prepared for a trip to the mountains. You educate yourself about the dangers that, though unlikely, you could possibly face, and you prepare for every possible scenario as best as you can. You pack matches, emergency gear, your hiking stick, a knife, etc. You are careful not to neglect taking the proper precautions when you are set to spend a day or longer in the mountains and you should do the same when you leave your home to go into the city.

Educate yourself on the possible dangers that you may encounter, although you know that these dangers are fairly rare. Know how to deal with these "emergency situations" should you find yourself caught up in one of these scenarios. Be prepared and aware. Don't wander mindlessly around town, anymore than you would mindlessly hike through the mountains. Sure, running into a street thug set on doing you bodily harm when you are going out to dinner is rare, but mountain lion attacks are also fairly rare, yet every year we read about people being killed in both situations.

I am always prepared. Trouble cannot catch me unaware.

July 12

Don't hit at all if it can be
avoided, but never hit softly.
Theodore Roosevelt

It is a principle of karate that you never attack first. The meaning behind this saying is that the warrior should not use his martial arts skills in a threatening or bullying manner. It goes without saying, that doing so is a dishonorable act and is not fitting for anyone who is traveling the path of the warrior. You should only use your martial arts skills in cases of self-defense or the defense of others, and then, only if you have no other recourse.

If at all possible, avoid a physical confrontation. Try to calm the other person down if he is in an excited mental state. Use your mind and mediation skills to resolve the problem. This is much harder to do than it sounds, and these types of skills should be a part of your training as a warrior. If your conversational skills fail, try and walk away if it is an option.

It is when your efforts to compromise or to resolve the issue peacefully have failed, that you may have to resort to using your martial arts skills. Although you should avoid this position if you can, once things evolve to this point, it is game on. Never strike softly as a warning. This person's chances to resolve things peacefully have been exhausted. When the situation degrades to a physical issue, strike hard, strike fast, and strike until there is no doubt left about the possibility of clear and present danger. Do what you can to avoid a fight, but once engaged, be deadly serious about coming out the victor. As Shaka Zulu said, "Never leave an enemy standing."

I walk in peace, but if attacked, I win, no matter what.

July 13

To subdue an enemy without
fighting is the greatest of skills.

Sun Tzu

We all train to improve our martial arts skills as warriors. We have confidence that we can defend ourselves and those who depend on us, but we should only use these skills when there is no other option available to us. In Sun Tzu's famous book, *The Art of War,* he tells us that it is a greater skill to subdue the enemy without actually having to resort to fighting. The word "subdue" means to pacify or control. We should try to pacify the enemy. We should try to defuse the situation with words or gestures. Do what you can to de-escalate the situation without fighting.

The hard part of pacifying the enemy, for the warrior, is swallowing some of your pride. It takes a lot of discipline and confidence to swallow your pride in order to pacify some rude, aggressive guy who you would rather lay out on the floor. But, as a warrior, it is one of those things which you have to discipline yourself to do. Nobody said that living the warrior lifestyle is easy.

Don't look at these situations like you are letting the other person get the best of you, but rather as a training exercise in the art of war. You are actually controlling the enemy without him even knowing that he is being controlled and manipulated. You are sharpening your arsenal of weapons. Study the art of verbal self-defense and learn how to diffuse potentially dangerous situations without resorting to the use of your martial arts skills. Victories of this kind are even more rewarding than physical conquests.

I perfect the skills of de-escalation. I win without fighting.

July 14

战
士

The true warrior ponders the future without
discarding the past while living in the present.

F. J. Chu

While it is true that the present moment is all that we actually have,
it doesn't mean that there is no value in the past or that we should not
plan for the future. What I mean when I say that you should live in the
now, is that you should focus your energy on the present moment; be
in the moment. The now is where you live, it is all that really exists,
but there is value in the past and you should definitely plan for the
future.

You can learn a lot from studying the wisdom and history of the
past. The warrior should read and study the wisdom contained in the
writings from throughout the ages. Don't discard these writings
because of their age. *The Code of the Samurai* states that the samurai
should constantly read the ancient records. This was one way that the
samurai maintained their focus on wisdom and integrity. There is
much to be learned from the wise men of the past.

It is also important to have goals and plans for the future. Think and
plan for the future, but do not worry or become fearful of what may or
may not happen. Goals are important for the warrior. The man who
does not plan for the future will come to regret it. It is part of the
warrior's duty to make sure that his family is cared for, both now and
in the future. This is impossible to do without making some
preparations for the future. Living in the present moment does not
mean neglecting to plan for the future or discarding useful wisdom
from the past. Think balance.

I prepare for the future, but I live in the present.

July 15

*The important thing is to be always
moving forward, little by little.*

Masutatsu Oyama

Always try to improve yourself every day. Even if it seems like you are not making any progress in your journey to become a warrior, you must continue to move forward. Just as an apple tree does not produce apples overnight, you will not be able to reach perfection as fast as you may like. It is a process and it takes time. The important thing is not to give up and quit, even if it seems like you are not making improvements as fast as you would like.

Improvements come in small increments. Little by little you move forward, sometimes so slowly that you will think that you are not moving at all, but you are. After several weeks or months you will be able to look back at where you started and see the tremendous change that has taken place in your life.

There is an old Chinese proverb which states that one doesn't plant a forest in the morning and cut logs in the afternoon. It takes time for the tree to grow. You must take care of it and keep the weeds from overgrowing it when it is young. The young tree needs water and nutrients in order to mature.

The same philosophy can be applied to your progress. You have to be patient and foster the traits and skills that you are trying to develop. Be patient and before you know it, you will find that you have improved in ways which will amaze you. The results will be worth your patience.

I am always improving. I never regress.

July 16

戦士

Dignity is not circumstantial.
Kotoda Yahei Toshisada

The dignity of a warrior is not circumstantial. Dignity is synonymous with self-respect and self-esteem. You do not want to put yourself into situations where your self-respect and self-esteem are compromised. Whether you realize it or not, if you lower your standards because of certain circumstances, you also lower your self-esteem. You must maintain your dignity whether you are alone, with friends and family, or with your greatest enemy. You determine your dignity, not your circumstances.

As with honor, you are in total control of your dignity. Nobody can take your dignity from you. Someone may put you in an awkward or embarrassing situation, but how you respond to that situation is totally up to you. No matter what situation or circumstance you have to deal with, you can decide to respond with dignity and honor.

For example, you may be performing a kata during a tournament and for whatever reason, you may slip down and fall flat on your face. Now, you can respond to that embarrassing situation by getting up, cursing, kicking, and just throwing a fit, which would be totally undignified.

The other choice, which I hope you would make, would be to get up, continue with your kata to the best of your ability, bow to the judges, and later, be a good sport about the whole thing when your peers start to tease you. This is just one example of responding with dignity, there are many more. The point is dignity is not circumstantial; it is an expected part of the warrior lifestyle.

I maintain my dignity no matter what is happening around me.

July 17

Trained fighters, much more than average people, have an obligation to employ their skills judiciously, to govern themselves and their emotions at all times.

Peter Hobert

Trained warriors have the ability to be much more dangerous than the average person and therefore have a sacred duty to be careful about the use of their skills. As warriors, we do not have the freedom to let our emotions or tempers run wild. We have to keep ourselves under control at all times. Allowing yourself to lose your temper just once can have devastating and long-lasting consequences.

When you are tempted to let yourself go and lose control, remember the damage that you could do and stop and think about the situation rationally. Is it worth all of the consequences that will come from a minute's loss of self-control? Is the thing that has riled you worth unleashing your wrath? Will you think that this is still important a month from now or a year from now? If not, it probably is not that important now.

Although there will be times when you have to act on the spot without regards to the consequences, the majority of the time you will have time to think before you act. Always remember that our justice system looks at martial artists in a different light than the ordinary man. The courts consider your hands and feet to be deadly weapons, therefore you have to be more careful when it comes to employing your skills than the average Joe. Self-defense means defending yourself from prosecution as well as from bodily harm. Be rational. Be self-controlled.

I only use my martial arts for self-defense.

July 18

You must be deadly serious in training.
Gichin Funakoshi

The above quote taken from *Karate-Do Kyohan by Gichin Funakoshi* pretty much says it all, but how many of us actually pay attention to his admonition? You must take your training seriously, or as Master Funakoshi said, "Deadly serious." He used the words "deadly serious" for a reason. The reason is, if you ever do have to use your skills in a life-or-death situation, your training was "deadly serious" whether you realized it or not. Your attitude and your attention to your training become extremely important at the time that you actually need to put your martial arts skills to use.

It is all too easy to just go through the motions during your training. There are times when you are not in the mood to train and you may be tempted not to workout at all. Remember, the warrior is not practicing martial arts for sport or for some part-time hobby. This is not some game or a fun activity that you participate in twice a week. Your training is about life and death, and you should take your training deadly serious.

If you read the writings of many of the older martial artists, those in their 70's or 80's, they leave no room for doubt that they don't consider practicing martial arts for sport as the true purpose behind the martial arts. Of course there is a place for martial arts competition in today's society, but there is a big difference between sparring for points and the philosophy of "one punch – one kill." The latter is the one in which the warrior should mainly be concerned with perfecting. He knows that when it comes down to the nitty-gritty, there had better be more to his skills than the ability to win a trophy.

I am always deadly serious in my training.

July 19

Focus on your one purpose.
Japanese Maxim

No matter what you are doing, you should focus on your one purpose; put all your attention into whatever you are doing at this very moment. Whether you are practicing your martial arts, studying wisdom from the masters, or gardening, focus on that one thing. There are so many things that vie for your attention today that it is very easy to get sidetracked. It takes discipline to maintain your focus.

There are a multitude of activities that are interesting and good to know something about, but you should always try to have one thing in which you are best. Find your purpose in life. Don't try to be a jack-of-all-trades. Find your one purpose and do your best to perfect that one thing, no matter what that may be.

For the warrior, his purpose is perfecting the skills that he needs to be a warrior. He realizes that being a warrior is his purpose in life. There are many different skills that he has to develop in the process of becoming the best warrior that he can be, but overall his main purpose is warriorship.

Don't try to learn everything about every technique, in every different style of martial arts. You should know a little about the different styles, but make sure you are proficient in your style before learning others.

Concentrate and focus. Concentrated energy is much more powerful than energy which is dispersed in different directions. If you want to achieve perfection, focus on your one purpose. Think about the power of a laser compared to the power of a light bulb. That is the difference in focused energy as compared to dispersed energy.

I always keep my one purpose in mind.

July 20

This is certain, that a man that studies
revenge keeps his wounds green, which
otherwise would heal and do well.

Francis Bacon

Revenge is not the way of the warrior. Although there are times when honor demands things be put right, this is a different situation from the act of revenge. Forrest E. Morgan does an excellent job of discussing this distinction in his book, *Living the Martial Way*. I highly recommend that if you haven't read it, you get a copy and read it. It is an excellent book for the warrior.

As for situations where honor does not require action, it is best to walk away from thoughts of revenge. When you dwell on the wrong that someone has done to you, you are only continuing to allow their action to hurt you.

It is as if they are getting the best of you over and over again. Don't allow this to happen. Be self-disciplined and control your mind. Get over it and move on with the goals which are important to you. If you allow these people to continually disrupt your inner peace, you are allowing them to win.

You will not be able to heal and move on if you are constantly remembering the offense and getting angry about it. Let it go. Focus on your goals. Know that by releasing this incident, you are allowing yourself to continue on your journey towards warriorship without this monkey on your back. Whatever happened, it was not important enough to allow it to interfere with your walk on the warrior path.

I have no use for revenge. I am busy improving myself.

July 21

Though we are powerful and strong, and we know how to fight, we do not wish to fight.

Cherokee Saying

This Cherokee maxim really describes the attitude of the warrior. The warrior is definitely powerful and strong, and he undeniably knows how to fight, but he would be completely satisfied if he went his whole life without ever having to fight. The true warrior does not look for the opportunity to prove his skills in battle. He longs for a peaceful life.

Never go out looking for a fight. This is something that a warrior should never do. In fact, you should do everything in your power, within reason, to avoid having to fight. There are times when you have to make the decision to get physical, but this should only be when all other options have failed and you have no other choice. The decision to fight should be taken very seriously.

There are different forms of doing battle. Remember that your goal is not necessarily to defeat your enemy by getting physical, but to defeat your enemy period. Avoidance, intelligence, and cunning are all alternative ways in which you can totally annihilate your enemy's strategy, and all without the possible ramifications of a physical confrontation.

Just keep in mind that your ultimate goal is to make sure that you are safe, and then to defeat your enemy, by the best means available. The majority of the time, fighting will not be the appropriate choice for the warrior, although this deadly ability is always lying in the background like a tiger in the bush.

I do everything possible to avoid a real fight.

July 22

*Opportunity is rare and a wise
man will never let it go by him.*

Bayard Taylor

A warrior must make the most of every opportunity. This is especially true in a confrontation. If you get the opportunity to use your intelligence to diffuse a situation, you have to grab it immediately. If the situation has deteriorated into a physical confrontation, it is even more important to take advantage of every opportunity. Once the decision to get physical has been made, don't hold back. Use whatever force you need in order to secure your safety.

You may only get one opening during a fight, but for the trained warrior that should be all that is needed. When you see your enemy make his mistake, you must exploit it without delay. Delaying your action could mean defeat. You have to be mentally and physically alert and ready to explode into action the second that the occasion requires you to act.

This takes discipline and courage, as well as good timing. When you have a chance, take it immediately. Strike hard and fast! This is not the time for doubts or second guessing; this is the time for action. There is little time to think at this point. This is what your training is all about.

You have to be mentally prepared and know what you should and should not do to keep yourself safe. If you have to slow down and think before you act in this situation, the opportunity may well pass you by before you get a chance to take advantage of it. Trust your training and go on instinct.

I never miss an opportunity. I always win.

July 23

Never interrupt your enemy
when he is making a mistake.
Napoleon Bonaparte

Given enough time, your enemy will make a mistake. Your responsibility is to be patient and allow your enemy the time to slip up. Whether it is a mental lapse, a physical mistake, or a loss of temper, sooner or later your enemy will make a mistake. Many times his mistake will bring about his defeat without much effort on your part.

Be patient and alert. Be ready to take advantage of his every blunder. There is no such thing as fighting fair in a real fight. Take advantage of everything and anything that will help you achieve your victory.

Use the weapons that you have available to you at the time. Using the enemy's mistakes is one of the skills that the warrior needs to perfect in order to come out of a physical confrontation on top. You only get one shot to take him down; don't fail to take advantage of it.

Be patient and let karma work in the lives of your enemies. There is no need for you to take revenge on your enemy. Men who lack honor and integrity will find that sooner or later, their mistakes will bring them down. What comes around goes around.

Just practice patience and be ready. Your enemy will make a mistake; it is just a matter of when, where, and how severe. When he does make his mistake, strike hard and strike fast. I said that he would make *a* mistake, but I didn't say he would make *multiple* mistakes. You may only get one chance; make it count.

I take advantage of every mistake my enemy makes.

July 24

*T*omorrow belongs to
those who prepare today.
African Proverb

I have already touched on being prepared for whatever you may encounter, whether you are going out for a day of recreation or going out on the town. Being prepared is extremely important and the only safe course of action for the warrior to take. You can prepare for some things at the spur of the moment. For example, if you start to walk out the door and it looks as though it may rain, you can turn back and get your umbrella just in case. Other situations take a bit more preparation in order to be prepared.

Self-defense is one of the things that you need to prepare for well in advance. You can't decide to go out to a late show, and just before you walk out the door, decide that you need to learn a few self-defense techniques just in case you run into trouble. This is ridiculous. As you know, it takes months or years of constant training to be competent to defend yourself. It is not something that you can put off until you happen to think about the possibility of needing it one night. You have to be prepared beforehand.

Your preparation in the area of self-defense has to be an ongoing process. If you want to be prepared for tomorrow's surprise encounter, you have to prepare for it today. This is what being prepared actually means. You are preparing now for what may happen sometime down the line. If you find yourself in a situation where you need your skills, they will be ready. If you find that you don't need them, they are still available to you. Either way, you are prepared.

I will win tomorrow because I prepare today.

July 25

*If you are a serious warrior, you'll
become a student of anatomy.*

Forrest E. Morgan

Become a student of human anatomy. Learning how the human body works gives you valuable information that you need for your life on the path of the warrior. There are two reasons for this. First, if you understand the fundamental way that the body is put together, you will realize how important it is to protect your body.

You will start to understand just how fragile the human body actually is. This will also give you valuable insight into which parts of the body need extra protection and why certain areas have to be carefully protected. There are some spots on the body where a knife wound would not be fatal and other spots where just a ¼ inch cut could cost you your life. This is important information to know.

The second reason that you should become a student of the human anatomy is the flip side of the coin. By studying how the body functions, and the structure of the body, you are better prepared to attack the body. Just as there are certain areas that need greater protection, there are also certain areas which are better targets.

There are spots on the body that can withstand a hard punch or kick, and there are spots on the body where a punch or kick could be a fatal blow. Martial arts skills are dangerous skills, and not knowing the human anatomy or not realizing how fragile the body can be, can make martial arts even more dangerous. Know how to attack the body and how to protect the body. Practice safe and fight smart.

My skills are dangerous, but only to bad men.

July 26

Whoso would be a man
must be a nonconformist.

Ralph Waldo Emerson

The warrior is a nonconformist. He refuses to lower his standards or his code of ethics to please others. The fact that other men may consider this action or that action to be acceptable, means nothing to the warrior. He is not interested in conforming to the opinions of others. He is only interested in living up to his own standards which he sets for himself.

If the warrior was the type of man that simply went along with the crowd, he would not be so rare. Anyone can bend their standards to conform to the standards of the day, but it takes a real man to stand firm concerning his ethics when all other men are trying to convince him to conform to their way of thinking. The warrior has to not only have confidence in his own code of honor, but also has to have confidence in his ability to walk alone against the tide of public opinion.

This attitude of independence is what makes the warrior a rare man of honor. He does what he knows in his heart to be right, independent of what anyone else says or does. He refuses to play the game of situational ethics. His ethics are set in stone.

Others may not be able to decipher his code or understand his way of thinking, but they know that the warrior is a man of principle. He is not a man that can be manipulated by popular opinion or moral fads. The true warrior is a true nonconformist and always has been.

I do not conform. My honor guides my path.

July 27

Your greatest weapon
is in your enemy's mind.
Buddha

During the 17th and 18th centuries, pirates terrorized the waters of the Caribbean. It was a common practice for these pirates to use psychological warfare on the ships that they attacked. This was the main purpose of the famous skull and crossbones flags that we associate with pirates today. These flags were meant to instill terror into the minds of the sailors aboard the other ship, and weaken their resolve to fight back once they were attacked. Pirates attacked the minds of their enemies first and foremost.

This is a common strategy in battle and has been employed, probably since the first men fought each other. It is even used today in sporting events. If you can defeat your enemy mentally, you own him. Once he allows fear or anger to enter his mind, he is primed for defeat. He is no longer thinking rationally, but allowing his emotions to control his actions. When he gets to this point, he will make a mistake, and then it is up to you to take advantage of that mistake.

There is also another, less violent side to psychological warfare which the pirates used. They were hopeful that their fear tactics would enable them to achieve their goals without having to resort to actual combat. This should be your goal also. Attacking the enemy's mind should not only be your greatest weapon, but your first line of defense. Learn to manipulate your enemy's mind in order to resolve things without having to resort to actual combat. Avoid having to fight by learning how to defeat your enemy mentally.

I defeat my enemy's mind and win with my strategy.

We are what we repeatedly do.
Excellence is not an act, but a habit.

Aristotle

Do you want to be a man of honor, integrity and character? Then you have to act like a man of honor, integrity and character. Not just once and a while, not just when you are in a good mood, not just around people who you consider important, but all the time. In fact, don't act like a man of honor, *be* a man of honor.

You have to get into the habit of living a life full of honor. It doesn't just happen automatically. You have to practice it and work at it. Sometimes you have to just plain grit your teeth and do it despite your feelings, until the time when acting with honor and integrity becomes automatic.

Aristotle also tells us that excellence is an art form and that it is acquired by training and repetition. You do not do the right thing because you have virtue, but rather you have virtue because you do the right thing. Your actions and intentions form your character. Later, when your character has been formed and becomes a habit, it determines your actions.

The warrior must be careful to make his actions and intentions right. He has to make a habit out of this until he has perfected his character. Once he has begun to perfect his character, acts of honor and integrity come naturally, without conscious thought. When you get to this point, living a life of excellence will become your nature. Your actions determine who you become; and even further what you are. What do your actions say about you?

I form good habits. Excellence is my ultimate goal.

July 29

He who lives without discipline
dies without honor.

The Havamal

It requires discipline to live a life of honor. It is not the easiest path, which is why there are so few people who choose to walk the path of honor. The man of honor makes certain sacrifices in order to live a life of honor, although to him, these sacrifices are more than worth it and are rarely seen as sacrifices at all. He doesn't understand how others live their lives paying little or no attention to the demands of honor. To him, it is unthinkable to live any other way.

Even so, this doesn't mean that a life of honor comes without hard work and intentionally cultivating it on a daily basis. Honor, like most other virtues, does not come automatically, but rather it has to be purposely developed over time. It takes discipline, discipline which most do not care to employ in their lives, and thus never really develop the character trait of true honor. To the common man, it is simply easier to live with "situational honor" where he is honorable most of the time, but his honor is not set in stone.

The warrior, on the other hand, looks at honor a bit differently. To the warrior, honor is not simply nice to have when it is convenient; it is an integral part of his life. Moreover, he takes pains to develop his code of honor and knows exactly what being honorable entails. He knows the truth behind the proverb above. He knows that if you live without discipline, you will have no choice but to die without honor because without discipline, there can be no honor. Live with discipline and leave this earth with your honor intact.

I will die with honor because I live with discipline.

July 30

He who is an ass and takes himself to be a stag,
finds his mistake when he comes to leap the ditch.
Italian Proverb

Don't be overconfident in your skills or abilities. Don't think that you are the toughest man around and nobody else can possibly be a threat to you. There will always be somebody out there who is bigger, stronger, tougher, and more ruthless. I'm not saying that you shouldn't have confidence in your martial arts skills, but make sure that your evaluation of your skills is honest and correct.

You don't want to find yourself in the position of believing that you are a great fighter only to find out in the middle of a violent street encounter that your skills are not quite as sharp as you believed them to be. It is better to discover your weakness in the dojo where you can strengthen your skills in a safe environment, than to discover your weakness in a life-or-death situation. Know your abilities and your limits.

It is very dangerous to have the martial arts skills of Barney Fife, but see yourself as having the martial arts skills of Chuck Norris. Judge your skills rationally and then train to strengthen your weak points.

It is no disgrace to have kicks or blocks which are in need of improvement. Everyone has weak spots that could stand some improvement. The shame is having too much pride in yourself to admit that you have some improvements to make, and carrying on a charade to hide your lack of skill. You will never improve your martial arts skills if you cannot realistically evaluate your skill level.

I see things as they are, not as I wish they were.

July 31

The wise hawk conceals his talons.
Japanese Proverb

It is unwise for the warrior to tell everyone about his weapons and his skills. Nothing good comes from bragging. If you actually are skilled in your martial art and you constantly talk about how great you do this or that, sooner or later someone will want to challenge you. They will want to find out how good you really are, and they will be prepared for all of the weapons that you have been bragging about so brazenly. This is just plain not smart.

Then, when you diffuse the situation with words, as you should, you end up looking as if you were lying about your skills, or that you are a coward. If you have been exaggerating your skills, as braggers tend to do, you find yourself in an even worse position. This should never happen to the warrior. It is wiser to avoid talking about yourself or your skills.

Your weapons are no one else's business. Don't give your enemies a "heads up" about your martial arts prowess. That is equivalent to the quarterback announcing to the defense what pass plays he likes to run before the game starts. Why would you possibly give your enemies an edge?

Next time you are tempted to brag or reveal information about your skills, think about why you feel the urge to open your mouth, and then think about the possible consequences. Do you really need someone else to approve of your abilities or pat you on the back in order to feel good about yourself? If you do, you need to do some soul searching and find out why.

My plans succeed because my skills are hidden.

August 1

Don't teach undesirable people.

Masaaki Hatsumi

In the past, martial arts masters refused to teach their art to just anyone who came through the door requesting to learn from them. Their arts were considered sacred, as were the dojos where they taught their students. The martial arts skills and philosophy that they taught were passed down from master to student over the years. Most of the teachers did not make their living by teaching martial arts. Gichin Funakoshi, for example, was a school teacher, and taught martial arts on the side.

It is totally different in today's world. The martial arts have become big business. There are dojos everywhere you look, and most will accept anyone who has the financial ability to pay their monthly fee and who will sign a long term contract. It is all about money for many people today. No one is turned away, and if they are turned away at one dojo, there are plenty of others who will accept them. This is not the way that it should be.

When you teach someone true martial arts techniques, it is the same as giving them a weapon and showing them how to use it. Sure there are plenty of dojos which are strictly for sport, but they are also teaching dangerous information. Someone's character should be discerned before they are given such weapons. A friend of mine, who happens to be a policeman, told me that dojos have financial concerns and can't afford to turn away paying students. My response was that, as a warrior, you have to put what is right before what is profitable. Always put what is right before what is profitable. Don't teach undesirable students the art of war.

My character, honor and integrity are worth more than money.

August 2

Let not the fruit of action
be your motive to act.
The Bhagavad Gita

The motivation behind your actions should be to fulfill your duty as a warrior. If you see that a course of action is the right course to take, you should take it. Don't be swayed to change your course because of the possible consequences, if you know that you are right. If you see a lady getting mugged on the street, you should step in. It would be wrong if you saw this happening and yet did nothing because you don't want to get involved. On the other hand, it would also be wrong for you to step in because you are interested in getting a reward or getting on the nightly news.

Your motive for doing the right thing should be the simple fact that it is the right thing to do, period. Don't let the outcome of doing the right thing trouble you. Be concerned with doing your duty, and let God take care of the outcome. All you can do is live as you should and take the right action when you determine what that action is. You have no control over the outcome.

Although doing the right thing without apprehension concerning the end result is a basic part of the warrior lifestyle, it is not enough. Your intentions have to be right. Your motives need to be pure. Remember, you must perfect your character, and your thoughts and intentions are a big part of the equation. Don't allow wrong intentions or dishonorable motivations to tarnish good actions. Make things right, inside and out. Do the right thing, for the right reason, at the right time. It has to be right on the inside, before it can be right on the outside.

What is right guides my actions. I live with honor.

August 3

You can also commit injustice
by doing nothing.
Marcus Aurelius

There are many ways in which a man can be unjust. The warrior's actions must be just. Justice is at the center of the warrior's thoughts. He strives to do what is right and just at all times. It is his aim to make all of his actions right according to the standards which he lives. He would never consider acting in such a way as to purposely commit an injustice on another human being. But he must consider that refusing to act is an action in itself.

This is a foreign concept to many people. Doing nothing is actually doing something. You are deciding that your action during a certain time period is to sit still, in essence, to not act, and you are just as responsible for the results of this action as you are for any of your other actions. For example, if you see someone get hit by a car and you are in a position to help, but you choose to do nothing, you are responsible for the consequences of that choice. You may not be held responsible by our legal system, but the warrior lives by a higher law than the law of the land.

This is what Marcus Aurelius is saying when he says, "You can also commit injustice by doing nothing." In the example above, you have committed an injustice to the person who was hit by the car. You did not run over that person. You did not take his wallet while he was lying in the street unconscious, but you did commit an injustice nonetheless, by doing nothing and refusing to help someone in need when you could have taken action.

I always strive to do what is right, even when I do nothing.

August 4

In critical times, one must be devoted
utterly to the cause of justice.
Gichin Funakoshi

Why did Master Funakoshi state that you must be completely devoted to the cause of justice in critical times? What makes critical times any more special than everyday times? The answer is simple. When your back is against the wall, and it is decision time, if you are not utterly devoted to justice, then you will falter and you will compromise your standards, your honor, and your character. It is these critical times which show your true character to the world.

The man who is not 100% devoted to justice, honor and integrity, will compromise himself when times get tough. Oh, he will justify his decision by saying things such as, "I had no choice. My neck was on the line." There are hundreds of ways to justify compromising your honor, but none of those justifications will placate the soul of the warrior who has just made concessions where his honor is concerned. Honor cannot be saved by excuses and justifying wrong actions.

You have to make a firm decision concerning your code of honor or code of ethics, and you must be totally devoted to being a man of honor, especially during critical times. Warriors take justice seriously, just as they take their honor seriously. There is no room for situational or counterfeit honor among those who profess to be true warriors. You are either a man of honor, or you are not. There is no middle ground. Be utterly devoted to your code of honor and to the cause of justice. Be a true warrior.

I am devoted to my code of honor and justice.

August 5

Individuals create karma;
karma does not create individuals.

Bodhidharma

Your actions create your karma, not the other way around. Karma is simply the law of cause and effect. Everything that you do, everything that you say, and everything that you think, carries with it some effect. There is a specific consequence connected to everything that the warrior does, no matter how small or how inconsequential. Nothing is immune to the law of karma, not even your thoughts.

Many people will argue this point and state that they can think whatever they please and there is no consequence connected to their thoughts, but this is not quite right. Your thoughts are strong forces. They have the power to change your emotions, the chemical make-up of your body, and ultimately they control your actions. This is just one example of how something as seemingly trivial as a thought, can have far reaching consequences that we never really consider.

Karma is like that in every part of our lives. Every single thing that happens in your life could be traced back to a cause if we had the ability or insight to do this exercise. Nothing happens without some cause behind it. People create karma. We are in control, not karma. If you don't like the things that are happening in your life, then change your actions, change your speech, change your thoughts, and you will change your future. Ultimately, you are in charge. You make the decisions, and ultimately, you have to live with the consequences of those decisions. If you needed yet another reason to live a life of honor and integrity – now you have it.

I have good karma because my actions are honorable.

August 6

We should know what our
convictions are, and stand for them.

Carl Jung

It is pretty hard to live by your convictions when you don't know what they are, much less have total faith that your convictions are right. Living by your convictions means that you live according to your beliefs. Your convictions are your firmly held beliefs about certain things in your life or in the world. These beliefs are part of what makes you who you are as a warrior, and you should be completely clear concerning your deeply held convictions.

You only truly understand your convictions completely when you take the time to meditate on your beliefs. You have to spend quiet time alone with your thoughts in order to really identify with your personal beliefs or convictions. Most people do not take the time to do this, and therefore, do not really know what they believe or what their convictions are and why they should stand for them. For this reason, the majority of people today either don't have strong convictions, or their convictions are molded by others.

If your convictions are dictated to you by other people, they aren't really your convictions. You have simply adopted someone else's beliefs as your own, and unless you take those beliefs and meditate on them, you will never truly make them personal. This is why so many people are willing to compromise their principles. They say that they believe certain things, but they don't know why they believe them. Therefore, they aren't actually personal convictions, but rather borrowed beliefs which they can take or leave.

I stand for my convictions and they guide my path.

August 7

Let the wise man take refuge in his silence.

Baltasar Gracian

The babbling buffoon – we have all seen him. He is not a rare creature. In fact, you can witness the behavior of this man almost anywhere that you go, whether it be the local restaurant or the grocery store, you are sure to find this amazing individual. He is easy to recognize, just use your ears and listen; his speech always gives him away. You will recognize him by his relentless jabbering about nothing and everything at the same time, and his willingness to repeatedly put his foot in his mouth.

Listening to this foolish man for long is tiresome and fairly fruitless. There is little wisdom that flows from his lips, yet he never tires of sharing what little information he has to impart. If he has read it, heard it, sensed it, or just plain imagined it, don't worry, he will freely communicate it to you at lightning speed, and he will embellish it free of charge. He wouldn't want you not to be entertained! He craves your attention, although there is little in what he has to say that is worthy of your consideration.

Throughout the ages, the sages have warned the wise man to not be like the man who talks incessantly without giving any thought or regard to what he is saying. Don't be like this poor creature who hangs himself over and over with the words from his own lips. Be like the wise man and take refuge in silence. It is not necessary to communicate everything that you know or everything that you think. In fact, it is unwise to do so. One of the traits of the true warrior is his ability to control his tongue. Think before you speak. Weigh your words carefully and make them mean something.

I always think before I speak.

August 8

Things are not always what they seem; the first
appearance deceives many; the intelligence of a
few perceives what has been carefully hidden.

Phaedrus

Don't take things at face value. Always take the time to hear both sides of the story before you make up your mind about something, especially something important. Even after you have heard both sides of the story, it is prudent to always remember that each of those "sides" is merely someone's recollection of what happened. Most people, even when they are trying to be honest, will recall things through their own perception, which may or may not be accurate.

Almost everyone tends to embellish or put their own personal spin on things, especially when they are trying to persuade others to see their point of view. Things are not always exactly as they have been presented to you. It is wise to not only hear both sides, but to also do a little investigating on your own, particularly when the matter at hand is very important. Don't rely on hearsay. Remember that a lot of people today see nothing wrong with lying to you if they feel it will personally help their cause.

Be wise enough to understand that things are often not what they seem. Don't be deceived. Be cautious concerning what you believe and who your trust. Always bear in mind that not everyone lives by the principles that the warrior lives by, principles of honesty and integrity. It is foolish to put your trust in those who do not hold honor and integrity in high regard. Don't depend on the honesty of others; depend on your ability to discern the truth.

I can easily discern the truth and see what is hidden.

August 9

The Universal Way is not just a matter of
speaking wisdom but one of continual practice.

Lao Tzu

It does no good to study wisdom or to sit around and talk about wisdom with your peers, if you do not practice wisdom. The same goes for honor, integrity, character, and all the other traits that are a part of the warrior lifestyle.

As Lao Tzu taught, the way is not simply a matter of speaking about things, but one of continual practice. If the traits of the warrior lifestyle are not put into action in the life of the warrior, they are worthless. Skills unused are of no benefit.

The warrior lifestyle in not about imagination or fantasy; it is about developing your life to the highest possible point. The warrior is a man of excellence in everything he does. He is a doer, not a talker. The man who simply talks a good talk, but never follows through on what he professes, is not a warrior, but rather a wanna-be warrior. He may know the language of the warrior, but he has not committed to live the warrior lifestyle.

On the other hand, the warrior takes his chosen path too seriously to merely talk about things such as honor and integrity, without making them a vital part of his everyday life. This is not a game to the true warrior; this is who he is. He is a man of wisdom, integrity and honor. He is sincere in his quest for the elusive perfection of character. He not only talks the talk, but he also walks the walk. Be a doer, not a talker. Take the path of the warrior seriously and it will reward you greatly.

I always practice what I preach. I am not a hypocrite.

August 10

Shun any action that will diminish honor.
Tiruvalluvar

When you have a decision to make and you are back forth about what to do, the first thing that you must look at in order to make the right choice is whether or not the action is honorable. If the action in question is dishonorable or will in any way go against your code of honor, don't even consider it. It is as simple as that. Any action that will diminish your honor is not the right path for you to take, even if it seems that it might be, for whatever reason. Never be deceived; a dishonorable path will never turn out good for you.

If your honor is compromised, you have chosen the wrong action. In order for your code of honor to be meaningful, it must be unbending. Don't compromise where your principles are involved. Don't be willing to put your honor on the shelf for a period of time in order to perform an action that you know full well goes against your code of honor. Doing this reveals that your commitment to honor is weak and that you don't really take it that seriously, but it is simply a convenience rather than an integral part of your life.

Your honor must be more important to you than the many other things that tempt you to act in ways which might cause you to violate your code. Men of true honor will place their honor above personal gain or profit. There will be things which they will refuse to do, even if they find them enjoyable or profitable, simply because their honor forbids them to be done. The warrior puts his code of honor first in his life, and by doing so he finds that everything else falls into place. Live with honor.

I shun any action that diminishes my honor.

August 11

The success of very important matters often depends on doing or not doing something that seems trivial.

Francesco Guicciardini

To the warrior, the trivial things are just as important as the crucial things. He strives to do everything that he does to the highest level. He is a man who seeks excellence, even in the smallest acts, which is a good thing when you consider this quote by Francesco Guicciardini. Many times it is the small things, which have been neglected, that lead to the failure of your goals or objectives.

Everything matters. Don't take the seemingly inconsequential things for granted because you believe that they don't matter. Strive to be complete. If something is worth doing, it is worth doing well. This includes the small things as well as the "important" things. By taking the time to ensure that everything is taken care of, every "t" is crossed and every "i" is dotted, you know that you have done the best that you can do.

Doing your very best in every undertaking gives you peace of mind. After all, if you have done the best that you can do, and have left nothing to chance, your conscience is free. You know that you have done all that you can do. What else is there?

Also, by approaching everything in your life with this attitude, you will find that you will have fewer hassles and more success. When the foundation is solid, the rest will fall into place. Take nothing for granted; that which seems trivial may be the cornerstone to your success.

Everything matters. I take the time to do everything with excellence.

August 12

Even if the stream is shallow
wade it as if it were deep.
Korean Proverb

Carelessness is the enemy of the warrior. How much trouble and how many hassles could be avoided if only we would do everything from the attitude expressed in this Korean proverb? The warrior should go about everything that he does both cautiously and confidently at the same time. Even the smallest things should be approached carefully to circumvent the possibility of a simple task turning into a nightmare of a mess. This can happen in the blink of an eye if you are not careful.

Have you ever had a simple chore to accomplish only to have it turn into this kind of nightmare? For example, maybe you were going to do something as simple as hanging a picture on the wall of your dojo. Instead of taking the time to measure, drill the hole, and use the correct hardware for the job, you hurried and decided to just hammer in a nail to hang the picture. In your haste, you made a hole in the wall that had to be repaired. Suddenly a very simple task has cost you much more time and work.

Wouldn't it have been better to slow down and take the time to do the chore correctly? Always approach everything that you do with an attitude of doing the best that you can do. Remember the old saying, if it is worth doing it is worth doing right. A little caution can save you a big headache. No matter how simple or easy the task at hand may be, it is important to perform that task with quality in mind. Keep in mind, haste makes waste. Slow down and make quality your signature. Always shoot for excellence in every area of your life.

I am careful in all my ways. I take nothing for granted.

In whatever position you find yourself,
determine first your objective.
Marshall Ferdinand Foch

Your objective is your goal or your purpose. As you may already know, in order for you to hit your target, you must first know what your target is. This is common sense. The first step in achieving your goal is knowing what your goal is. Without knowing what your goal or objective is, how would you determine what needs to be done in order to reach your objective. Different objectives require different actions in order to successful.

This principle applies to everything that you do. The first step in any endeavor should be to determine your objective. This is particularly important to the warrior and yet another of the traits which sets the warrior apart from the man who is only a street fighter. The street fighter will not let an insult go unnoticed or unaddressed. His foolish pride will not let such an offense slide. He has a warped sense of honor which tells him that he must put this guy in his place or he will lose face over the situation.

The true warrior, on the other hand, takes into account his objective in this situation. Is his objective to save face, or is his objective to keep himself and those under his care safe in this situation? I think you know the answer. Knowing what his situation is, he knows what his response must be. Different objectives require different responses. It is only when you know what your objective is that you can know what your action should be, and once you have determined your objective, the appropriate actions are much easier to discern.

I always know my specific objective. I do not shoot in the dark.

August 14

Take away the cause, and the effect ceases.

Miguel de Cervantes

There is no such thing as luck. Everything happens for a reason. The law of cause and effect is the way of nature. Every action, no matter how small, has a ripple effect. Everything that you do, from the boldest action to the smallest thought, has a consequence that follows along with it.

The consequence may be so small and insignificant that you do not notice it, but it is still there. There is a cause for everything. Take away that cause and you take away the effect.

This is why it is so important for the warrior to keep a watchful eye over himself at all times. You must keep this in mind. There is nothing that you can do, nothing that you can say, and nothing that you can think, that will not affect your life in some way. Everything matters. It is important that you live every minute to the best of your abilities. Live according to your code of ethics, whether you are alone or out in public.

If you find that you are constantly dealing with unpleasant consequences, find the cause of those consequences and change it. Change your actions, and you change the consequences. The old saying that it is crazy to continue to do the same things over and over, and expect different results, is true. If you want different results, you have to change what you are doing. If people challenge you and become aggressive every time you go out, you should take a close look at yourself to discover the cause. Take away the cause, and the effect ceases.

Everything has a cause and effect. I am careful with all my actions.

August 15

To be prepared for war is one of the
most effective means of preserving peace.
George Washington

No bad guy wants to attack a warrior. The mugger or thug looks for an easy target. These people do not have any honor. They don't want to test their skills against someone who might be able to pound them into the ground. Just like any other predator, they prey on the weak. Therefore, by being in shape and prepared to defend himself, the warrior is actually preventing other people from attacking him. As I said, no one in their right mind wants to tangle with a prepared warrior.

I can already hear some of you saying that this is a contradiction to the Japanese proverb which states, "The wise hawk conceals his talons." But this is not really a contradiction. I'm not saying that you should go around telling everyone how prepared you are as a warrior.

You don't have to say anything. Criminals are experts at sensing who they should and should not target. They have a pretty good idea whether or not you are prepared to defend yourself, and those who don't could be in for a rude awakening if you are truly prepared.

George Washington knew that other countries would prey on the United States if they perceived us as weak. When you portray yourself as weak, you are actually doing more to cause violence because predators will be tempted to attack you; but by being prepared for battle, they are deterred. Preserve peace; be prepared for battle. Never allow yourself to be caught unprepared.

I am prepared for war, therefore I walk in peace.

August 16

A man can compromise in his actions
without compromising his principles.
Bohdi Sanders

In everything you do, you must first think about your final objective. What is it that you really want to accomplish? Once you are able to answer this question, then, and only then, will you know the right actions to take. If you act without first knowing what your final objective is, you are simply shooting in the dark, and you may find that the final outcome is something that you never intended.

There is a right way and a wrong to do everything in life. Even when you know the right thing to do, you can still do the right thing in the wrong way. For example, the doctor may prescribe a certain medicine for your medical condition. It is the right medicine and it will heal your body if you take it. But, you can still take the right medicine the wrong way.

One of the tenets of the Noble Eight-Fold Path of Buddhism is right action. You can have the right intentions, the right effort, and the right heart, but if you take the wrong action, it can nullify all of your efforts. And, if you take the right action, in the wrong way or at the wrong time, it can also cause you to fail.

A man can compromise in his actions without compromising his principles. You must do the right thing, at the right time, and in the right way. If one of those foundation stones are not right, it can cause you to fail and can even cause unforeseen consequences that can lead to even greater problems than the one that you were trying to solve to begin with. See things from every angle before you act.

I will compromise in my actions, but I won't compromise my principles.

August 17

Make yourself a sheep,
and the wolf is ready.
Russian Proverb

There are a lot of bad guys out there and they, as I have said before, are predators. They look for the easy target. Wolves like to attack sheep, not grizzly bears. There is a reason for this; sheep are weak and can't defend themselves, grizzly bears are strong and not only can, but will defend themselves. Sheep are also not the smartest animals on the planet; they tend to wander around aimlessly, making themselves an easy target.

People who have sheep-like characteristics are exactly what the human wolves are looking for in their prey. They wander around aimlessly, oblivious of their surroundings. They tend to not use their brains when they are out and about, either because they are distracted or just too busy. They appear weak and unable or unwilling to defend themselves from any possible attack. When these people leave home, the wolves smell dinner.

Lt. Col. Dave Grossman has likened the warrior to the sheepdog. He states that it is their duty to protect the sheep and confront the wolves. He goes on to say that, in general, the sheep do not like the sheepdog, because he looks much like the wolf in that he has "fangs and the capacity for violence."

The difference is that the sheepdog would never harm the sheep, but is there for the sheep's protection. The wolf, on the other hand, preys on the sheep. Make yourself a sheep and the wolves will be ready.

I am a sheepdog. I will never be a sheep or a wolf.

August 18

It is foolish to try and live on past experiences. It is a very dangerous, if not fatal habit, to judge ourselves to be safe because of something that we felt or did twenty years ago.
Charles Spurgeon

Being a warrior is an ongoing lifestyle. It is not a goal in the sense that once you achieve the status of a warrior, you can then relax because you now have all the weapons and training that you could ever need. After all, you have a black belt that you earned, how could anybody ever stand up to you in hand to hand combat? Too many people believe that they are prepared to defend themselves or others because of their past training.

Martial arts training is like paddling your boat up a river; as soon as you stop paddling, you begin to go backwards. If you have ever developed your martial arts skills to a level where you felt you could easily defend yourself, it is hard to imagine that your skills have dissipated and you are no longer at the same level. In your mind you still see yourself as a force to be reckoned with, even if it has been years since you actually practiced your art.

Moreover, many people, even if they were promoted to black belt, were never actually prepared to defend themselves in the first place. Their black belt had more to do with sports and memorization than it did with self-defense. There is also a big difference between a practicing black belt and someone who earned their black belt and then quit working out all together. You either continue to practice and move forward or you regress. See things as they are; not doing so can be a very dangerous illusion.

I see things realistically. I do not live in a fantasy world.

August 19

He does not guard himself well
who is not always on his guard.
French Proverb

A warrior should always be on his guard. This doesn't mean that he has to walk around constantly looking over his shoulder for trouble. It also doesn't mean that he has to be uptight and uneasy whenever he is out and about. What it does mean is that he is aware of his surroundings. He is not oblivious to what is going on around him.

When you are leaving the movie or restaurant at night, be aware of your surroundings. Check out who else is around the parking lot when you go out to your car. Just be aware.

Also, don't overindulge when you are out on the town. If you have just eaten enough for three men or you happened to drink a little too much, both your awareness and your ability to defend yourself, if the occasion arises, will be compromised.

It is important to maintain your readiness anytime you are away from home. Stay on guard and be ready for the surprises of life. Awareness is the key. Just being aware of your surroundings can keep you safe. Predators are able to take most people by surprise simply because most people are not aware of their surroundings.

They wander around with their heads in the clouds and their minds going in 20 different directions. If you are not always alert and aware when you are away from home, you are not guarding yourself as well as you should be to avoid predators. This is even more important in today's world which is filled with scum such as Islamic terrorists who kill indiscriminately. Guard yourself well!

I am always aware of my surroundings. I guard myself well.

August 20

The master warrior is a man of character,

a man of wisdom and insight.

Forrest E. Morgan

No man is born with all of the traits in the above quote. These traits have to be developed over time. You have to make a conscious decision to work at acquiring these traits.

This means that there is hope for everyone who wants to be a man of character. It is up to you. You make the decision concerning your own character.

So, how do you become a man or woman of character, wisdom and insight? First, you need to make a firm decision about your own standards. Decide what you stand for and what you won't stand for in your life. Then stick to your decision.

Study the writings from the men of the past who were men of character, wisdom and insight. Don't just casually read through these texts as you would a newspaper, but actually study what they are trying to teach you. Then put what you have read into action; don't just read it and forget it – live it!

For the true warrior this is not a nice addition to his life. This has to be an integral part of his being. He has no choice about this. He has to be a man of character, wisdom and insight. Martial arts training, without this part of the equation, does not produce a warrior; it produces a dangerous menace to society. Character is the cornerstone for the true warrior; character is the cornerstone for the true human being.

My wisdom expands daily. My character is true.

August 21

Deal with a dangerous situation while it is safe.
Eliminate what is vicious before it becomes destructive.

Lao Tzu

One of my favorite books is the *Tao Te Ching*. This book is packed full of wisdom. In the *Tao*, Lao Tzu tells us that it is best to deal with dangerous situations while they are still safe. This is exactly what the warrior should attempt to do when things start to get heated between other people. We all realize that a physical encounter can be a very dangerous and destructive situation. Things can get violent very quickly.

Your duty as a warrior is to try your best to stop circumstances from getting to that point. Take control before tempers start to boil. Deal with the situation and handle it with your psychological skills. Attack your opponent's mind without him ever knowing that is what you are doing. Manipulate the situation without allowing others to see that you are in control. Taking these subtle actions before things get to the point of no return can eliminate a vicious threat before anyone else even recognizes that there was imminent danger.

Train yourself to recognize a dangerous situation before it occurs. Don't allow your pride to get in the way of your victory. Sun Tzu taught that the best victory is won without fighting. This is what he was talking about. Learn to fight using subtle techniques, so subtle that your enemy doesn't even realize he has been in a battle, much less that he has been completely defeated. These techniques come from using your mind, not your muscles, but they can be just as effective. Learn the art of winning without fighting.

My mind is my greatest weapon and I keep it sharp.

August 22

Whatever you think, be
sure it is what you think.

T. S. Eliot

Independence is an important trait of the warrior. Many times the warrior's view, whether on ethics or actions that have to be taken, differ from that of the average person. He is an independent spirit and must have the courage to stand by both his thoughts and his convictions. The warrior shouldn't allow himself to be swayed by the voice of public opinion or outside pressures from people who do not share the same ethics as he does.

A warrior's thoughts have to be his own. He must determine what is right and wrong by the strict code of ethics which he has set for himself. Nobody else can do that for him. Very few people share his convictions concerning right and wrong, good and evil, or honor and integrity, therefore he must think for himself. If you allow others to influence your thinking, instead of thinking rationally for yourself, you have given away part of your freedom, the freedom to think and decide for yourself.

The majority of people in our society today do just that. They allow the government, the news media, the schools, or their family members to think for them. They are too lazy to take the time and think about a subject rationally and then make up their own mind about the issue. It is much easier for them to allow the radio shows or television hosts to tell them what to believe. The problem is that this is also much more dangerous. Others control you when you allow them to think for you. Make sure that what you believe is what *you* believe.

I think for myself and I seek the truth.

August 23

Having the idea is not living the reality.

Rumi

In our world, which has become dominated by the internet and all of the various online entertainments, many people find themselves living a type of fantasy life. They have "friends" online which they have never met. They carry on conversations with people who may or may not be real, and believe that they have numerous friends, but when they meet someone face-to-face, they find that the social skills which work so well for them online, don't really transfer into the real world. There is a big difference in the real world and the little fantasy world which they have created.

In the same way, many people read books on the subject of martial arts and watch videos on how to defend themselves. Many go to dojos to learn how to defend themselves with the skills of a true martial artist, but never have used their "skills" beyond the safety of the choreographed moves which most dojos practice for their self-defense training. Mentally they believe that they know what they are doing when it comes to self-defense, but do they really? Can you learn to fight without ever being in a real fight?

As Rumi tells us, having an idea about something is not the same thing as living the reality. Sparring in a safe environment with a familiar partner, is much different from a no rules street fight where your life is on the line and the other person is trying his best to do as much damage to your body as possible. You can't live your life in your own little bubble and expect to be prepared for real life when you finally get the courage to go out into the world. Train for authenticity and be ready for the reality of the streets.

I see things as they truly are, not as I wish they were.

August 24

If you live in the river you
should understand the crocodile.

Indian Proverb

The mind of the predator is so foreign to the majority of people walking around today, that they can't even imagine how predators think. You hear them make comments such as, "People are all the same," or "People are just people." They have no concept about the mindset of someone who is capable of committing murder or assaulting an elderly lady.

The criminal mind is different. People are not all the same. Predators have different values than the average person. They don't value human life the way the normal person does. Expecting someone, who does not value human life, to act the same as the average person or to behave as an upstanding citizen, is absurd. There are people out there who would kill you over pocket change and not give your passing a second thought. Predators are different!

If you live by the river, you need to understand the ways of the crocodile. Even if you only visit the river occasionally, you still should understand the dangers which it holds. You need to know what to look for and how to avoid those dangers. You need to know how to respond and what to do should you come face-to-face with the dangerous predators that live on the river. If you live in an environment where these type people live, you need to understand who they are and how they think. Don't be caught off guard by a naive world view. Not everyone you run into is going to be just another nice person.

I make sure that I understand the predator. I know my enemy.

August 25

Those who play with cats
must expect to be scratched.

Cervantes

Have you ever played with a cat using a string or some other toy? If so, you know that no matter how careful you are, you usually get scratched. That is just the nature of cats. They are not careful about where their claws strike. They just instinctively claw at things, and many times they hit you instead of the toy.

The same principle goes for people. If you are going to hang around with thugs, street punks, or people of low character, be prepared to be scratched. That is just their nature. There is no honor among thieves, and there is no true friendship among people of low character. I know that this statement will be offensive to some people, but it is true. You cannot trust people who do not esteem virtue and character; and it is a mistake, many times a dangerous mistake, to put your trust in them.

All of the sages throughout history tell us that it is vitally important to choose the right people to associate with and to allow in your life. Choosing the wrong people to be "friends" with, people of low character, can cause major problems for you, and at the least, will not help you on your path of warriorship.

The wise man should choose to associate only with those who will help him on his journey. Why would you choose to associate with someone who has nothing positive to offer you, but potentially could cause you a lot of trouble? The man who associates with the sage becomes wise; the man who associates with the cat gets scratched.

I am able to read people and see their true character.

Be your friend's true friend.
The Havamal

The true warrior is the best friend you could possibly imagine finding in your lifetime. He understands the value of true friendship, as well as understanding the difference in a friend and an acquaintance. Because he is a man who takes his word, his honor and his character seriously, he is the kind of friend that you can count on to be there when the chips are down. He is not a fair weather friend. It is in his nature to stand by his friends in times of trouble and to go to bat for his friends when they need him.

His understanding of what a friend should be is far beyond that of most men. Once you are truly his friend, you have a friend for life. Moreover, you have a friend with character, honor and integrity, one who will help you on your journey, and not be a hindrance. He is a friend who appreciates the type of lifestyle that you are working so hard to manifest in your life.

The warrior is a friend by the true definition of the word. He will stand side by side with you, should you need his aid. The whole idea of turning his back on his friend is so repulsive to the warrior, that the thought of it never enters his mind.

During your life, you will have many acquaintances, but very few real friends. Don't get the two confused. There is a tremendous difference in both the definitions and the reality of the two. Once you have a true friend, you should be a true friend in return. Your friends should know that you are there for them, no matter what. They should know what it means to have a warrior as a friend. Anything less is dishonorable.

I am my friends' true friend. I am the best friend someone could have.

August 27

Snakes follow the way of serpents.
Japanese Proverb

Snakes follow the way of snakes, and fools follow the way of fools. I have talked a lot about how the warrior should act; now let's look at the antithesis of the warrior, the fool. There are characteristics which define the fool, just as there are characteristics which define the warrior. The sages tell us that fools are full of pride and find pleasure in evil deeds. They are ungrateful, unintelligent, short-sighted, and always in the majority.

Fools are not fond of study, but rather they waste their time in other people's business, and participate in malicious gossip. Though they have a shocking lack of wisdom, they esteem themselves as wise. They refuse to listen to advice from the wise, but find pleasure in airing their own opinions. Although the fool may acquire knowledge, he never acquires understanding. Hypocrisy is the trademark of the fool; he is rarely sincere.

These unwise men believe whatever they are told, except when it comes to real wisdom. They are easily led astray and make easy targets for predators and swindlers. Speaking without thought is common with these men. Fools are quick to offer an insult, and even quicker to become angry and willing to fight. The *Book of Proverbs* says that fools die for lack of judgment.

These traits do not paint the picture of a warrior. The warrior lifestyle is a completely different road than the one that the fool travels. If you find that any of these traits are present in your life, it is time to make some changes. Think about this.

I follow the way of the warrior.

August 28

To generalize is to be an idiot.
William Blake

There are very few statements which are absolute. Things are not always black and white; in fact most things are not black and white. Therefore it is unwise to make generalizations, but every day there are examples of people who make absolute statements in our media. One of the statements often heard, especially in our schools today is that there is never any reason for violence; violence never solves anything.

The word never implies that it never happens. The people who make such statements usually don't believe them themselves. Does anyone believe that violence has never solved anything? It certainly has served to save many lives. World War II is a perfect example. Yes, many lives were lost during World War II, but think about how many more lives would have been lost without a violent intervention.

Self-defense, many times involves violence, and I can assure you that there is a very good reason for violence when you are being attacked and your life is on the line. Furthermore, I doubt that these same people who state that there is never any reason for violence, would not fight back if they were being attacked and their life was being threatened.

Don't make blanket statements. To anyone who is thinking rationally, generalizations demonstrate, at the very least, a lack of thought, and in the worst case scenario, a lack of intelligence, neither which is fitting for a warrior. Think rationally and think before you speak. Generalizations are not the way of the warrior; they are the way of the idiot.

I do not speak in generalizations. Absolutes are rare.

August 29

Don't easily trust anyone on this
earth because there are all kinds.

Bruce Lee

During your lifetime you are going to run across a lot of different kinds of people, and the sages have always taught that the majority of the people that you meet will not be people of the highest character. People are different; they don't all have the same character traits or the same standards. Many of the people you meet will not think twice about lying to you in their business dealings. As amazing as it seems to the warrior, a lot of people lie, cheat and steal whenever it suits their purpose.

Traits such as these are foreign to the warrior and his lifestyle, but he must be aware that they are common in the world. The way of the warrior has always been rare, but is even more so in today's society. Knowing this, it is wise to be careful concerning who you trust. As the Russian proverb goes, "Trust but verify." Don't just blindly trust everyone that you do business with in this world. If you do, I can assure you that you will be sorely disappointed.

The warrior must be able to discern the honest man from the dishonest man. See things as they really are and look beyond the charade. Be prepared to be tested by people who will look you square in the eye and lie through their teeth, without blinking or missing a beat. These kinds of people are becoming more and more common, and you will have to learn how to deal with them. Be prepared to deal with those who don't live by a code of honor, and deal with their lack of integrity with the same high standards in which you deal with all people.

I am very careful and selective about who I trust.

August 30

*Hold yourself responsible for a higher
standard than anyone else expects of you.
Never excuse yourself.*
Henry Ward Beecher

To the warrior, laws are pretty much worthless. Laws are for men
of low character who need someone else to keep them in line with the
threat of punishment. This is not to say that warriors do not have to
obey the laws of the land, at least most of the time. What it does mean
is that the warrior's code of ethics is actually stricter than any law of
the land. His standards require him to keep a closer watch on his
actions than any law could.

The warrior holds himself to a higher standard than anyone else
expects of him, just as Henry Ward Beecher suggests that you should
do. He doesn't bend his "rules" as one does with discretionary laws
such as speed limits, etc. For this reason, he finds most laws useless.
The true man of character doesn't need laws in order to do what he
should. He simply does what's right regardless of whether or not there
is a law to guide him.

Moreover, even if there were no laws, the warrior would still live
the same lifestyle of honor and integrity. The point here is that the
warrior sets his own law. That law is his code of honor or code of
ethics. He decides what is right and what is just, and lives accordingly.
You may be thinking if everyone did that we would have anarchy, and
you would be exactly right. Everyone is not a man of honor. That is
why we have to have laws – for lesser men who will not discipline
themselves.

I hold myself to a higher standard.

242

August 31

Hated by Many ~ Confronted by None!

Have you ever noticed how true warriors are hated by many, but confronted by none? There are many people out there who will bad mouth you behind your back, but who never seem to be able to manage the courage to confront you face-to-face with their hollow opinions.

People like that are sheep. They would like to be tigers, but they do not have the courage to face their prey. They will babble endlessly about the ways of the tiger, but only when the tiger is nowhere in sight. When the tiger appears, they are as silent as a winter's night, and do their best to hide in the shadows – big talkers with no spines.

They are cowards to the core, but they hate the warrior so much that they still find ways to attack him. These people are much like the little lap dog behind the chain link fence. These little mutts bark and bark as the noble sheep dogs walks by the fence. They act all tough, but in reality, they are nothing more than noise. Their bark is worse than their bite.

If the sheep dog ever gets annoyed enough to stop and move towards the fence, these barking, paper "tigers" turn into yelping road runners, running as fast as possible to the safety of their home. They act tough, but can't back it up when push comes to shove.

Don't let the opinions of such people bother you. Not everyone's opinions matter. It is the opinions of those who you respect that are to be valued, not the opinions of mealy-mouthed cowards who talk behind your back. Strive to be a true warrior and you will be hated by many, but most likely confronted by none.

The opinions of others do not bother me.

September 1

Doing it halfway is no good; you have to do it all the way, give yourself wholly to it.

Taisen Deshimaru

It is easy to get into the habit of thinking about "this, that, and the other thing" when you are in the middle of a workout. This is the result of an undisciplined mind. If you find yourself focusing on other things during your workout, stop yourself and refocus on why you are working out in the first place.

Thinking of other things, instead of focusing your energy on your workout, is definitely not taking your training "deadly serious." Your training is too important to do half-heartedly. Focus all your energy on the task at hand.

Arnold Schwarzenegger pointed out during his bodybuilding years that your muscles actually increase in size and get bigger if you concentrate and visualize this happening as you workout. Now, if concentrating on your weight training increases the effectiveness of your workout, why wouldn't the same be true concerning your martial arts workout? What you concentrate on matters. Our mind has much greater powers than we give it credit for having.

Do you want to increase your flexibility? Visualize your muscles lengthening and becoming more flexible and stronger as you stretch. If you want to make your front kick stronger, visualize yourself going through each part of the kick. Focus totally on your kick when you are practicing it. If you are not including your mind in your workout, you are leaving out a vital part of your training.

I do everything to the best of my ability. Excellence is my goal.

September 2

When you step beyond your own gate,
you face a million enemies.

Gichin Funakoshi

Every time you leave your home and venture out into the world you should be aware of your surroundings. Be aware that there are bad guys out there. You may or may not recognize them as your paths cross, but they are there. As a warrior, you should recognize this fact and not walk around in a daze when you are in public. Many times it seems as if people walk around in a semi-hypnotic state, unaware of their surroundings or the people around them. This is unwise and dangerous.

Discipline your mind. Stay aware of both your surroundings and what is going on wherever you may find yourself. This doesn't mean that you should see everyone as your enemy when you leave home, but you should realize that many of the people that you see are not going to be upstanding people of good character. Be careful and aware when you are outside of the security of your own gate.

Learn to recognize the character traits of the predator and be aware of anyone who displays these traits. Also, realize that predators are very skilled at disguising these traits. Not everyone who displays the behavior of a predator is going to be a threat to you, but it is always best to play it safe. The key is always being aware of your surroundings. Don't be caught unaware of your surroundings and find yourself in a bad situation. Keep this little piece of wisdom from Master Funakoshi in the back of your mind whenever you leave home, as a reminder to be alert and attentive.

I am always aware when I leave my home.

September 3

In the midst of men who hate us,

let us live without hatred.

The Dhammapada

The old adage that you fight fire with fire is a good analogy for many things, but it is not for hatred. *The Dhammapada* states that hatred can only be combated with love, not more hate. When hatred is met with more hatred, it only fosters a continuing cycle of hatred among men. Fight hate with love, but take care that you realize what this means and that you think about this rationally.

You are responsible for your actions, not someone else's actions. If someone has a malicious hatred towards you, this doesn't give you a license to hate them back. You must still walk the path of warriorhood by the same standards of integrity and honor, no matter how someone else acts. Too many people live with the idea that if someone crosses them, the gloves are off and anything goes.

The warrior does not have the liberty to set his honor and integrity on a shelf just because someone wrongs him. He is required to live by his code of honor. Even if everyone around him hates him, he still must live without allowing hatred to be a part of his mindset. The warrior holds himself to a higher standard, no matter how others live.

This doesn't mean that he doesn't fight back when action is required. Warriors can use their martial arts skills against an enemy without hating that enemy. The fact that the warrior tries all else before resorting to violence, attests to the reality that the warrior is not acting out of hatred, but out of necessity. Think about this.

I am not responsible for the actions of others, only mine.

September 4

But here we may wonder what he would
do if nobody knew anything about it.
The Code of the Samurai

What would you do if you knew that there was absolutely no possibility that anyone else would ever find out about your actions? According to *The Code of the Samurai*, this is a question that every warrior should ask himself. Would this fact change the way that you think about things or would you continue to live by the standards that you have set for yourself? This question is the true test of your character.

The real warrior would live the same way and adhere to the same high standards whether anybody else knew about his actions or not. Even if all laws were abolished and we had a world of complete anarchy, his standards would not change.

To men of character, their standards are not flexible. Their honor is not negotiable. Whether they are alone or in the middle of thousands of people, their character is set in stone. They know that their character is a part of their being and they refuse to allow it to be tarnished for any reason.

To the samurai, this question was an insinuation of hypocrisy. If a man is sincere about his beliefs and his code of ethics, he doesn't just live by them on some occasions, while at other times completely ignoring them. He lives the life of the warrior seven days a week, regardless of who is watching. Keep a check on your character. Ask yourself, "What would I do if nobody else knew about it?" Be honest. If he answer is not what you want to hear, you have some work to do.

I live and act with honor, even when I am alone.

September 5

The angry man will defeat
himself in battle as in life.
Samurai Maxim

If you will pay attention as you go through life, you will see many people who allow their anger to defeat them. They will get angry and say or do the wrong thing. I have seen anger cost people jobs, friendships, money, the list could go on and on. Don't be defeated by your anger. Don't give your enemy an easy victory. An angry mind is never a conscious, rational mind.

I have seen many fighters at tournaments that have fought well until they lost their composure. It is fairly easy to tell when a fighter has lost his composure and has given in to his anger. His punches, instead of being controlled and focused, become wild and erratic. His kicks also become sloppy and frequently miss his targets, while at the same time leaving him open to his opponent's counter attacks. It is obvious from his behavior that he has lost his poise and is trying to inflict a painful blow just as much as he is trying to score points.

I have rarely seen someone win a match, who has allowed his anger to take control of his thinking and his actions. More often, the person who loses his cool loses the match, along with a portion of his dignity and respect. It is self-deception to believe that you are unstoppable when you get really angry. I believe that if you think back to the times in your life when you have allowed your anger to control your actions, you will find that your anger did not win you any victories. On the contrary, the angry man usually ends up defeating himself. Don't allow your anger to defeat you!

I control my anger at all times. Anger cannot defeat me.

September 6

Do not seek to follow in the footsteps
of wise men, seek what they sought.

Basho

Too many people idolize the martial artists or great philosophers of the past. They put them on pedestals almost like they were gods. They want to be like them; they are almost obsessed with them. You shouldn't focus so much on the person, but on what that person tried to teach. What was it that these masters sought and what did they want to teach others? What thoughts did these wise men have and why?

Warriors do not try to imitate someone else. They shouldn't try to be exactly like Bruce Lee or Lao Tzu. What they should do is seek the perfection that the great men of the past sought. Seek the perfection of your martial arts skills. Seek the perfection of your character.

Seek wisdom, discipline, knowledge, and honor. Dedicate yourself to seeking what they sought, not to the man himself or any specific philosophy. Men are just men, no matter how great they were; seek the Source. Seek what they sought.

If we were able to actually sit down and engage in a conversation with the great teachers of the past, I believe that they would tell us this exact same thing. They would say, "I am nothing special. You should seek wisdom and knowledge. Do not seek to be my disciple."

Great teachers will teach their students how to think, not just what to think. It is with this knowledge that we should read the wisdom of the elders. Wisdom is not about repeating quotes and clichés, but about internalizing true knowledge and using your mind.

I cultivate wisdom and the perfection of character.

September 7

The hunter can make many mistakes, the hunted, only one.
Native American Maxim

Most criminals are predators. They "hunt" for the weak, the unaware, and the unprepared. They can afford to make some mistakes and still survive to "hunt" another day. It may take several "hunts" for the criminal to bag his prey, but he learns from his mistakes and continues to hunt, perfecting his skills as a predator.

The "hunted" on the other hand, cannot afford to make a mistake. He may not get a chance to learn from his mistake. The "hunted" has to remain alert at all times, being aware of his surroundings and constantly watching for the predators who seek to prey on him. One mistake may cost him his life.

This fact actually makes it more important for the warrior to have sharp self-defense skills. You don't have the luxury of learning from your mistakes on the streets.

Those mistakes could be a permanent lesson. The warrior has to be ready for the attack. Even if the predator makes a mistake and fails in his quest, he can still do some serious damage to his prey, if his prey is unprepared.

The warrior has to be alert and aware of his surroundings at all times. He cannot afford to let down his guard. The pressure is on the prey, not the predator. The predator can always live to hunt another day; the prey cannot afford to be careless. Why does the warrior need to be alert and aware at all times? The Native American maxim above summarizes the answer to this question perfectly. Think about it.

I am not prey. I will destroy every predator that comes against me.

September 8

Your reality check must be done long before you actually find yourself confronted with a life and death, kill-or-be-killed situation.

Dirk Skinner

It is very important for the warrior to judge his skills and readiness to deal with a violent conflict honestly and accurately. You need to know ahead of time how much force you are willing to use and in what circumstances you are prepared to use that force. You have to decide how far you will go in defending yourself and those who depend on you. Are you mentally prepared, as well as physically prepared, to do what it takes in an actual self-defense situation?

Being mentally prepared for a confrontation is just as important as being physically prepared. All the training in the world will do you no good if your mind panics in a life-or-death situation. For the warrior, being ready means that he is prepared in every area of his life – spiritually, mentally, and physically. Train your mind as well as your body. Know what you are prepared to do and what you are not prepared to do, before the occasion arises.

This is where your visualization practice can come into play. Visualize different attacks in different circumstances, with different people, and then see yourself responding to each one in the way which you feel is right. This practice will establish your response in your mind. Essentially, it is like you have already experienced this attack, although it was only in your mind. This is part of your mental training, a very important part.

I know what I am willing to do, and I have the will and the skill to do it.

September 9

Gratitude is the sign of noble souls.

Aesop

Character is one of the traits of the true warrior. In fact, character is one of the most important traits of the warrior. Without character, there really is no warrior, but rather just a person who should have never been given the gift of martial arts training. Character is vital to warriorship.

Gratitude is an important part of good moral character, and the warrior never takes gratitude lightly. When someone does a favor for you, no matter how large or how small, you are indebted to that person until you have repaid that favor.

The Japanese have a term for this; it is called giri. Giri is your duty to repay your debts. You should not just say thank you and then forget about it. This is not the way of the warrior. You have incurred a debt and not paying that debt is an act of dishonor.

It doesn't matter if it is a small favor or something much more important, a debt is a debt, and the warrior is honor bound to return the favor. It is really very simple. If someone does something nice for you, you must return the favor. Don't allow any good deed to go unnoticed or unappreciated.

Hold yourself to a higher standard than the average person. Live by your own set of standards, standards that require gratitude and appreciation to be shown when someone else helps you in any way. Be a noble soul. Never fail to express your gratitude, even for the smallest things.

I am grateful for every blessing in my life.

September 10

To respond immediately to an angry
person is like throwing fuel on a fire.

Spanish Proverb

The true warrior should become an expert at handling an angry man. Most times, in a conflict, the angry man can be calmed down and the situation can be handled without things getting physical.

Angry people will usually calm down pretty quickly if they are handled correctly. Never respond to an angry person with a fiery comeback, even if he deserves it. This will only increase his anger. As the proverb above states, this only adds fuel to his fire.

Instead, remain composed and try to calm his anger. You already know that you have him defeated, because he has allowed anger to get the best of him. This is a perfect time to practice the skill of defeating your enemy without fighting. Don't allow his anger to become your anger. If you can't control this situation without things becoming physical, use his anger against him to defeat him physically. Either way, his anger has defeated him.

You may fight fire with fire, but you don't fight anger with anger. In fact you shouldn't fight at all if you are angry. Allow the angry man time to catch his breath and think. Most people will calm down after they have had time to think about things. Don't respond immediately if you can avoid it. If you have to respond immediately, respond with a soft, but dignified reply. Remember, your goal is to defeat your enemy, not to appear as though you got the best of him verbally. Think about this.

I see angry people as a chance to practice my de-escalation skills.

September 11

Trust in today's friends as if
they might be tomorrow's enemies.

Baltasar Gracian

Never put too much trust in your friends or acquaintances. No matter how good a friend you think you have, you should not trust them with enough information that they will have the ability to use it against you in some way. Today's best friend can turn against you faster than you can imagine. People that you think will never ever turn on you, could be your worst enemy tomorrow.

You can still have good friends without arming them with information concerning your private affairs. No matter how good of a friend you think you have, not everything should be discussed with him. Use discretion with everyone.

If they turn out to be your tried and true friend, great, if not, then you have avoided arming them with any weapons that could be used against you. The bottom line is that you should always watch what you say. Don't say too much. Keep personal and private information to yourself.

Not everything is other people's business. Don't feel the need to share every single thing about your life with others. Some people feel the need for the approval of others to confirm that they are on the right path. The warrior should know he is on the right path independent of whether or not others approve of his lifestyle. He doesn't need their stamp of approval to live by the standards that he has set for himself. Have confidence in yourself.

Fake friends are bountiful. I am careful who I trust.

September 12

If you wanna live life on your own terms,
you gotta be willing to crash and burn.
Motley Crue

Living the warrior lifestyle is definitely living life on your own terms. There are very few people left in this world who live their life by a specific code based on honor, character, and integrity. Therefore, when you live by the code, you walk alone much of the time.

The life of the warrior is very independent. You must be an independent thinker. You must live your life, your way, without conforming to the lifestyle that everyone else approves of or believes to be "normal." And, when you live your life in this way, you will find that it seems to rub many people the wrong way.

You will have people just waiting for you to crash and burn, as your lifestyle makes them see their own faults. They would love to have your character, your honor, and your integrity, but they are not willing to walk that path. They want the reward without the work. They want what you have, but they aren't willing to make the sacrifices to earn it.

If you want to live your life protecting those you love, and willing to protect those around you, you have to be ready to crash and burn, because that is always a possibility. When you put your life on the line, you are never assured that you won't lose it.

While this is all true, live by your own code anyway. It is better to live one day as a tiger than 100 years as a sheep. Live life on your own terms and be ready for whatever comes your way.

I live my life my way and I accept the risks and earn the rewards.

September 13

Embrace the snake and it will bite you.
Bulgarian Proverb

There is an old Japanese folk tale about the farmer and the snake which would serve you well to remember. The farmer was out working on his farm one day, getting ready for the winter snows to set in. It was already cold and snow was on the ground. While doing his chores, he came across a snake lying in the snow, nearly frozen to death. Feeling benevolent, the farmer wrapped the snake in his coat and took it inside his home to see if he could save the poor creature.

The farmer laid the snake on the floor in front of the fireplace to warm it up and see if he could revive it. He checked on it often to see if it was going to live or not. As the snake started to show a bit of life, the farmer went into the kitchen to get some water for his new friend. Coming back into the room with the saucer of water, the farmer leaned over and placed the water in front of the snake. In a split second, the snake lunged out and bit the farmer in the neck, rendering a lethal dose of toxic venom.

As he lay on the floor, dying from the venomous bite, the farmer looked at the snake and asked, "Why did you kill me after I saved your life?" The snake coldly said, as it slithered away, "I can't help it, it's just my nature."

Learn to judge the nature of others. There are many bad people out there who will take advantage of any help you offer, and then stab you in the back. Help others when you can, but be selective about who you help and what you get yourself into. See things as they really are.

I am always alert and careful with dangerous people.

Do not forget great kindness,
even for a single meal.
Emperor Wen Di

People in today's world seem to feel that the world "owes" them something. They have the attitude that they are somehow special and deserving. Gratitude is something that many people pay lip service to, but never really understand what it actually means. Sure, it is common to hear someone say "Thank you," but are they actually grateful for the kindness that they have received?

You should remember that no one "owes" you anything in this world. They don't have to hold the door open for you. They don't have to return your lost dog. They don't have to do anything for you at all. It is only out of the kindness of their heart that people do nice things for other people, and you should be sincerely grateful when someone does do something nice or kind for you.

As a teacher, I see ungratefulness on a daily basis, especially in younger people. Someone will do them a favor or go out of their way to help them, and they couldn't care less. When I lecture them about how lucky they are that someone was willing to help them, I hear things such as "Well, it didn't cost them anything," or "It was no big deal." People have lost the attitude of gratefulness.

This should not be the case for the warrior. The true warrior knows that if someone does something for him, he is indebted to that person. At the very least, he should show sincere gratitude, but what's more, he owes that person for their kindness.

I never forget a favor or a kindness. I am an honorable man.

September 15

Men flourish only for a moment.
Homer

Nobody is promised tomorrow. All of the sages have taught that your time on this earth is very short; it goes by in a flash. From the earliest wisdom writings to the Native Americans and the samurai, every warrior culture knew the importance of using the time that you have on this earth wisely. This is even truer for the warrior because the warrior lives life on the edge, never knowing when duty may require him to put his life on the line, and when fate may dictate that his time here is finished.

Juvenal put it this way, "The short bloom of our brief life flies fast away. While we are calling for flowers and wine and women, old age is upon us." Time is extremely deceptive. While you go about your day to day routine, the sands of time continue to flow to the bottom of the hourglass. Knowing that you don't have all the time in the world, you should take pains to live right, today. Don't delay. If there is anything that you want to learn, study, or do with your life, do it now, as you don't know when later will be too late.

The samurai warriors recognized the importance of this in their lives. A samurai's daimyo, feudal lord for whom the samurai was employed, could require that the samurai warrior commit suicide at his will, and the samurai was obliged to do so. Samurai warriors understood, that because of their lifestyle, tomorrow was never guaranteed to them. Therefore, they made sure that they were prepared for death. They lived their life by strict standards of honor, and they took life seriously. You are only here for a moment. Now is the time to live the warrior lifestyle; later may be too late.

Life is short; I am living my life to the fullest.

September 16

People hate those who make them feel their own inferiority.
Lord Chesterfield

Have you ever noticed how, if a football team evolves into a dynasty, everyone wants to see them get beat? This is because nobody likes to feel inferior to anyone else, and a team who has practiced, worked, and grabbed hold of excellence, makes those who have not, feel inferior. The same principle applies to individuals. Those who have developed their lives to the point of excellence, make others who have not, feel inferior, unless they are very careful about how they carry themselves. This can also lead to hard feelings and jealousy.

The warrior should develop his life to the point of excellence, while at the same time living in such a way as to not make those who haven't, feel inferior. Yes, this is a tall order on both accounts. It is hard enough to live the life of the superior man, who has worked to develop his character through many hours of discipline and training, but once you start to feel that you are making progress, it can be even harder not to make others feel inferior. You have to watch what you say and how you treat those who have no honor.

How do you live a life of excellence and honor without making others feel inferior? The answer lies in respect. You have to treat them with respect, even if you don't really respect their lifestyle choices. This is not being hypocritical. It is simply treating others as you would have them treat you. Inside, you may know that men of honor, who live the warrior lifestyle, deserve more respect and reverence, but this fact doesn't mean that you shouldn't treat others respectfully.

I am wary of those who may be jealous of me.

September 17

It is easier to prevent bad
habits than to break them.

Benjamin Franklin

Part of the duty of the warrior is to develop good habits in every area of his life, spiritually, mentally and physically. Essentially, the development of the right habits is what *BUSHIDO* is all about. Honor, character, and integrity have to be practiced and studied until they become a habit. In the same way, your workouts and your meditation time have to become a habit; they have to become a part of who you are, not just something that you do.

As demanding as this duty may sound, it is much easier to develop these traits and make them your predominant habits, than it is to allow bad habits to take root and then to try to break them. Bad habits will have to be dealt with in order to live the lifestyle of the warrior.

Just as noxious weeds are contrary to your goals if you are a gardener, many bad habits are directly contrary to the qualities that you need to foster on the path of the warrior. Therefore these bad habits have to be rooted out.

If you have ever done any gardening, you know how much easier it is to put down mulch or fabric to stop weeds from ever growing in your garden, than it is to allow weeds to grow for weeks and then try to get rid of them. Once the weeds have developed strong roots, they are extremely hard to eliminate. The same principle applies to bad habits. It is easier to not develop bad habits than to break them. Prevent them before they develop strong roots in your life.

I consciously form good habits and weed out bad habits.

September 18

When you arise in the morning, give thanks for
the morning light, for your life and strength. Give
thanks for your food and the joy of living. If you see
no reason for giving thanks, the fault lies in yourself.

Tecumseh

Spirituality has always been a part of the warrior lifestyle, and so have the character traits of gratitude and appreciation. Tecumseh tells us that each morning you should be thankful for all of your blessings. Be thankful for your health, your family, for having enough food and water, for living in a peaceful, free society, or simply for the fact that you are alive.

There are any number of things in which you can be thankful for in your life. Even if you are running into hard times at the present moment, you can find much to be thankful for, just meditate on the blessings that you have in your life. Tecumseh certainly did not have a life of leisure at the time he taught this. He was at war for the very existence of his people, and yet he continued his teaching with the statement that if you don't see a reason to be thankful, the fault lies in yourself.

If you find that you have a bitter attitude toward life and the things which are unfolding in your life, it is time to do some soul searching. The samurai taught that we should cleanse our hearts morning and night. Don't allow bitterness to reside in your heart or mind. Meditating on the things in your life which you appreciate is one way to keep resentment and bitterness out of your heart.

I find something to be thankful for each day.

September 19

*Ikken hisatsu – one punch kills – is the essence of karate.
Put everything – your whole life – into one punch.*

Masami Tsuruoka

In our politically correct society, we don't hear the phrase "one punch – one kill" much anymore. You are much more likely to hear things such as strike here, there, and here, and you will score a point, but if you draw blood you will be disqualified. Martial arts have become more of a sport than what they were meant to be, which is a way to defend yourself against deadly assaults. They were never meant to be a sport or a fun activity for kids. The martial arts were deadly serious; they weren't meant as some sort of game, but that is exactly what they have become in today's world for many people.

Many of today's martial artists see traditional arts as either strictly a form of art or just boring and outdated. They neglect the fact that when these arts originated, they were not for competition, sport, or hobby; they were for combat. The fact that many people see traditional martial arts as outdated simply shows their lack of understanding of these arts. Has the art of hand-to-hand combat changed so much that old techniques are only useful for tournaments?

The old techniques were not developed to look flashy or to show one's flexibility. They were developed to destroy one's enemy as efficiently as possible. The "kiai" of the warrior was not originally meant to be yelled as loud and as long as possible to earn points in a tournament, but rather to focus all of one's energy into a single blow, a blow meant to kill. Don't confuse a sport black belt with the black belt of a true warrior; there is a huge difference between the two.

I know exactly why I train in the martial arts.

September 20

Thatch your roof before rainy weather;
dig your well before you are thirsty.
Chinese Proverb

You have to be prepared for what you may have to deal with long before you actually find yourself face to face with the challenge. The warrior can't wait until he is face to face with an attacker before he thinks about whether or not he is in shape to defend himself. You don't wait until the ruffian is at your door. When the thug has entered your space, you cannot call "time-out," stretch, and warm up. You have to be ready. This is why warrior training is vital. You never know when you will have a situation for which you must already be prepared. Always plan ahead.

If you wait until you are thirsty, and have no water, before you think about digging your well, you may likely die of thirst. If you wait until the storm comes before you fix your roof, you are assured that your roof will not protect you from the rain. If you wait until you have no choice but to fight for your life, to hone your martial arts skills, you may very well lose your life. You have to prepare for tomorrow's battle today.

Think ahead and plan for the future. Be disciplined. Don't start thinking that your training doesn't matter because you may never actually need it. Today may be the day that your training saves your life or the life of your loved ones. Train hard, don't put it off. Make sure that you are prepared for whatever may come. Being unprepared, for whatever reason, is simply leaving your life to chance. This is not the way of the warrior. Be a warrior – be prepared.

I think ahead and prepare for the hard times.

September 21

Defeat is a state of mind; no one is ever defeated until defeat has been accepted as a reality.

Bruce Lee

Nothing is over until it is completely over, and you can't be defeated until you declare defeat. My friend, Don, is a retired lawman who worked in a large border town. Don has many colorful stories, but the one that I am about to tell you really demonstrates this quote.

Don had been called to this bar late one night, as lawmen often are, to take care of a bit of business. Business concluded, he was on his way out the door, headed home, when a huge guy in a cowboy hat and boots, blocked his path with his leg. This guy looked at Don with a cold stare and said, tonight, I'm going to kick your ass. Don said that by the look of this man, he knew that he meant it, and he also knew that he could get the job done. The following was Don's response.

You may kick my ass tonight, but tomorrow night I will be back with a deputy, and if we can't set things right, I will be back the next night with two more deputies. We have 465 lawmen in this county, and I will come back as many nights as it takes to make things right, and then, on top of that, you will be going to jail. The man simply removed his leg and let Don pass.

Then Don told me, "You know Bohdi, the Creed of the Texas Ranger is what I believe in, no man in the wrong can beat a man in the right that just keeps coming." Defeat is a state of mind. Losing one battle does not equal a lost war. You decide when to declare victory or defeat. Don't declare victory too soon, and don't declare defeat at all.

I do what I know is right and I don't worry about the rest.

September 22

Never separate yourself
from the Way of the Warrior.

Miyamoto Musashi

When one reads this statement written by Musashi so many years ago, the first thought is Musashi is just trying to say how great it is to be a warrior, but this statement takes on a deeper meaning once you really understand the way of the warrior. The way of the warrior should be the life that everyone lives. It is the way that human beings were meant to live. It means much more than just training physically in a martial art.

Departing from the way of the warrior is departing from the way of character, honor, and integrity. It is abandoning the spiritual connection which the warrior has with his Maker. Leaving this path means discarding your code of ethics and your sense of right and wrong. For those who separate from the way of the warrior, filial duty is no longer a priority in their lives. Self-discipline and self-reliance goes by the wayside.

Why would anyone want to separate from the way of the warrior, but then again, why doesn't everyone live the warrior lifestyle? The answer is that they do not have a true understanding of the benefits of this lifestyle. All they can see is the discipline that it takes to walk this path. They are shortsighted, not being able to see past their instant gratification. Warriors know that the training, discipline, and work it takes to live this lifestyle are worth it. They know that this lifestyle is not just something that they do, but is something that they are. You cannot separate yourself from something you are.

The way of the warrior is ingrained in me. I will always the path.

September 23

If your temper rises, withdraw your hand;
if your hand rises, withdraw your temper.

Gojun Miyagi

Allowing your temper to control your actions is always a bad decision. This statement is even truer when it comes to physical confrontations. So many people believe that they become some kind of unstoppable force when they get angry and explode. For some reason, the feeling that they get when they feel that rush of adrenaline through their body, translates, in their minds, to the equivalent of Popeye popping open a can of spinach. And they aren't shy about letting people know this.

I cannot even count the number of times I have heard someone warn someone else with the words, "You had better not get me mad!" Well, simply put, this is unwise and faulty thinking. What these people are actually saying is that if you continue to push their buttons, they will lose control and allow their emotions and anger to dictate their actions. It is music to the ears of the trained warrior when he hears his enemy say this, because at that time he knows his enemy is well on his way to being defeated.

Taunting an enemy to the point of losing control is an ancient battle tactic. It has been used throughout the centuries to defeat one's enemies. Losing your temper doesn't make you stronger or more dangerous, at least not more dangerous to your opponent. It merely demonstrates your lack of control. Once you lose control, you don't think rationally. In a physical confrontation, you must be able to think rationally. If you find that you have no choice but to fight, keep your temper in check.

I keep my temper under control at all times.

September 24

Treat every encounter as a fight to the finish.
The Eight Essentials for Novice Swordsmen

The human body is very fragile. Any physical encounter should be taken seriously, as there is always the chance of being injured when you find yourself in a combative situation. Even if you win, the old saying holds true; when two tigers fight, one will be killed and the other will be injured. Never underestimate your enemy or his ability to do bodily injury to you. Treat every violent confrontation as a possible life-or-death situation.

Treating every physical encounter as a fight to the finish ensures that you are in the right frame of mind for the fight. You must have your mind focused on the task at hand, which is to make sure you are safe, and to destroy your enemy's will to continue to be a threat to you or those around you. Don't allow overconfidence to slip into your mind. There are no small enemies. Overconfidence can lead to your demise. Every fight is a serious fight. If it isn't serious, you have no business fighting.

I'm not suggesting that by treating every physical threat as a fight to the finish, you should kill your opponent whenever you enter into a fight. This should be common sense. What I am saying is that you should enter that fight with the mindset that your enemy wants to kill you, and act accordingly in your self-defense applications.

Never count on someone's mercy or self-control in this type of situation. Make sure that you are safe, not because your enemy is unwilling to really hurt you, but by ensuring that he is unable to hurt you.

I will only fight if I am forced to, and then, I will finish it.

September 25

When the world is at peace, a
gentleman keeps his swords by his side.

Wu Tsu

We are very blessed to live in a time of peace and stability in our country. For the most part, our citizens live in a peaceful world, at least while they are close to home. It has been this way for years in our country, but if history has taught us anything, it is that this world is constantly changing. Countries rise and fall. Peace is disrupted by war. Governments are overthrown and replaced. Nothing stays the same for very long.

Change is the one thing that you can count on in this world. It doesn't pay to become complacent just because you are now living in peaceful times. The wise man will stay as prepared as possible, in order to meet the challenges of this changing world. He realizes that peace rarely lasts for long, and that when times change, they often change violently and without notice.

What Wu Tsu is trying to tell us in this quote above, is that during times of peace, the warrior should keep his weapons ready, by his side. Don't become lazy and allow your weapons, your martial arts skills, to become rusty.

Stay prepared and keep your weapons in good shape. Remember, even in the sheath, the knife must be sharp. Take care to keep your skills sharp, even in times of peace. The skill which is not practiced deteriorates. It is part of the warrior's duty to keep his skills sharp and to practice his art and to be ready.

Even in times of peace, I will continue to train hard.

September 26

*It is not only what we do, but what we
do not do, for which we are accountable.*

Moliere

You are accountable for both your actions and your lack of action. As a warrior you are expected to do the right thing; you are expected to make your decisions in accordance with your honor. There are times when you can do wrong by taking no action at all.

For example, if you see a lady being harassed by two thugs, and you decide to do nothing and walk on by, you are accountable for your lack of action. You are a warrior and you have the duty to get involved and protect this lady. Your lack of action would be against your code of honor.

A warrior has a greater duty than the average man. He has a responsibility to protect the weak and those in need. Not doing so, when he has the opportunity, is a dishonorable act. If you see an injustice and take no action, is that a sign of courage or cowardice?

How do you think the "real" warrior would react in this circumstance? Would a true warrior be indifferent to a travesty that he could stop by stepping in and taking action? Of course not! He would use the skills he has developed to protect those who needs his protection.

Take action when action is needed. Don't let fear or indecision cause you to simply do nothing when duty is screaming for you to act. Live the code that you profess. Be able to rationally explain both your actions and your inactions. Make sure that you have a rational reason for all of your actions and intentions.

I am responsible for what I do and for what I fail to do.

September 27

To see what is right and
not to do it is cowardice.

Confucius

Sometimes taking the right course of action seems as though it will cost you dearly, but the true warrior will put what is right over what is profitable. To put what is profitable over what is right, shows a lack of honor and integrity.

Your duty as a warrior is to do what is right, not to worry about the consequences of doing the right thing. Honor requires that if you *know* what you should do, you do it. Doing the right thing takes courage. It takes fortitude, especially when the majority is against you. It is a test of your dedication to your principles.

Doing the right thing is a trait of the warrior. There have been many examples throughout history where an army or a group of men have been outnumbered to the point where they had virtually no chance of survival if they decided to stand up and fight.

Staring death in the face, they still made the decision to stand and fight. They chose to stand for what they felt to be right, at all costs. To them, doing otherwise would have been cowardly and that was not an option.

This is the type of conviction that the warrior should have concerning doing what is right. Once he has decided what is right in a certain situation, he should stand on the side of what is right at all costs. Yes, this does take a lot of courage and fortitude. It takes self-confidence and integrity beyond the average man. In short, it takes a true warrior.

When I know the right action to take, I take it!

September 28

A man's word is his honor.
Okinawan Proverb

Your word is your honor. In today's world there doesn't seem to be many people who think this way. People will say whatever gets them what they want, whether it is true or false, right or wrong. Most people don't seem to care about their "word," but then again, most people do not have a clue what true honor is either. You should think before you speak and you should honor what you say.

Honor consists of multiple parts. It is a complex idea in which intention plays a huge role. Think about the intentions behind your words and your actions. What is the purpose behind your words? Do your words even have a purpose?

The Code of the Samurai tells us that the warrior should carefully consider every word that comes out of his mouth. Be conscious of your words and make your word mean something. Don't babble endlessly like a fool. Speak when you have something to say and be silent when you don't have anything important to say.

As a warrior, your word should be as binding to you as any written contract. If you say that you will do something, do it. If you make a promise, you have a debt to fulfill. If you promise someone that you will do something, do it! If you are not going to do something, then don't say that you will.

Those who take honor seriously will always honor their word, and warriors take honor seriously. Make your word your bond. Make your word your honor. Say what you mean and mean what you say. Those who do not honor their word are not true warriors.

My word is my honor. I always keep my word.

September 29

Don't appear just; be just.
Aechylus

It is part of your duty to build your character and to be just. Many people in this world appear just, but behind the veil they are really people of low character. They will lie and cheat, and will do virtually anything to get what they want.

We constantly see politicians who fit this image. They talk about their good character and honor. They seem like upstanding men and women. Then one day, when the scandal breaks, we find out the truth about these people. Their character was just a charade. It was all for show – an act for their unsuspecting audience.

Don't be an actor. Don't pretend to be something that you aren't, especially in the area of your character. You should not have the appearance of being a man of character and virtue in public, but in private live a different way. Don't fake character; build character from the inside out.

Nobody respects a hypocrite, nor should they. La Rochefoucauld taught that hypocrisy is the tribute that vice pays to virtue. This means that people can see the value of being a just man, but they aren't willing to make the sacrifices that it takes to truly obtain this character trait.

If they couldn't see the value in being just, they wouldn't pretend to have this quality. Take the duty of perfecting your character seriously. Be a man of real honor, not counterfeit honor. If you don't have a certain character trait that you would like to have, work to develop it, don't pretend to have it. Don't appear just; be just.

I am just in all my ways. I always seek what is right.

September 30

You cannot talk to a frog in a well about the
vast sea; he is limited to his area of space.
A summer insect has no knowledge of snow;
it knows nothing beyond its own season.

Chiu Shu

You will find that the majority of people out there will not be able to understand much of the warrior lifestyle or why you would chose to live this lifestyle. This is becoming even more evident as the moral character of our world seems to continue to degenerate. People just can't understand why you would risk your life to defend a stranger or why you won't lower your standards just for the time being or just until the deal is done.

People who do not take honor seriously cannot comprehend why anyone would put their character and honor ahead of their comfort or finances. It just does not compute for them. They think that this is ridiculous. These people have no concept of true honor and therefore can't understand the warrior lifestyle. Talking to them about the standards of a warrior is about as productive as talking to them about quantum physics.

Be selective with whom you share this information. Understand that not everyone will be sympathetic to your quest. There are but few who are able to understand the way of the warrior, and fewer still, who are able to live by the warrior ideals. Just as a summer insect cannot understand the concept of snow, they cannot comprehend the warrior lifestyle.

Even in a world of dishonor, I will still act honorably.

October 1

One should have learning on the left
and the martial arts on the right.

Hojo Nagauji

The warrior should not be some uneducated brute. There is a difference in someone who merely knows how to fight or who has a sufficient amount of shear strength, and someone who is a true warrior. Balance is an important part of the warrior lifestyle, and learning and education is part of that balance, especially in today's world. Without education, whether formal or otherwise obtained, the warrior is at a distinct disadvantage today.

Learning doesn't have to come from years of college experience. There are many forms of education and many ways to obtain a well-rounded education. Many times a college education doesn't equate to true education. If someone truly wants to educate themselves on a subject, it can be done from books and from the internet. The point is, no matter how you choose to go about it, you should make sure that you balance your life with learning, as well as martial arts, character training, meditation, etc.

Spend time learning about things that interest you. Become well read. Study the subjects which apply to the warrior lifestyle, as well as staying informed about worldly affairs. The key to education, as with most other things in this life, is balance. You should know something about finances, investments, business, etc. You should know how things work around your house. It is impossible to be self-reliant and self-sufficient without the proper knowledge. A well-rounded education will serve you well.

I cultivate knowledge, wisdom and perfection of character.

October 2

How often do we supply our enemies
with the means of our own destruction.

Aesop

Have you ever noticed how many times on reality television shows people get into hot water because they say too much? They tend to hand their competition exactly what they need to defeat them in the game. I see it over and over; people just can't seem to keep their mouths shut. They begin to talk without thinking and their enemies take advantage of it. It never fails.

You should not reveal any more personal information than is absolutely necessary. The more information that you give someone about yourself, the higher the chances are that you will give them something that they can use against you somewhere down the line. And make no mistake about it, your enemies will make note of every little thing that they can possibly use to defeat you or hurt you.

Small things mentioned in casual conversations can be turned around and used against you if you aren't careful. Don't supply your enemy with the weapons that he needs to destroy you. Be discreet in your conversations, but do so without appearing too secretive.

Nobody likes to feel like something is being kept from them, especially your friends. Although it is important that you keep some things private, it is just as important as to how you go about doing so. This is a balancing act that requires you to actually think before you speak. Learn the art of keeping private things private without appearing to be secretive.

I have many enemies; therefore I am careful about what I say.

October 3

Warriors aren't born, and they aren't made. They create
themselves through trial and error and by their
ability to conquer their own frailties and faults.

Philip J. Messina

It takes a lot to live the warrior lifestyle. You will make mistakes and fall short at times as you work to perfect each area of your life. What is important is that you never quit working to improve yourself. Continually work to perfect your character. Hone your martial arts skills to a fine edge and then keep them sharp. Slow down and take time to keep your mind calm through meditation and study.

Confucius stated that he wasn't born with the knowledge that he had; he worked hard to obtain it. In the same way, no one is born with all the traits of warriorhood. They have to be developed over time, through trial and error and hard work. Living the life of the warrior is a decision that one makes. Once the decision is made to walk the path of the warrior, then the real work begins. Making the decision to live the life of the warrior is only the first step in a long, endless process that will continue throughout your life.

Victories begin to be won as you conquer your shortcomings and overcome your mistakes. Each time you resist the temptation to lower your standards or to slack off in your training, you add another notch in your belt. You are constantly creating your character as you live the warrior lifestyle. Men can be taught to fight, but they develop character through their own efforts. As Gichin Funakoshi stated, "The ultimate goal of karate is the perfection of character." This is also the ultimate goal of the warrior lifestyle.

I choose to live the warrior lifestyle. I will not dishonor myself.

October 4

You cannot step twice into the same river.
Heraclitus

Change is the one thing that you can count on in this life. It doesn't matter what the situation may be, it is sure to change over time. If you currently find yourself in bad times, take heart, the bad times will not last. Nothing stays the same for long, everything is in flux. You may not be able to recognize that things are changing, but be assured, change is taking place. True, things may not be changing as fast as you would like, but they are changing.

Yes, it is hard going through these changes, but "hard" is not impossible. What doesn't destroy you only makes you stronger. Don't let the changes which time brings about destroy you. Take them and use them to build your strength and character. Know that nothing stays the same. Bad times will not stand! There is a purpose for everything in this life. Find the purpose in the changes that you are going through.

There is never a time in this life for the warrior to be complacent. In bad times, you must work to improve your standing. In good times, you must strive to maintain your position. The warrior is always wary of the changes that inevitably come around as the winds of time silently weave threads of transformation through our lives.

Don't become complacent when times are good, and don't give in to despair when times are bad. No matter what changes time brings to you, deal with those changes like the noble warrior that you are. As Hemingway put it, "Grace under pressure." There is a purpose for everything in this life. Find the purpose in the changes that you are going through.

Everything changes, but my honor is always intact.

October 5

Carelessness is a great enemy.
Japanese Proverb

Carelessness can defeat even the most skilled warrior. No matter how great your skills are, if you get careless or overconfident you can find yourself in trouble. Pay attention to even the smallest details. Don't take anything for granted. Everything matters. For the prepared warrior, it is carelessness in the small details which can get him in trouble. Stay alert and stay focused.

I once found myself in a physical confrontation where I discovered the truth contained in this proverb firsthand. Although I tried every possible thing that I could have done to stop this encounter from getting physical, this guy's mind was set on using my face as a punching bag. Drugs played a major part in his decision, as they often do with violent trouble makers. He insisted on attacking me. I'm sure that he felt confident in the fact that he could thrash me since he was at least six inches taller than me.

After a short struggle, I was able to end the encounter with one punch, but carelessly my punch was just off target. My careless punch, although it ended the fight, left me with a broken hand. The punch was only off by an inch, but carelessness in even the smallest details can cost you big time.

That one little mistake cost me months of pain and some major down time, not to mention the doctor bills. The ring finger on my hand still, to this day, will not straighten out like it should without effort. Carelessness is one of your worst enemies and an enemy which must be defeated.

I discipline myself to be careful in all my ways.

October 6

To spare the ravening leopard is
an act of injustice to the sheep.
Persian Proverb

As a teacher I have had to deal with several menacing students over the years. I had one student who was constantly disruptive, threatening and abusive to both teachers and students. Other students were afraid of him. He disrupted the education of students who actually wanted to learn and make something of their lives. This student made threats to teachers and students alike.

With all of this going on for months, the administration refused to expel this student because they wanted to be "compassionate." The other side of the coin is that their compassion for this student was actually an act of injustice to all of the other students and teachers.

The same thing goes for our justice system. When our justice system has mercy on the violent criminal and gives him a light sentence or probation, it is really an injustice to the next person this criminal assaults. People don't understand that it is impossible to be compassionate to both the leopard and the sheep at the same time.

Warriors are by nature compassionate people, but there are limits to their compassion. When a wolf is killing your sheep, is it your duty to be compassionate to the wolf or to the sheep? A decision has to be made. Do you spare the wolf or protect the sheep? You can't do both. The obvious answer is that you ensure that justice is carried out. The warrior should always stand on the side of justice. Those who do not have the spine to enact justice on the wolf are unjust to the sheep.

I protect the sheep from the predators.

October 7

The best armor is to keep out of range.
Italian Proverb

The best self-defense tactic is to stay away from places where trouble is likely to happen. If you are careful about where you go and when you go there, you may live your whole life without ever having to call on your self-defense skills in a real-life situation. Don't hang out where the thugs and trouble makers prefer to congregate. Associate with people of character. As a rule, you usually do not find people of character and thugs in the same place.

Years ago I found myself at a party that could be classified as one of those places where the thugs hung out. I found that there were several people at this party who seemed to have an extreme dislike for me. Out of the blue, I found myself being grabbed from behind and a folding razor blade being held to my throat. Now, once you get yourself in that kind of position, you are at your enemy's mercy; this is not a good position to be in to say the least.

The point here is that if I had been at the movie theater instead of this party filled with thugs, my safety would have been assured, or at least in my own hands instead of depending on the mercy of a thug who was too high to be rational. My lack of judgment led to my being within a ¼ inch of the spirit world. It turned out alright that time, but it could have just as easily turned out very badly for me.

If you are not in the places where trouble is usually found, you can be fairly assured of your safety. Keep out of range of trouble. Don't tempt fate. Stay clear of people of low character, and you will stay out of range of their attacks.

I stay clear of people of low character and I stay out of their range.

October 8

It is truly regrettable that a person will
treat a man who is valuable to him well,
and a man who is worthless to him poorly.
Hojo Shigetoki

It is not honorable to treat people with respect only when you feel they are, or could be, valuable to you in some way. This has probably been a common practice ever since men began to socialize, and it is also a hypocritical practice. If you are treating someone in a respectful manner only because they could be useful to you at a later time, you are not being sincere, but being manipulative. Don't use or manipulate people in order to serve your own selfish purposes.

The warrior should treat everyone he meets with respect, whether he sees them as valuable to him or not. He treats people with respect because treating people with respect is part of the lifestyle which he has chosen. The warrior lifestyle is a lifestyle of honor, and it is honorable to treat everyone you meet with due respect. If you want to be respected, respect others. You should treat others as you would have them treat you. Treating someone with respect has nothing to do with whether or not they actually deserve respect.

Warriors may have to manipulate certain circumstances at times, but he still treats everyone he meets with respect, even those who do not deserve his respect. His actions are determined by his own code, and not how others live their lives. He treats others in a certain manner because that is the kind of man that he has decided to be, not because they do or do not deserve to be treated with respect or kindness. Respect is given out of a sense of honor.

I treat every man and woman with courtesy and manners.

October 9

Every action we take, everything we do, is either a victory or defeat in the struggle to become what we want to be.

Anne Byrhhe

This is a very strong statement for the warrior to consider. Every action, everything you think, everything you say, and everything you do, is either bringing you closer to your goals or further away from your goals, on your quest for warriorship. Every little thing matters. This is a very powerful thought. Just think about that. There are no insignificant decisions.

Did your actions last night bring you closer to your goals or take you further away from your goals. I'm not talking about whether or not they were right or wrong, but only were they helpful or a hindrance. There is nothing wrong with going out to dinner, but if you go out and load up on unhealthy foods, along with excessive amounts of alcohol, your actions definitely did not bring you closer to your goals as a warrior.

Start looking at each action with this quote in mind, and ask yourself, "Is this action going to make me a better person, spiritually, mentally, or physically?" If the answer is no, then maybe you need to reconsider this action. It takes practice to slow down and think about your actions and the consequences that each of them will have on your goals. This is not an easy thing to do, but just as your martial arts skills are difficult at first and then become easier, so shall your struggle to become what you are trying to become, a man of excellence who has perfected his character.

Everything I do matters; I seek excellence in every way.

October 10

We ought to do everything both
cautiously and confidently at the same time.

Epictetus

The warrior should always be aware of his surroundings. This doesn't mean that he is constantly walking around, nervously looking for trouble, but that he is aware of what is going on around him.

He observes the people he encounters and pays attention to their behavior. When dealing with others, he reads between the lines and is cautious about believing what he sees. It is in his nature to be cautious because he knows the nature of most people.

At the same time, he acts with confidence. His cautious nature allows him to go through life with confidence. He is aware of what is going on around him. He has done his homework and therefore is a confident player in the game. Being cautious is not being fearful or cowardly; it is being safe and prepared. Only when you feel prepared are you able to feel confident in different situations.

Your martial arts training gives you confidence in dealing with violent situations, but you still have to enter into any physical confrontation with extreme caution. This is a good example of doing something with both caution and confidence at the same time.

You have confidence that you can defeat your attacker, but you are still cautious. Being overconfident and careless can cost you your life. No matter how sharp you believe your skills to be, always enter every confrontation with the utmost caution.

I do everything both cautiously and confidently, with honor.

October 11

Tomorrow's battle is won
during today's practice.
Samurai Maxim

Sun Tzu taught that you should win first and then enter into battle. For most people, this doesn't make much sense, but it makes perfect sense if you take the time to understand it. In order to win, you must first be prepared. You must prepare yourself physically and mentally to meet the challenge at hand.

Most people want to neglect their preparation and just jump right into the fight. They do the exact opposite of what Sun Tzu taught; they want to enter into the battle and then figure out how to win. This strategy depends largely on luck. Warriors don't depend on luck; they depend on their preparation. The warrior wins tomorrow's battle today because he spends today preparing for victory.

Your preparation is not simply working on your martial arts skills and staying in shape. There is much more to securing victory than being in good shape. Many a warrior has been in the best shape of his life and has still lost the battle because he was unprepared for his enemy. You have to not only be prepared physically and mentally, but you also have to prepare your strategy and know something about your enemy's strategy.

Sun Tzu also taught that you must know your enemy, know his strategy and how he may attack you. When you have an enemy to defeat, make it your business to know him. Know his character, the way he thinks, and know how he most likely plans on attacking you. Then prepare for your victory.

I win tomorrow's battle during today's practice.

October 12

*Rely not on the likelihood of the enemy's not coming,
but on our own readiness to receive him; not on the
chance of his not attacking, but rather on the fact
that we have made our position unassailable.*

Sun Tzu

You don't really have any control over whether or not some predator decides to mug you or assault you. While it is true that presenting a certain image of confidence and awareness can deter many predators from seeing you as an easy target, you really have no assurance that some low-life will not try to attack you for whatever reason. You can't rely on the enemy not coming. The only thing that you really have total control over is whether or not you will be ready, if and when someone does decide to attack you.

How do you make yourself unassailable and ready to repel an attack from a predator? To start with, make sure you have not neglected your training. Keeping up with your training will continue to keep your self-confidence in your martial arts skills high. This self-confidence will shine through and will not only serve as a deterrence for predators, but will also make them rethink their decision should they actually confront you.

I know that I have said it before, but it is worth repeating ad nauseam. Be aware of your surroundings. This is probably the most important factor in making yourself unassailable. If you allow a predator to catch you by surprise, you have put yourself at an automatic disadvantage. Take nothing for granted; make yourself as ready as possible.

I prepare for my enemy and he cannot hurt me.

October 13

Instead of worrying, a
strong man wears a smile.

Japanese Proverb

Worrying serves no purpose whatsoever. It is a total waste of time. The warrior should not allow his mind to be clouded by worrying about what may or may not happen in the future. He must think rationally. If you can do something about the situation at hand, then make a decision about the right course of action and act. If the situation cannot be changed, then let it go and focus on something else. Either way, worrying will not help you resolve your problem; it will only drain your mental energy.

This is another instance when you have to discipline your mind. Controlling your mind is a skill that is just as important to you as your martial arts skills. Actually, if you can't control your mind, your martial arts skills will falter in a life-and-death situation. You must control your mind. Do what you can do about the situation, know that you have done your best, then let the chips fall where they may. When you have done all that you can do, what else is there?

Realize that you have done your best to live according to your principles. After you have done your best, whatever is going to happen, is going to happen. Worrying will not change that. Calm your mind and know that whatever happens, you will be able to deal with it. When things change, you will see what steps you need to take next, and you will again act to the best of your abilities. For the warrior, life is a series of evaluating the situation, deciding on the right course of action, and then taking the right action.

Instead of worrying, I wear a smile. I act; I don't worry.

October 14

No matter what the warrior is doing, he must
conduct himself in the manner of a true warrior.
Bushido Shoshinshu

Always maintain your dignity, no matter where you are or what you are doing. It doesn't matter what situation you find yourself in, you should always conduct yourself in the manner of a true warrior.

This is excellent advice from this ancient samurai text, better known as *The Code of the Samurai*. Whatever you are doing, do it with class. Don't lower your standards. Treat everyone you meet with respect and good manners.

Realize that people do watch how you conduct yourself and that they will judge you according to your actions. Everything that you do is contributing to your reputation, either in a positive way or a negative way. Know how a warrior should conduct himself and then make a point of acting that way until it becomes a natural part of your being.

The warrior doesn't change what he is because of what somebody else is or because of what somebody else does. He remains the same regardless of his environment. The actions of other people do not influence his actions, as far as his code of conduct goes.

His character doesn't change according to the company he happens to find himself surrounded by at the time. No matter where he is or what he is doing, he conducts himself according to his code of ethics, and in the manner of a true warrior. He lives according to his own code regardless of how anyone else lives.

No matter what I am doing, I conduct myself as a true warrior.

October 15

To stand still is to regress.
Gichin Funakoshi

No matter how far you paddle your boat up the river, if you stop paddling you will start to float backwards. You may have a goal to get to a certain place up the river, but once you get to that place, you cannot stay there unless you continue to work to maintain your position.

The day you don't feel like paddling to maintain your position, you will find that you have lost some ground and that it will take some work to get back to where you were. You will also find that when you quit paddling, you will go back down the river much faster than you paddled up the river.

There is no standing still in the river. You are either moving toward your goal or you are moving away from your goal. It takes discipline and work to maintain your goal, even after you have obtained it. You never achieve perfection; the best that you can do is to continually strive for perfection each and every day.

The warrior is never satisfied achieving his goal and then stopping. You don't get to a certain point in your training and think that you are set for life. Continue to train for perfection and excellence in every area of your life.

When you stop training, you start to regress. The more you regress, the less prepared you are to meet your enemy. Continue to train hard and maintain your level of preparedness. Don't let your skills, which you have worked so hard to achieve, disappear with the current of inactivity.

I refuse to regress; I am constantly improving in every way.

October 16

Never do anything against conscience
even if the state demands it.

Albert Einstein

As a warrior, your own conscience should be so highly developed that it becomes the ultimate factor in determining your every action. This will not happen automatically. It takes study, practice, and correcting the many mistakes that you will make along the way, but once you have accomplished the task of perfecting your character, your conscience will be your most reliable guide. When you get to this place in your training, all you have to be concerned about is living by the dictates of your conscience.

It is vital that you don't do anything that goes against your conscience. This is equivalent to breaking your code of ethics. If you feel inside that an action is not the correct action to take, then don't take it. Learn to trust your instinct or your intuition. Once you have developed your conscience through time and patience, it will not steer you wrong, but you must trust it enough to act on what you feel.

This also takes a lot of practice, as well as courage. It takes courage to go against the majority just because you don't feel right on the inside about the issue at hand. Start listening to your intuition in small matters. Slow down, quiet your mind, and listen to your intuition. Then follow what you feel. Develop this skill in small, non-essential matters, and it will serve you well when more critical situations suddenly appear in your life. The warrior lifestyle has many components, and each must be developed through training and discipline. Listen to your conscience.

I always listen to my intuition and follow its instruction.

October 17

Highly evolved people have their

own conscience as pure law.

Lao Tzu

As a warrior, you have to consider what is right in all your actions. Legal does not necessarily equal right, and illegal does not necessarily equal wrong. There may be times when the warrior has to decide between what is right and what is legal. Yes, sometimes the warrior has to do things which may be against the law. Conversely, there are many things which are considered legal according to our laws, which the warrior will consider dishonorable according to the code by which he lives.

This may sound strange to many of you, but it is reality for the warrior. An example that many people can relate to would be the issue of abortion. Abortion is legal in this country, but there are millions of Christians in our country who would not consider abortion an ethical option. It goes against their principles. In the same way, there are many things which are legal which go against the warrior's code; and his code always trumps what is legal according to the politicians.

Einstein said that one should "Never do anything against conscience even if the state demands it." This describes the warrior perfectly. He never goes against his code of honor. His honor is his law. He must do things which are illegal at times in order to hold fast to his integrity and honor. The warrior doesn't need laws to keep him in line. His own sense of right and wrong, and his sense of honor and integrity keep a tighter rein on his actions than any outside law. Even if there were no laws at all, the warrior would still do the right thing.

My conscience is my ultimate law because I am highly evolved.

October 18

It is not the oath that makes us
believe the man, but the man the oath.

Aechylus

It seems that not many people keep their word in today's society. People will lie straight to your face in order to get what they want, and they will not even feel bad afterwards. Today, when someone gives you a promise, unless you are dealing with a man of honor, that promise is virtually meaningless. It is not the promise or the "oath" that gives us a sense of security, but rather it is the honor of the man who gives you his word.

With most people, it is wise to get any agreement in writing, and even then, have that written contract checked for loopholes which will give dishonorable people a way to not live up to their promises. Their word is almost worthless. This in turn gives us insight into their character. If their word is worthless, so is their character. Never trust the word of a man of low character. To do so is not only unwise, but it is simply foolishness.

The warrior is a man of character, honor and integrity. He is a man of his word. His reputation precedes him and people know that when he gives his word, they can rely on him to back it up with his actions. You don't have to worry about a man of honor not keeping his word. To do so would be against his standards. We know that we can believe the oath because we know that we can depend on his honor. This is one of many traits which set the true warrior apart from the rest of society. Your word should be your bond; your word should be your honor.

My oath is good because I am a true warrior – a man of honor.

October 19

The superior man is watchful
over himself even when alone.

Chung Yung

Although the number of people who do not observe manners in public is drastically increasing, the vast majority of people seem to behave well when they are away from home. They are watchful over their behavior and manners when they are out on the town, but at home or alone, they tend to live differently. This should not be so for the warrior. The warrior should be aware of his actions at all times, whether alone or in public.

Chung Yung reiterates the teaching of Confucius and tells us that the superior man, the warrior, is watchful over himself at all times, even when he is alone. This doesn't mean that the warrior doesn't relax at home or that he is constantly uptight. It means that he is careful to do what is right, whether he is out in public, around his family, or home alone where no one else sees his actions. The point to this teaching is that the warrior should live according to his standards at all times.

Time, place and company do not affect the warrior's dedication to his code of honor. He remains true to his code regardless of where he is or who is with him. Even alone he is careful to do what is right. He is not acting for the benefit of others. The opinions of others are not what concern him. The warrior is concerned with his duty and doing the right thing. His conscience guides him and he knows that he must answer only to himself, but to the man of honor, that is the highest authority, besides God.

I do what's right, even when I am alone.

October 20

The word friend is common, the fact is rare.
Phaedrus

An acquaintance is simply someone who you know or who you are on friendly terms with, whereas as the term friend has a much deeper meaning. To me a true friend is a very rare person to find today. A friend is someone who will stand by you through thick and thin. When the chips are down, your friend will support you.

When the wolf is at your door, your friend is standing inside the door with you, ready to put his life on the line, side by side with his brother. He will stand by you, right or wrong. When you win the lottery, your friend is sincerely happy for you, just as if he had won it himself. Are you getting the picture?

I consider a friend to be much more than an acquaintance. In truth, you are lucky to have one true friend in your life. If you have more than one, you are truly blessed. Realize this and don't make the mistake of thinking of your acquaintances as your true friends. This is a common mistake that people make. When their back is against the wall, they are shocked to find that they really don't have friends, but only acquaintances that can disappear like a dove in a magic show.

Strive to make sure that your true friends are men of character, honor, and integrity. Warriors are the best of friends because they live by a strict code of ethics. They refuse to let their friends down in their time of need. This would go against their nature and their code. When you have developed a true friendship with a warrior, you have a trusted friend for life, a friend who you can actually count on through thick and thin.

True friends are rare, but I am a true friend.

October 21

It is no easy thing for a principle to become a man's own unless each day he maintains it and works it out in his life.

Epictetus

Developing your character takes work. It takes patience, dedication and perseverance. It is not an easy thing to do, at least not at first. There will constantly be temptations to step away from your principles. This is why the perfection of your character is a never-ending process. The opportunities to slide backwards are also never-ending; therefore the opportunities for new victories over yourself are endless.

Each day you have to work at maintaining your character. You have to work at developing your principles. It will become easier and easier as your principles become second nature to you, but you will still have temptations to compromise those principles, even once you have made them your own. Developing your character and living by a set of principles is not a goal, but an ongoing process. It takes work and discipline to resist the many temptations to compromise your standards.

You can liken this to the wise fish who never takes the bait. This fish has learned the strategies of the fishermen. He recognizes all the various baits and lures that he has been tempted with over the years. Yet no matter how many times he resists the newest temptation that the fishermen cast into his pond, the next day he can be assured that he will be presented with another one. It only takes one bad decision for the wise old fish to end up in the frying pan, only one! Think about this.

I maintain my principles every day; they are a part of me.

October 22

The superior man does not give up good conduct
because the inferior man rails against him.

Hsun-Tzu

The warrior is a man of principle. He doesn't set his principles aside when they seem inconvenient. Today many people do just that. They use the actions of others to justify their own bad behavior. Statements such as, "Well I wouldn't have done that if he hadn't shoved me, cursed me, been rude to me, etc." are commonly heard to justify bad behavior. The warrior should not allow the behavior of others to affect his own behavior, at least not as far as doing things that are against his principles.

Of course, as a warrior, there may be times when the actions of others may cause you to have to take action, but this is different than allowing someone else's actions to affect how you respond as far as your principles are concerned. The warrior must respond, not react. Even if you have to take physical action in a specific situation, you can still do so without lowering your principles. The true man of principle can't set his principles aside. They are a part of him, a part of his spirit and who he truly is as a human being.

Someone else being what they are, whether it is an obnoxious thug, a criminal, or whatever, should not cause you to forget the fact that you are a man of principle. Don't allow the actions of others to cause you to compromise your principles. This is an easy trap to walk into, and a flimsy excuse for poor behavior. The warrior never forgets what he is and never sets aside his principles. Think rationally and remember who you are and what you are.

I won't change my actions because inferior men attack me.

October 23

Let them know a real man,
who lives as he was meant to live.

Marcus Aurelius

The vast majority of people think that the term "man" and the term "male" are synonymous, but the sages throughout the ages have always disagreed with this. Many of the great sages taught that there is a difference in being a male and a true man. Confucius made this distinction with the terms "superior man" and "inferior man." Marcus Aurelius made this distinction by referring to a man of honor and integrity as a "real man."

In today's society, the mere mention of the "real" man is met with sneers and ridicule, usually followed by rude and crude comments. Most people can't wrap their minds around the concept that you earn the right to be called a man. Just because you are born a male doesn't necessarily mean you are a man. The term "man" can be synonymous with the term "true human being." When looked at in this way, there is a big difference between being a male and being a man. That difference is how someone lives their life.

This distinction is really only recognized by those whose philosophy leans towards that which is found in the warrior lifestyle. Warriors know that there is a difference in the way a real man lives as compared to the inferior man. Real men live a life of character, honor and integrity. They take care of their family and filial duties. They serve and protect those around them. They live by a strict code of standards. In short, they are warriors. Let the world know a real man; don't sell yourself short. Live the warrior lifestyle.

I live with honor and integrity.

October 24

*A successful samurai should put his heart in order
first thing in the morning and last thing at night.*
The Hagakure

The warrior has to "cleanse" his heart just as he has to clean his weapons and keep them in good working order. What I mean by this is that you have to continually make sure that your spirit is free from feelings and emotions that can, and will, move you away from the warrior virtues.

Make sure that you do not harbor hate, fear or unforgiveness in your heart. Continually examine yourself to make sure that your motives are pure and just. This can be especially hard to do when you have enemies who have really wronged you.

As the samurai maxim from *Hagakure: The Book of the Samurai* tells us, one way to do this is to examine your heart first thing in the morning and last thing at night. Take time to pause and look inside. Are you living according to the warrior ideals? Are you upholding your character as a warrior should? Is your heart right? If not, take steps to put your heart in order.

Focus on what your ultimate goal is and determine what needs to be done in order for you to continue on your quest. The journey of the warrior is a never-ending path and requires constant vigilance in order to continue to move forward. Spend time meditating on your actions, your motives, and your thoughts. If you find weeds in your garden, don't just try to keep them under control; remove them completely from the roots.

I cleanse my heart every morning and every night.

October 25

The warrior is always in training, and to some extent, at some level of consciousness, training is always on his mind.

Forrest E. Morgan

At first glance this statement seems ridiculous. How could anyone always be in training? But when given closer thought, this makes perfect sense, knowing the character of the warrior. He may not be always training physically, but at *some level of consciousness* he is training.

If he is driving down the road, he may be visualizing self-defense techniques in his mind or visualizing a dangerous encounter and how he would handle the situation. This is a form of training. Mental training is as important as physical training for the warrior.

There are many examples of warrior training that do not involve actual physical training. While in the movie theater, the warrior may be practicing awareness of his surroundings, while at the same time he is critiquing what the hero could have done differently in order to have ended the conflict better, again a form of mental training.

When you look at training in this light, the admonition by Musashi in, *The Book of Five Rings,* to train more than you sleep becomes a possibility even in today's world. To the warrior, the training possibilities are endless, no matter what he is actually doing. Next time you are doing something other than working on your skills, think about how you could be integrating training into what you are doing. When you look at training in this light, always training at some level becomes a very real possibility, even in today's world.

I am always training in one way or another.

October 26

Outside noisy, inside empty.
Chinese Proverb

Just as a jug that is empty makes more noise than a jug that is full, people who talk too much usually have less wisdom than the people who say little. People who continually chatter on and on about nothing, have very little wisdom inside to draw from, thus the saying outside noisy, inside empty. The same can be said concerning people who brag about their martial arts skills.

People who go on and on about how tough they are, or how good a fighter they are, usually are trying to convince themselves that they have the skills which they in fact lack. They want you to think that they are something special.

In reality, they know that they are not that tough and that they don't have the skills that they wish they had. Outside they present the image of being this great martial arts expert while inside they have the skills of a novice martial artist.

The master warrior, much the same as the master sage, will not brag about his skills. He does his best to perfect his art and leaves it at that. Obtaining the admiration of lesser men is not high on his list of objectives.

He is not concerned with the appearance of being tough or the appearance of being a master; he is focused only on what is, not what appears to be. "Outside noisy, inside empty" refers to the pretender. "Outside quiet, inside secure" refers to the warrior. Think about which type of man you have respect for.

I am careful with my speech and my words have meaning.

October 27

All warfare is based on deception.

Sun Tzu

The principles in Sun Tzu's classic book, *The Art of War*, have been applied to everything from business practices to martial arts philosophy (which is actually what it was written for to begin with). Like many books on wisdom, the principles contained in *The Art of War* can be meditated on and applied to many different areas, even if those areas are not what the original author was referring to in his text. Here we can liken warfare to dealing with your enemies in general.

People who wish to hurt you or disrupt your life are indeed your enemies, and your interaction with these people can be a form of warfare. If all warfare is based on deception, we can deduce that deception is an essential part of defending yourself from your enemies. You do not want your enemies to know exactly what your strategy is or what is happening in your life because you can be assured that they will use this information against you. Therefore, deception in these areas is not only advantageous, but essential.

Don't misunderstand what I am saying here. I am not advocating lying or compromising your integrity. What I am saying is that secrecy and misdirection is an indispensable part of defending yourself against the malicious intentions of your enemies. You have to look at your interaction with your enemies as a game, a game likened to warfare if you will. It is a game of strategy much like the game of chess. Anyone who knows the game will tell you that it is based on deception and misdirection. Think about this.

I use whatever it takes to defeat my enemies.

October 28

Knowing is not enough, we must apply.
Willing is not enough, we must do.

Goethe

You may have the knowledge concerning what it takes to live the warrior lifestyle, and you may think that you are willing to make the sacrifices that it takes to follow through with that lifestyle, but that is not enough. It is not enough to have the knowledge about something without putting that knowledge to use. It is not enough to be willing to do something; you must actually take action.

Too many people read book after book, gaining a little knowledge on this and a little knowledge on that, without ever putting anything that they learn to use.

We have more information available to us today than at any time in human history, yet ignorance is still rampant. It does you no good to learn something if that knowledge is not going to be put to use in some constructive way.

The warrior should have knowledge about various things, but he should also make use of that knowledge. He must apply what he knows to the warrior lifestyle. Knowledge without action is like having money without ever spending it. It does you no good.

You continue to earn money so that you can use that money to provide for yourself and your family. Likewise, you should continue to increase your knowledge so you can use that knowledge to better yourself and your life. Don't hoard knowledge, apply it. You can have all the money in the world in the bank, but it is totally worthless to you if you don't actually use it to better your life.

I apply what I learn to my life and do what's right.

October 29

The superior man seeks what is right;
the inferior one, what is profitable.

Confucius

Today it is very rare to find a person who will think about what is right instead of what is "best" for him personally. As I have discussed, the warrior should be a superior man, a man of excellence. Confucius tells us that the superior man will seek what is right, not what is profitable.

This doesn't mean that the warrior never seeks what is profitable for himself and his family. What it does mean is that the warrior will not seek what is profitable while at the same time disregarding what is right.

The warrior thinks first about what is right, what is justified, and then what is profitable. You should always seek to do what is right. Sometimes this may not be the most profitable path for you to take.

It is easy to profit if you have low standards. Drug dealers profit every day. In fact they make huge profits because they are only concerned with making money, not doing what is right.

The warrior on the other hand is restrained by his ethics and character. He is not free to seek profit by any means available. He answers to his code of ethics.

If he feels that an action is not right, he will not act, no matter how profitable that action may be for him. He always puts what is right first; it comes before everything else, even making money. Put what is right before what is profitable; be a superior man.

I seek what is right and only profit if it can be done honorably.

October 30

Each action of the warrior is performed from a
place of fundamental wisdom. It is completely
different from the ordinary behavior of a fool.
Even if it looks the same, it is different on the inside.

Takuan Soho

This is a very important statement for anyone who seeks to live the warrior lifestyle to contemplate. Every action of the warrior is performed from a place of fundamental wisdom; even if it looks the same on the outside as everybody else's action, it is different. How is it different? It is different on the inside, the intention is different, the spirit is different. You have to look below the surface. Not everything is as it first appears. In fact, things are seldom completely as they seem from the outside, especially where the warrior is concerned.

The warrior may be having a drink with a friend at the local pub and at first glance, he may look the same as the weak-minded fools that are surrounding him in the bar, but even though he may look as though he is the same on the outside, this is just an illusion. He is as different from the others as night is from day. He is coming from a totally different place, a place of fundamental wisdom.

He is different, even though he seems the same. The differences may be hard to distinguish for the ordinary person, but they are there, cloaked behind his unflinching poker face. Don't be too quick to judge someone. You only see what he allows you to see. You don't see the fundamental wisdom contained in his thoughts nor do you know the purpose and intention behind his actions. Think about this.

My actions come from a place of deep wisdom.

October 31

Great winds are powerless to
disturb the water of a deep well.

Chinese Proverb

The warrior should not get annoyed or upset at every little thing that goes wrong in his life. Small things affect small minds. Don't allow things to dictate to you what your emotional state will be.

You may be thinking that this is easier said than done, after all, when something bad happens, it is supposed to make you upset or put you in a bad mood. Well, it doesn't have to upset you or affect your mood.

You have to stay calm in your mind. Don't let the winds that blow outside enter your mind and affect your peace and tranquility. You decide what your emotional state will be. It is up to you. As a warrior, you must remain in control.

Don't give the control of your emotions to any other person or circumstance. Look at things rationally and calmly, and decide how to handle each situation. Respond, don't over-react. Remain in control at all times.

What's the difference between responding and reacting? Reacting is acting in response to something or someone according to the feelings that are aroused in you, by whatever has happened. Essentially, it is allowing your emotions to dictate your actions. This can get you in trouble. Instead of reacting, you should take rational action. This means that you rationally determine what the right course of action is and then act. This is the way of the warrior.

I am not disturbed by those who come against me.

November 1

Do nothing to make you lose respect for yourself.
Baltasar Gracian

The respect that you have for yourself can't be taken away from you by anyone else. You are the only person who controls the level of respect that you do or don't have for yourself. Other people can try to hurt you, embarrass you, humiliate you, etc., but they can't control your own feelings toward yourself. You control your self-respect just as you determine your own honor.

So if others can do nothing to cause you to lose your self-respect, how do you lose respect for yourself? Obviously it can be lost or Gracian would not have admonished us to be careful about losing self-respect. The answer is that you lose self-respect when you lower your standards or do not live up to your own code of conduct that you have set for yourself. The warrior knows inside his spirit if he is living up to his code of honor or not. Only he can determine that.

When he knows inside that he is not living up to his own standards, he starts to lose a bit of his self-respect. If he refused to help someone because of fear, then that action would eat away at him until he made it right. This is because of the strict standards which he sets for himself. He knows that he must do what is right in order to feel at peace with his own actions. Anything less and his conscience will not let him be at peace. Warriors esteem their honor too highly to allow themselves to lose self-respect because of weakness or laziness. When you live up to your code of honor you never lose your self-respect. Don't chip away at your self-respect; live with honor and integrity.

I do nothing that causes me to lose my self-respect.

November 2

The pebble in the brook secretly
thinks itself a precious stone.
Japanese Proverb

No one likes to feel inferior to someone else. This little gem of wisdom is one that should be filed under "good to know" in the warrior's mental files. Because the true warrior is a man of excellence, it can be natural that others may feel inferior in his presence unless he makes a conscious effort to make them feel at ease. I have talked with many men who I consider to be true warriors and they have actually confided in me that it seems as if other people are intimidated when they are in their presence.

Superior men radiate a certain type of energy. A person in the presence of a true warrior can sense this energy, and although they can't really explain what it is that they are sensing, they can sense that there is something special about this man. Most, it seems, sense this energy and are slightly intimidated by the warrior's presence. To them, they don't really know why, but they feel that this man is not someone to cross; they feel that he would be a force to be reckoned with and that he should be treated with respect.

The true warrior is a man of humility as well as honor. He must also remember that even the lowest of the low secretly think that they are something special. Almost no one truly thinks deep in his heart that he is beneath most men. Everyone secretly thinks that he or she is special, no matter what the ugly truth may be. The warrior is a finely cut diamond in a brook full of river rocks which secretly think that they are rubies and emeralds.

I do what's right, no matter how anyone else lives their life.

November 3

When the time comes that foes pose as friends,
keep a friendly face but banish their
brotherhood from your heart.

Tiruvalluvar

Things change constantly, and this includes your acquaintances and those who would like to see you destroyed. People, who you once considered your enemies, may later reconcile and offer their hand in friendship. Be careful when this happens. I'm not suggesting that you should be unfriendly or hold a grudge, but you should definitely not consider those people true friends whom you would confide in and take into your confidence.

While you should always conduct yourself with courtesy, it is unwise to think that a leopard will change its spots. A previous enemy may outwardly seek to be on friendly terms with you, but it is likely that he will still hold resentments deep in his heart where you are concerned. Be on friendly terms if you wish, but always be aware of what information you share with this person, and don't put too much trust in what this person says or does.

Consider a reconciled foe as an acquaintance, not a friend. There is a big difference in the two. Don't hold resentments against this person, but at the same time don't be naïve and think that he now has your best interest at heart either. Forgive, but do not forget. This does not mean that you should dwell on what happened in the past, it only means that you should keep that information filed away in your mental computer for later reference if needed. Be careful not to be conned; enemies have many deceptive ways to hurt you.

I forgive, but I do not forget.

November 4

Kill the spider and you
will destroy the cobweb.
Maltese Proverb

Everything in life is governed by the principle of cause and effect. Nothing happens without a reason, even if you don't know what that reason may happen to be. Whether you call it karma or the law of reciprocity, one thing always leads to another. Everything in your life has some cause behind it which brought it about. There is nothing that you can do which does not have some accompanying effect. If you don't like the results that you have been getting, change the actions that brought about those results.

This is the wisdom behind this Maltese Proverb. If you don't like cobwebs, get rid of the spider. When you kill the spider, there will be no more cobwebs, at least not from that specific spider. If you simply remove the cobweb itself, the spider will only spin more of them, and the cycle will continue endlessly, until you finally address the underlying cause – the spider. When you remove the primary cause, the effect will cease to exist.

This same principle applies to any problem that you may have in your life. If you can figure out what the underlying cause is for that specific problem, you can make a rational decision concerning how to eliminate that cause, therefore getting rid of the problem. Remove the root and the weed will cease to exist; kill the spider and the spider web will cease to exist. If you don't like the results that you have been getting, change what you have been doing and do something different. Different actions bring about different results.

When I change my actions, I change my results.

November 5

Trust in God, but tie your camel.
Arabian Proverb

There is a story about an old lady who lived in a town where there was a great flood. People all over were stranded and being rescued from the rising waters of the overflowing river. The flood waters had risen so high and so fast that this lady had climbed to the roof of her house to avoid the rising waters. She sat silently on her roof, praying for God to rescue her and get her out of this mess. Soon a boat came by and the man in the boat told her to get in, but she responded, "No thank you. God will rescue me."

Later another rescue boat came by and offered the lady a ride. Once again the lady responded, "No thank you. God will rescue me." The man in the boat argued with her to no avail, and then sped off to help others in need. The water continued to rise and was just a foot from covering the entire roof where the lady sat, when a helicopter flew over and hovered above her rooftop. The chopper pilot drop a ladder and a rescue worker dropped down to help the lady board the chopper, but the lady refused.

For the third time she said, "No thank you. God will save me." The lady drowned as the flood waters overtook her rooftop. When the lady got to Heaven she asked God, "Why didn't you save me? I prayed over and over, and yet you let me drown!" God replied, "I sent you two boats and a helicopter and you refused to do your part. You drowned because you would not act." The moral of the story is obvious; it is good to have faith, but God expects you to do your part. Not even God respects someone who will not take action when action is needed. Do your part!

I trust God, but I always do my part.

November 6

Depend on others and you will go hungry.
Nepalese Proverb

The warrior should be self-sufficient, at least as much as possible. It is much better for others to depend on you, than for you to have to depend on others for what you need in your life. Dependence on others can put you in a tricky position at times. When you depend on someone else for something, you are giving that person a certain amount of power or control over you, and this is even more true if you have to depend on someone for something important.

It is much better to be self-sufficient. Do what you can to become as self-reliant as possible. Don't leave yourself open to the whims or mercy of others. While it is true that in today's society the majority of us are dependent to a large extent on others, whether it is for your income, your food, your heat, or whatever, not many of us are totally independent. In fact, unless you have your own farm, with your own water supply and food supply, you are not truly self-reliant.

Most people never really think about this point, but the warrior should give thought to the future and to making sure that his family is safe and provided for, no matter what changes occur. Besides buying your own farm and raising your own food, there are many ways that you can make yourself more independent.

Do some research on what goes into making someone safe and ready for an emergency situation. Think about what you would need to keep yourself and your family safe should you find your normal sources of food and water are no longer available to you. Be as prepared as possible.

I work to be self-sufficient. I will depend on no one.

November 7

Great spirits have always encountered
violent opposition from mediocre minds.

Albert Einstein

Don't expect everyone to see the value in your quest to live the warrior lifestyle. People who do not respect the qualities of integrity, character and honor, will most likely not respect your decision to live by warrior values. They don't see the value in living a life of excellence or aspiring to high ideals. To them it is folly to live according to a code of standards which puts honor ahead of profit, comfort, or personal gain. Most people's first concern is what is "best" for them.

It never enters their mind that maybe the best thing for them is to live by a code of honor. Sometimes making profits or being comfortable is not really what is best for you. The warrior realizes that it is always best in the long run to make your decisions according to your code of honor, even if those decisions cost you a business deal or some profits. It never profits you to go against your standards, even if it seems like it will. All of the sages taught this truth, but few people today understand the reality of it.

This realization only comes through deep reflection on the value of your code of honor. The warrior understands this and makes time to really reflect on his standards. He realizes that he is a man of excellence, a great spirit, and that those with mediocre minds will not understand his way of life. For this reason, he is careful with whom he discusses his code of honor. He knows that the majority of people will belittle his goal of perfection of character as simple arrogance. Expect opposition and excel anyway.

I excel, no matter who comes against me!

November 8

The warrior backs up his words
with conviction and action.

Tony L. Jones

It may seem to many of my readers that I spend a great deal of time considering the importance of exercising diplomacy when speaking, and I do. There is a simple reason for this, your mouth can get you into more trouble, faster than anything else that I know of, and it doesn't have to be that way. There is a simple solution to this potentially dangerous problem – think before you speak, and mean what you say. Although this is a pretty simple way to stay safe, at least where this one danger is concerned, it is easier said than done.

Controlling your urge to give someone a severe tongue lashing can be a challenge. It is all too easy to vent your anger and say things that you neither mean nor would have the conviction to back up if you did mean them. This is an area where the warrior has to constantly monitor himself, especially when he is upset or angry. Anger has a way of escaping in the form of nasty, hurtful words, which later require apologies and which will probably cause you future problems.

The warrior has to defeat his personal temptations to put someone in his place. One way to do this is to remember that your words should mean something, that you want people to see you as a man of your word, not some hothead who allows his anger to dictate his speech. There is no way to back up your words with conviction and action if you allow yourself to spew out emotional garbage, filled with anger. In order to back up your words with conviction and action, they must be calm and rational. Think about this.

I do what I say and say I do. My word is my bond.

November 9

*A hundred lifetimes may not be enough to
rectify the mistake made in one short morning.*
Chinese Proverb

It takes a long time to build a reputation of being a man of honor and integrity. Building your reputation is something that you have to work at continuously. You cannot afford to let your guard down when it comes to your character. It takes a lot of effort, forethought, and determination, to not only build a good reputation, but to make that reputation true – to walk the walk, and not just talk the talk. Those who only talk the talk are soon found out.

While it can take a lifetime to build your reputation, it may only take minutes to destroy it. Like many things, it is much easier to obliterate your reputation than it is to build it. A good analogy would be finishing a beautiful room in your home. It takes a lot of thought, material, planning, and labor to finish a room in your home. The walls must be measured and built to certain standards. Then they have to be covered and painted. A lot of time and money goes into the final product.

It can take weeks to finish the walls for one room, but think about how fast those same walls can be destroyed by one unskilled buffoon with a sledgehammer. It takes very little to ruin what took many hours to build. The same principle applies to your reputation. It takes thought, planning, and work to build a good reputation, but it can be completely destroyed in just a few quick minutes by thoughtless actions. Be careful to maintain the character and reputation that you have worked so hard to build.

I am careful to keep my reputation and character spotless.

November 10

A promise is a debt.
Irish Proverb

Many people make promises without any consideration for their words. Their word is absolutely meaningless to them. A promise from them is to be taken with a grain of salt. It usually means little more than they are in a desperate state at the time and they are willing to say anything to get whatever it is that they need for the moment.

Once they have what they are after, their promise is quickly forgotten. They never consider that a promise is a debt, after all, who is going to force them to live up to their word?

The warrior, on the other hand, is a man of his word. If he promises that he will do something, he does it, period. He doesn't make empty promises just to get his way, this would be dishonorable. He takes his word of honor seriously. To him, a promise is indeed a debt, and a debt that will be repaid. Warriors feel honor bound to make their word good. People who make empty promises lose the respect of those around them, and the warrior realizes this.

He is not willing to compromise his word or the respect that his character affords him. To the man of honor, a promise means as much as a written contract that is signed and notarized. His word is good whether it is written on paper or written on the wind.

Your promise is your word of honor. It should not matter whether or not your promise is legally binding in a court of law. The warrior lives by a higher law than the law of the land; he lives by a code based on honor and integrity.

When I make a promise, I keep it!

November 11

Victorious warriors win first and then go to war,
defeated warriors go to war first then seek to win.

Sun Tzu

Preparation is vital when it comes to a physical confrontation. You can't wait until the thug is at your door to go learn some martial arts techniques, lift some weights, and do some stretching. You will never be successful if you wait to study for the test until you walk into the classroom, sit down, and receive your test. That would be ridiculous. You have to be prepared for what you may have to encounter long before you actually encounter it. You must think ahead.

This is the way of the victorious warrior. He knows that he must be prepared to meet the wolf anytime that he leaves his house, and possibly without leaving his home. He realizes that the skills which he will need to keep himself and his loved-ones safe take time to develop and perfect. They do not just magically appear like a genie from a bottle. It takes months and years of hard work to acquire the skills, techniques, and mental toughness that you will need when confronted by a skilled street fighter.

Don't do like so many others and go into battle unprepared, thinking that the adrenaline that they feel, from their anger, will pull them through to victory. This is what Sun Tzu meant by defeated warriors going to war first and then seeking to win. They enter a conflict unprepared, and then seek to win by whatever means they can. The victorious warrior on the other hand, prepares for victory long before he enters into battle. He knows when to fight, and how to fight, and therefore he ends up victorious, even without fighting.

I win first, and then I fight. I always win!

315

November 12

Perfection is attained by slow degrees;
she requires the hand of time.

Voltaire

I have stated many times that the ultimate objective of the warrior is the perfection of character, as Gichin Funakoshi stated in his book *Karate-Do Kyohan*. The perfection of your character is not a simple thing. It actually is very complex and consists of various intertwined parts which are personal for each person. Perfecting your character is not a concrete goal in which once you have done a, b, and c, you have achieved success and can then move on to a new goal. It is a lifelong objective.

It is a never-ending quest for excellence, and it takes time. As Voltaire stated, it is attained by slow degrees, not overnight. You must make a decision to work at perfecting your character on a daily basis. There are opportunities every day to either move forward toward your goal or to slip backward away from your ultimate objective. Many people seem to be caught in the ebb and flow of this struggle. They move one step forward and two steps back.

In order to achieve this goal, or any other goal for that matter, you cannot afford to allow the tide of life to move you back and forth. You must be focused and determined to achieve any objective, this includes perfecting your character. In fact, it is even truer when it comes to your character. Each step backward not only takes you further from the perfection of your character, but it also makes it easier to compromise the next time, which makes achieving your goal in the future even more difficult. Be disciplined and patient.

I will keep living the warrior lifestyle until I reach perfection.

November 13

The steadfastness of the wise is but the art of
keeping their agitation locked in their hearts.
La Rochefoucauld

Everyone gets angry and frustrated at times. This is a normal part of being human, but while certain things have a way of rubbing you the wrong way, you don't have to make that information public. La Rochefoucauld taught that the wise man will keep these things private – locked in his heart. This is where his appearance of steadfastness comes from and why people see him as a man of self-control and restraint.

He does not express his displeasure with everything that annoys him. Like anyone he can become upset, frustrated, and angry, but he has the wisdom and insight to keep his emotions private unless he has a specific reason for expressing those emotions. Everything the wise man, the warrior, does is calculated. No action is performed out of thoughtlessness. This includes making a decision concerning when and how to express his anger over specific things.

This especially includes allowing his temper or frustration to control him. He is a master of keeping his emotions in check. His agitation is kept locked in his heart, at least until he decides it is time to release it to achieve his objective if need be.

No one has respect for a man who cannot control his temper or who walks around with a negative attitude concerning every little thing which has annoyed him. You must command respect, and in order to do so, you must be worthy of respect and act in a respectful manner.

I keep private things private.

Those skilled at making the enemy move do so by creating a situation to which he must conform.

Sun Tzu

You must become an expert in the art of winning without fighting. This may sound strange to you, but once you understand, it makes perfect sense. To illustrate I will use a scene from one of Bruce Lee's movies, *Enter the Dragon*. During a short boat ride with other fighters, Bruce Lee is accosted by another fighter, who is, of course, obnoxious and rude, and who wants to fight Lee. He pushes and pushes until Lee agrees to fight him. Lee suggests that they fight on a nearby island that can be seen from the boat.

The man agrees and Lee suggests that the two men board a small boat for a short boat ride over to the island. Again, the rude man agrees and heads toward the row boat, with Lee right behind him. As the pushy fighter makes his way into the row boat, Lee simply unties the rope, which was holding the row boat to the side of the ship, and lets it drift away without oars, thus defeating this enemy without fighting. The enemy lost, not because of Lee's martial arts skills, but because of his superior strategy.

This is a great example of making the enemy move by creating a situation to which he must conform. This thug would have looked like a coward had he refused to fight on the island after challenging Lee. Thus he had to agree to take the row boat over to the island and fight. Lee created a situation to which he had to conform, and the challenger did so freely. Lee made his enemy move, and at the same time defeated his enemy without fighting.

I defeat my enemies with my mind and my strategy.

November 15

It is you who must make the effort;
the sages can only teach.
Ralph W. Sockman

Just as you can tell who your true friends are in difficult times, you can also judge someone's true character in times of crisis. It is easy to have friends when you are prosperous and times are good, but these so-called "friends" seem to disappear at the speed of light when your fortune turns on you. Your character is much the same. It is easy to talk the talk when things are going well and there is no pressure on you, but it is in times of crisis that you know your true character.

This does not mean that if you slip and falter during a crisis, that you aren't a man of integrity. Everyone makes mistakes and everyone can give in during a time of weakness, this doesn't mean that you are a man of low character. One action does not define a man, although it may in the eyes of others. Only you know who you truly are and whether or not you are a man of character and honor, but at the same time, a man of character will exhibit those traits, both on a daily basis, and in times of crisis.

In order to maintain your character during a crisis, when everyone and everything seems to be against you, you have to be prepared beforehand. This is why the warrior works to perfect his character on a daily basis. If you do not train and hone your martial arts skills before the predator attacks you, you will not be able to defend yourself. You will be unprepared. If you do not work to build your character during your daily life, you will not be strong enough to maintain that character when your back is against the wall.

I make the effort and I am always successful.

Surprise defeats strength and speed.
Glenn Morris

An enemy surprised is half defeated. This is a common statement seen in many martial arts books. I don't care who you are or how advanced your martial arts skills may be, there are people out there who are bigger, tougher and more talented. They will be stronger and faster. Even if you are the best there is today, that will change next year or in the next ten years. Some day you will find that you are no longer the best of the best, if you ever were.

When that day comes, you will have to find ways to compensate for the fact that there are many bad guys out there who you cannot stand up to toe-to-toe in a physical confrontation. One of the ways to counteract the current of the river which keeps pulling you downstream is to develop superior strategy.

Using the element of surprise is one of the strategic moves that can give you the edge that you need. As the Ninja Master, Glen Morris, stated, surprise defeats strength and speed.

This is a very good thing for the aging warrior because as we age, our strength and speed regress. The element of surprise makes the battle ground even, or even tilts the odds in your favor. This is even truer if you are still at the peak of your skills as a martial artist. If you are still among the best, think how much harder you will be to defeat if you integrate the element of surprise into your arsenal. Don't rely solely on your techniques, your speed, or your strength, throw in the element of surprise and all the rest will be more devastating and you will be victorious.

My strategy always beats my enemy's strength and speed.

November 17

For when moral value is considered, the concern
is not the actions, which are seen, but rather
with their inner principles, which are not seen.
Emmanuel Kant

Can the right action be wrong? At first this may seem like a very simple question with a simple answer, but is it really? When you stop to think about this question, it becomes a little more involved. The answer depends on whether you are judging only the action itself or the moral intentions behind the action. According to Kant, the true test of whether an action is right or wrong lies not in the action itself, but in the principles behind the action.

This is also what the warrior should be concerned with when it comes to his actions. The warrior can do the right thing, but if he does it for the wrong reason or with evil intentions, is he really following his code of honor? I don't think so. The intentions or the "inner principles" behind the warrior's actions are very important. This is why many times it is impossible for someone else to truly judge another's actions as right or wrong.

Only the warrior knows if his intentions are just and honorable, and even if they are, he still has to make sure that his actions are right. You can have honorable intentions and still make the wrong choice as far as your actions go. For example, you could want to help the poor, but robbing a bank would be the wrong way to accomplish this goal. On the other hand, you can do what others may perceive as the right thing, but have less than honorable intentions, which can spoil the true integrity of your actions. Both intentions and actions have to be right.

I make sure my intentions are right, and then act.

The man of principle never forgets
what he is, because of what others are.

Baltasar Gracian

This is one of my all-time favorite quotes from one of my favorite authors. The warrior is a man of principle. He doesn't set his principles aside when they do not seem convenient. Today many people do just that. They use the actions of others to justify their own bad behavior.

Statements such as, "Well I wouldn't have done that if he hadn't shoved me, cursed me, etc." are commonly heard to justify wrong behavior. The warrior should not allow the behavior of others to affect his behavior, as far as doing things that are against his principles.

The warrior never forgets who he is or what he is, because of what others are or what others do. If someone is acting like a jerk, that doesn't give you a free pass to set aside your principles. Someone else's actions have nothing to do with you. You are responsible for your actions, not someone else's actions.

Someone else being what they are, whether it is a jerk, a criminal, or whatever, should not cause you to forget who you are, and that is a man of principle. You must live independently from the actions of others. Don't allow the actions of others to cause you to compromise your principles. This is an easy trap to walk into.

Think rationally and remember who you are and what you are. You have a code to live up to. That code is not dependent on what other people do or do not do. It stands alone, unaffected by the act of others. The man of principle never forgets what or who he is.

I never forget what I am, because of what others are.

November 19

Deliberate Often – Decide Once.
Latin Proverb

The warrior has to be decisive. He has to spend time meditating on his values and his standards, and he has to know who he is deep down inside. This information gives him a moral compass as to how to live his life and how to make the important decisions that have to be made throughout his journey. Everyone has important decisions which have to be made in their life. Your choices determine your destiny.

It is vital that you make the correct choices because every choice carries with it a set of consequences. For this reason you have to look at all the possibilities when you are deliberating what you should and should not do.

Examine the pros and the cons. Look at the possible consequences for each choice. Don't rush your decisions. Take your time when possible, and don't make a decision until you feel confident on the inside that your decision is correct.

Once you feel that you have made the best decision that you possibly can make, stick with it. The time for debating the issue has passed. You have spent time meditating on your options, you have thought about the different outcomes, and you have made the best decision that you could make.

Have confidence that you have done the best that you could do to make an intelligent decision. Don't second guess yourself over and over again. This only causes doubt and stress to cloud your mind. Deliberate often – decide once, and then stand firm on your decision.

I deliberate often but decide only once, and then follow through.

A wise man, in great or small matters, must act
with due consideration. Whether attacking a hare
or an elephant, the lion has no time for indecision.

Sakya Pandit

The warrior has no time for indecision. He must know the right course to take, and then act accordingly, without delay. Indecision can bring about defeat. It can cloud the mind and confuse the thought process. Indecisiveness is a sign of weakness in the warrior. Have confidence in your judgment and act decisively.

Deliberate often, but decide once. Once your decision is made, follow through to the end. Going back and forth, and changing your mind time and again, accomplishes little more than to add to your uncertainty concerning what you should do.

It doesn't matter what you are debating or what the issue at hand happens to be, habitual indecision only makes things worse. This doesn't mean that you should rush to make a decision. On the contrary, timing is essential. The right decision at one moment may be the wrong decision just a few minutes later.

Even small matters require your full consideration. A small slip while in the middle of a violent confrontation could cost you dearly. When you see it is time to strike, you must strike immediately. Things change constantly in battle and delaying your attack may render your attack useless. Once the opportunity is gone, it is gone forever. Indecision can defeat you both in battle and in life.

No matter how small a problem, I take it seriously.

Efforts and enemies, if left unfinished, can both ravage you like an unextinguished fire.

Tiruvalluvar

When you start something, finish it. Don't leave anything undone. The warrior must strive for excellence in all that he does. He must give his best all of the time, every time. Tiruvalluvar is trying to stress the importance of this in the above quote.

Warriors realize the importance of making sure that your enemy is completely defeated before you stop your attack, but by combining "effort" and "enemies" in the same category, Tiruvalluvar is demanding that we look beyond our enemy to the bigger picture.

You must grapple with the fact that your lack of effort and attention can derail your goals on the path of the warrior, just as an unfinished enemy can overturn your victory during a physical confrontation. The warrior lifestyle requires both attention to details and constant effort in order to make it part of your being. Without the proper effort towards this lofty goal, it will remain unobtainable.

Finish what you start. Don't leave things half-way done. Anything worth doing is worth doing well. Whether you are getting a hard workout or going head to head with a dangerous adversary, stay focused to the end.

Niccolo Machiavelli taught in this book *The Prince,* that you should never leave an enemy standing. When you have a fire to put out, make sure you leave no danger of it re-igniting. Put it out once and for all! Give some thought to this.

I leave nothing undone; I finish what I start.

November 22

When you see a rattlesnake poised to strike, you do
not wait until he has struck before you crush him.

Franklin Delano Roosevelt

Gichin Funakoshi stated that there is no first attack in karate, but what exactly does this mean? Does this mean that you cannot throw a kick or a punch until your enemy has tried to kick or hit you first? No, this is a misconception. An attack does not necessarily have to be physical.

Many times, waiting until the first kick or punch has been thrown is a mistake. It is rare that an enemy just walks up and throws a punch without any warning. There is usually a verbal or a visual attack that precedes an actual physical attack. The warrior should be able to sense imminent danger.

When you have determined that you or someone else is in danger, the first attack has already occurred. Once you have reached that point, you decide when it is time to strike. Don't wait for the enemy to set the pace or make his move. You be in control. Read the situation and take the appropriate action at the appropriate time.

Use your intuition and your environmental awareness. Learn to read the intentions of other people. This is almost like a sixth sense that alerts you when something is wrong. When you know that danger is imminent, and that an engagement is unavoidable, then it is time for you to act. Be decisive and crush your enemy before he can harm you. Be aware and learn to sense danger. Listen to your inner spirit and have the confidence to act on what it tells you. Don't wait for the rattlesnake to strike before you act.

I know when it is time to strike, and I strike hard.

He who plants a forest in the morning
cannot expect to saw planks the same evening.
Chinese Proverb

The warrior lifestyle takes time to perfect. It takes time to develop your character, to learn to automatically live by your code of honor, to serve and protect others when you would rather be minding your own business, and to develop the overall discipline that this lifestyle requires. All of these things do not come naturally; you have to work for them, and this takes time. Developing any worthwhile skill is a process, and developing your character is no different.

Voltaire taught that perfection is attained by slow degrees; she requires the hand of time. It doesn't matter what you are trying to perfect; nothing goes from the foundation to flawlessness over night. It takes time for a seed to grow into a full grown plant.

It takes time for a baby to grow into a man. And it will take time for you to develop all of the skills and character traits that are a part of warriorhood. Knowing this, you must be patient with yourself when you miss your mark at times.

One of the main ingredients in success is determination. You must be determined not to give up. Don't quit! If you find that you have made a wrong move, and you will, don't throw in the towel and think that you can never measure up to the true warrior. Everyone makes mistakes. This is just part of the learning process of the warrior lifestyle. You will make mistakes. Learn from those mistakes and do better next time. You are never defeated until you declare defeat.

I move forward every day. I will not quit!

November 24

No weapon is sharper than the mind;
even the finest sword is inferior.

The Masters of Huainan

No matter how much weapons training or martial arts training you have had, your best and most reliable weapon is your mind. That's right, your mind is your first weapon of self-defense, and just like any other weapon, and you have to practice using it in order to be proficient with it when you need it. You have to train your mind concerning how to respond to certain situations, just as you have to train your body through strength training and martial arts training to be prepared to defend yourself.

Once you have trained your mind to remain calm, no matter what condition you may find yourself in, you have taken a huge step in the preparation of your mental arsenal. You must learn to stay calm in the storm. A calm mind is a mind that can think rationally. It is sharp and focused. Stress, anxiety and panic all hinder the mind's ability to function properly and thus renders your most important weapon useless or at least not functioning at its peak.

There are several techniques that the warrior can use to train his mind to remain calm. Realistic martial arts training is a good way to accomplish this, as is meditation. Your martial arts training should be as realistic as possible. You have to learn how to control your mind under stressful situations such as when someone is in your face yelling and threatening you. This type of training technique enables you to feel what it is like to respond to a real threat. Keep your most useful weapon sharp and ready.

My best weapon is my mind. I win with my strategy.

November 25

The wise pursue understanding;
fools follow the reports of others.
Tibetan Proverb

It seems it is getting harder and harder today to find an unbiased source for news. No matter which television station you watch, radio show you listen to, or news page on the internet that you read, it seems that they all have an agenda.

It is foolish to blindly follow the reports of others, especially when those sources have hidden agendas which you are not privy to. With this in mind, you may ask, "What is a person to do if he wants to understand world events?"

That is a hard question to answer. The best you can do, if you do not have personal knowledge or have trustworthy friends with personal knowledge of what is going on, is to get your information from several different sources. This is akin to hearing both sides of the story. If you hear only one side, you will find that you are in the dark, as far as your understanding goes. Don't take things for the truth just because they are on television or because they are in writing.

Facts and statistics can be slanted to demonstrate whatever someone wants them to illustrate. Many people are experts when it comes to twisting the truth to fit their own personal agenda. Don't take what they say as gospel. No matter what the topic may be, strive to achieve an understanding of the issue. Trusting in the reports of others can prove dangerous and misleading. The warrior has to depend on the truth, not the spin.

I find out the truth; I do not follow theories or gossip.

November 26

He is the best man who, when making his plans, fears and reflects on everything that can happen to him, but in the moment of action is bold.

Herodotus

Some people have a false idea about who the warrior is as a person. They think that he is this brute who has no fear of death, or that he doesn't think before he acts, but rather acts out of pure adrenaline, not considering that he may be killed. This is not an accurate picture of the warrior. The warrior knows better than most, how fragile the human body is and how easily it can be destroyed. He has intricate knowledge about what can and does happen in physical encounters.

He knows the risks that he takes when he steps up to help someone who is being attacked by a mugger. He fully realizes what could happen if things go wrong. Warriors understand how much they have to lose and the consequences that certain situations could have on them and their family. They aren't born with some superior form of courage that makes them immune to fear. They develop their courage to the point that they are able to overcome their fear.

The warrior has the same human emotions as everyone else, but elects to control those emotions instead of being controlled by them. He realizes all of these things, but in the moment that someone needs his protection, he rises above all of these thoughts and emotions, and takes bold action. Warriors don't wait for someone else to take care of things because of their fear; they step up when they are needed. Herodotus said that this is a trait of the best men, and he is right, the true warrior is the best man.

I act when it is time to act. I overcome all of my fears.

November 27

What lies in our power to do,

it lies in our power not to do.

Aristotle

You don't have to do anything. People are constantly saying, "I have to do this or I have to that," but the reality is that nobody *has* to do anything. You choose to do everything that you do. Now you may be thinking, that is not true, I *have* to go to work or I *have* to pay my bills, but you really don't *have* to do either of these. The simple fact of the matter is that you don't have to do anything; you *choose* to do these things.

It's true; you don't have to go to work. Work is something that you choose to do either because you like having money or because you find it rewarding, but either way you make the choice to get up and go to your job each day. Nobody is forcing you to go to work. No one is forcing you to pay your bills. You choose to pay them in order to keep living the lifestyle that you have decided to live.

Likewise, nobody forces you to get angry or to lose your temper. Again, you *choose* to get angry or to lose your temper, and just as you choose to allow these things, you can also choose not to allow them. What lies in our power to do, it lies in our power not to do.

You choose each and every one of your actions – all of them. There are no exceptions. The choice is 100% yours. You don't *have* to do anything. This is precisely why we are each responsible for all of our actions; we *choose* them therefore we are responsible for them. Think about this.

I always have a choice. I am responsible for everything I do.

Even in the sheath the knife must be sharp.

Finnish Proverb

Your martial arts training must be kept sharp. It is one of the duties of the warrior to keep his skills ready at all times. Don't neglect your training. It is easy to fall into the mental illusion that you may never really need to use your martial arts skills in "real life," but as a warrior, you cannot think this way.

As the above proverb states, "Even in the sheath the knife must be kept sharp." The same goes for your martial arts skills; even if you are not using them, and they are "just in the sheath," they still must be sharp.

You don't wait until you need your knife to clean it up and sharpen it. After you use it, you clean it, sharpen it and store it in good shape for the next time you need to use it. It must be ready when you need it, especially if it is needed in a self-defense situation. Thus the saying, even in the sheath the knife must be sharp. It is not being used in the sheath, but it is ready to be used.

In the same way, you don't wait until you need your martial arts skills to make sure they are developed, sharp and ready to be used. You keep them sharp and ready to be used when you need them. Procrastination can be a deadly habit. If your skills are not ready to use at a moment's notice, you could be in big trouble.

The warrior's weapons are kept sheathed the majority of the time, but they still have to be kept sharp. You don't want to find that you need to use your "knife" and when you take it out of the sheath, it is dull, rusted, and couldn't cut hot butter. Think about this.

I work to keep my skills sharp.

November 29

Lay down for yourself, at the outset, a certain stamp and type of character for yourself which you are to maintain whether you are by yourself or are meeting with people.

Epictetus

You may be thinking that it must be exhausting having to make all these decisions every day concerning what is right and what is wrong, as you walk the path of the warrior. But that is really not the way it is. The warrior does not have to mentally debate every issue that comes along to decide which action is right or wrong. The issue of how the warrior will live has already been decided. He has already set the standards that he will live by, and he knows what he stands for and what he will not stand for. These decisions have already been made.

What the warrior must do on a daily basis is *actually live* by the standards that he has set for himself. He knows what is right and what is wrong, and he knows that it is his duty to maintain his character and to have the courage to do what is right. His code is not for show. He doesn't use it to impress people. It is his way of life. It is who he is.

The warrior knows all of this. All that is left for him to do is to put all these things into action. Whether he is alone or with others, he must live up to his standards. He has determined the type of character that he wants for himself, and he knows in order to develop and maintain that character, he must make it a vital part of who he is, whether alone or with other people. Make a firm decision concerning how you will live your life, and stick to it.

I decide what my character will be and I choose to be a warrior.

November 30

Hear all sides and you will be enlightened.
Hear one side and you will be in the dark.
Wei Zheng

Everyone perceives things through their own lens. There are very few people who can give you an unbiased opinion on any subject. If you have five people who witness a fight, you will get five different accounts of what happened, maybe not on the main points, but they will differ concerning the details. For this reason, it is always wise to hear all sides of the story before you form any opinions.

True life court shows on television demonstrate this fact. They will go through the evidence and present the prosecution's side of the case, and you think to yourself, "this guy is guilty as sin," but when the defense presents their case, many times you start to see things in a different light. Don't be too quick to form a decision. Once you have heard all sides of the issue, then you can form your opinion concerning the matter at hand.

Strive to see things as they really are, not as they appear. Look for the truth. Too many people make decisions without having all of the pertinent information needed to come to a wise conclusion. Without all the information, you're just guessing.

Don't be too quick to totally trust the information that you receive from someone else. Trust but verify. Don't be duped, hear all sides before you make important decisions. Make sure that what you think is truly what you think, and not simply someone else's thoughts which have been seeded in your mind.

I hear all sides before I act.

December 1

Because a human being is so malleable,
whatever one cultivates is what one becomes.

Lao Tzu

Lao Tzu tells us in the *Tao Te Ching*, that whatever you cultivate, whatever you practice, you become. You have to be careful of your thoughts and your actions. Your thoughts become your actions, your actions become your habits, and your habits become your character. Be aware of what kind of character traits you are cultivating and make sure that they are the character traits of a warrior. If you have cultivated something in your garden that you don't want growing there, take steps to remove it from the roots. Keep your garden weed free. Don't keep the weeds under control, remove them.

Science tells us that it takes anywhere from 30 to 45 days for something to become a habit. That is, if you want to make something a part of your life, practice it for 30 to 45 days, without skipping a day. This fixes that behavior in your mind and causes it to become a habit. It doesn't matter what the behavior is. Your mind and body do not discriminate. They will accept whatever you decide to cultivate.

For this reason it is important that you carefully consider your actions, especially the actions which are part of your daily routine. Bad habits are easy to develop; quality habits take more discipline, at least in the beginning. After something becomes a habit, it takes very little effort to continue to make it part of your life. It becomes natural and essentially automatic. This is the point that you want to reach in your character training, as well as the other vital parts of the warrior lifestyle.

I cultivate courage, honor, and integrity.

December 2

In the beginner's mind there are many possibilities,
but in the expert's mind there are few.
Shunryu Suzuki

This is an interesting quote and can be applied to the warrior's mind. In the mind of the ordinary person the possibilities concerning how to conduct himself are endless, but to the warrior the possibilities concerning how to conduct himself are few. He is bound by honor and integrity. The same goes for the world's view concerning right and wrong. The world views right and wrong as an endless parade of possibilities depending on what is best for specific issues. The warrior views right and wrong in more concrete terms.

To the beginner, there are many possibilities, but the expert knows that there are only few possibilities because he has wisdom concerning what should be done and what should not be done. He knows what will work and what won't work. It is the same with the warrior. He knows that "give peace a chance" doesn't work when confronted with a violent situation. There is definitely a time and a place where violence is the only answer.

Of course there are always many possibilities, but what Shunryu Suzuki is referring to is *viable* possibilities. The warrior knows that there may be many options in a violent situation, but there are only a few that will keep him and his loved ones safe. This is the difference between an experienced warrior and a novice. The expert warrior knows what must be done in any given situation, or is able to discern what must be done quickly, whereas the beginner is unsure concerning the "many possibilities." This is where constant training comes into play. Think about this.

I am careful about who I trust.

December 3

*Only one who continually reexamines
himself and corrects his faults will grow.*
The Hagakure

Anyone seeking to perfect his character has to continually examine himself in order to correct the things in his life that need to be corrected. All men have faults. Every man has his own personal shortcomings, yes, even the best trained warriors and men of honor have faults that they need to continually keep in check and correct. This is just part of being human. One of the differences between the warrior and other men is that he continually tries to correct his faults, instead of just ignoring them. He is not satisfied allowing them to control his life or parts of his life.

He continually examines himself and molds his life in the way that he knows he should live. Every morning, recall the code that you strive to live by, and every night reflect on whether or not you have been successful in living up to your code of honor. Look for ways in which you have fallen short in your quest and determine what you should have done differently, and know that you will handle that situation differently the next time. Strive to improve your life and your character every day.

Little by little your character will be perfected, just as drop by drop the water wears away the stone. Be patient with yourself and continue with your quest. Successes, whether in the warrior lifestyle or any other endeavor, consist of not giving up. Don't quit, just continue to press on with each new day. Every day is a new chance to start with a clean slate.

I reexamine myself regularly and correct my faults.

December 4

If you calm your own mind and discern the inner mind of others, that may be called the foremost art of war.

Shiba Yoshimasa

I have talked a lot about how the warrior should keep a calm and tranquil mind no matter what situation he may find himself in, but I haven't elaborated much on discerning the minds of others. This is another important skill for the warrior to learn. Shiba Yoshimasa calls the combination of these two skills the foremost art of war. They are both necessary for success. You have to develop, not only the ability to remain calm in adverse conditions, but the ability to sense when others mean you harm.

One of the advanced black belt tests in ninjutsu is called the sword test. The master stands behind a student, who is kneeling in meditation, with a bokken, ready to attack with a downward cut to the top of the head. The student is required to "sense" the attack and move to the side, avoiding the blow, at the exact moment of attack. If he moves too soon, he fails the test; if he moves too late, well he will have a tremendous headache.

Students who have successfully passed this test have a hard time putting into words how they avoided the blow of the sword. They simply say that they just moved. The purpose of this test is for the student to learn to sense the energy of someone who wants to do them harm. In order for this to work, the master has to truly be willing to hurt the student and he gives off this violent energy. Being able to sense danger before it comes is a great advantage to the warrior.

I keep my mind calm and think clearly at all times.

December 5

Truth is not a matter of personal viewpoint.

Vernon Howard

The truth is the truth no matter what anyone thinks about it. Truth doesn't change because the majority doesn't agree with it or doesn't want it to be so. It is independent of all outside influences. Personal viewpoints play no part whatsoever in determining truth. People will debate the truth and then say things like, "It depends on how you look at it," but in reality, it doesn't matter how you "look at it." The truth doesn't change because you look at it one way or another.

The truth may seem elusive in many cases, but it is not. The truth simply is the truth, period. What is elusive, is people's ability to discern the truth, whether it is because of their prejudices, preconceived notions, or their simple refusal to accept the truth as the way things truly are. People tend to see what they want to see, whether it is the truth or not. Many people live in their own pre-constructed fantasy world where the truth holds little value.

This should not be the case for the warrior. The warrior can't afford to live in a fantasy world. He has to be rational and see things as they truly are in order to make rational decisions concerning his life. Refusing to see the truth for what it is, is just a form of escapism for those who do not want to deal with the realities of life.

These are the people who will tell you violence never solved anything, while at the same time depending on the warrior to be prepared to defend their rights by violent means if necessary. Don't hide from the truth; embrace it and meet it head on with the determination of a warrior.

My mind is open to the truth. I always discover the truth.

339

December 6

Don't follow any advice, no matter how good,
until you feel as deeply in your spirit as you
think in your mind that the counsel is wise.

David Seabury

The wise man listens to the thoughts of others, but always makes his own decisions. Ultimately, you are the only person responsible for your actions. Nobody else will be held accountable for the choices which you make. Since you, and you alone are responsible for the choices that you make, shouldn't you actually be the one who decides what those choices are. Make sure that your actions are based on your choices, not the choices of other people.

It is good to listen to the advice and admonitions of others at times, but don't automatically take the advice of others to be the gospel or to be more enlightened than your own thoughts. Meditate on the right choice until you feel deep in your spirit that you know which road to take. Don't simply rely on your mind to figure things out. Spend time in quiet meditation. Clear your mind and listen to your intuition or your spirit.

Buddha taught the same principle to his followers. He said that you shouldn't believe anything merely because someone tells you this or that. You should examine things for yourself, think about them, and not act on them until you know inside that they are right; then act on what you know is right. The warrior knows that he is solely responsible for his decisions in life, and therefore he is not content to act without giving thought to his actions beforehand. Listen to the counsel of the wise, but make your own decisions.

I listen to my intuition. I am led by my spirit.

December 7

Do not let trifles disturb your tranquility of mind.
Ignore the inconsequential.

Grenville Kleiser

The warrior should strive to do the best that he can do in every area of his life. It is a part of his nature to try to make every part of his life as perfect as possible. He strives for excellence in every area of his life, but no matter how hard he tries, there will always be times when things will not go as planned. Everyone has stumbling blocks that they have to maneuver around on their journey. Don't focus on the stumbling blocks; focus on your actions and your response to these challenges.

Everything matters, but not everything is important enough to get upset over. Don't let these small glitches disturb your mind. If something is inconsequential, don't spend time thinking about it, and even if something is momentous, don't let it rob you of your peace of mind. Whether the challenge that you have to face is small or monumental, maintain your composure and strive to keep a tranquil mind. Worry is worthless in your quest to overcome your problems.

I'm not suggesting that you just ignore your problems and hope that they somehow mysteriously disappear. Things don't change simply because you don't want to deal with them. What I am saying is don't sweat the small stuff. Not only should you not sweat the small stuff, but don't let the larger things bother you either. Simply do the best that you can do in each moment to deal with the issue at hand and move on to the next moment. The way of the warrior is in rational action, not immobilized worry.

Nothing disturbs my peace of mind.

December 8

Think like a man of action,

act like a man of thought.

Thomas Mann

How does a man of action think? Well, to start with, he thinks about what can be done to solve the problem at hand or to make things better. The man of action is a go-getter. He doesn't wait to see what others think or depend on others to step up while he minds his own business. The man of action wants to get things done and make things right. His thoughts center on accomplishing his goals, and doing so in the most efficient manner possible. "Do it now and do it right" is his mantra.

The man of thought on the other hand, likes to think things through before he makes a move. He examines all the possible outcomes of his actions and tries to see the situation from all sides. Realizing that there is more to most things than meets the eye, he delves deeper into things in order to develop a true understanding of them. He searches for the truth so he can make decisions based on facts rather than emotions. Justice and honor are foremost on his mind.

The warrior should find balance between the traits of the two types of men. Think like a man of action, but act like a man of thought. Be ready for action and know what action is needed should things come to that, but at the same time, be calm, collected and rational like a man of thought. Think things through before you speak or act. Don't be rash. Integrate these traits into one and find a sense of balance between the two. A calm, rational mind which is always ready for action is a trait of the true warrior.

I think like a man of action. I act like a man of thought.

December 9

Take a deep breath of life and
consider how it should be lived.
Don Quixote's Creed

Don Quixote's creed contains a lot of wisdom that we can all benefit from if we will only slow down and listen to it. Slow down and take a look at your life and consider how it should be lived. It seems that the majority of people just go through life randomly reacting to whatever comes their way. They don't appear to have any set ideas about how they should live their life. They simply go through the motions day by day.

The warrior should take the time to retire to a quiet place and meditate on his life and how he should live his life. He shouldn't just go through the motions, but instead he should consider the value of life and how quickly it disappears. Life should be lived to the fullest each and every day, and not only lived, but lived with character and honor.

Take time to consider how your life should be lived. How should a true warrior spend his time? Are you truly living your life to the fullest or do you walk through your days on autopilot? If your self-examination reveals that you haven't been living life to the fullest, it is time to make a change. Don't wait another day; start living today.

Determine what it is that you want from life and what you need to do to manifest the kind of life that you want. Don't wander through life with no idea of what you want or who you want to be. Sit down and map out your life. Determine how your life will be lived, and then live it, every day.

I choose to live my life with gusto. I choose to live as a warrior.

December 10

A hero in old age never lets go of his principles.
Cao Cao

The warrior lifestyle is built on specific principles which the warrior makes his own. These principles actually become a part of who he is as a man. They are not something that he uses when he needs them and then puts them in a closet until the next time that he finds he needs to pull them out and apply them. The principles of warriorship become as much a part of the warrior as his arm or his leg. They become ingrained in his spirit.

Knowing this, the above quote by Cao Cao appears very obvious. The hero doesn't let go of his principles as he ages. His principles actually become more embedded in his spirit as he gets older. They are a part of who he has become over many years of training and learning from his mistakes and his triumphs. The aging warrior has learned the value of character, integrity and honor, and knows the importance of maintaining his standards.

He would consider it ridiculous to let go of his principles after many years spent honing them to perfection. Instead of letting go of his principles, the warrior in his old age elects to pass on his wisdom to those who will listen. He is able to see the mistakes which the younger people are making because he has seen the same mistakes before, and he knows what must be done to correct and deal with these mistakes.

The wise man will listen to the aging warrior's wisdom and learn. With age comes insight, especially in those who have been wise enough to develop the traits of the warrior. Listen to their wisdom and learn from their experience.

I will never let go of my principles; they are a part of me.

December 11

My enemy is not the man who wrongs me,
but the man who means to wrong me.

Democritus

Every enemy has the capability to disrupt your life, some in a small way and others to a much larger capacity, but not many of them go to the effort to cause you harm. The fact that you don't openly see enemies attacking you physically, verbally or discreetly behind your back, doesn't mean that you do not have any enemies. It simply means that your enemies are not malevolent enough or energetic enough to make the effort to cause you harm, but their lack of effort should not be mistaken for a lack of malevolence toward you.

As Democritus taught, just because a man does you no harm, it doesn't mean he is not your enemy. You have to look deeper than that. You have to read between the lines. Your enemy is not only the man who wrongs you, but also the man who longs to see you wronged. He is the man who is happy when you are hit with misfortune, the man who celebrates your downfall. Your enemy is the person who wishes you calamity, even if he doesn't have the courage to openly state the fact or to actually try to act on it.

Be careful who you trust. You don't always know who your enemies are. They are not always those who openly oppose you. The enemies of a good man are usually not men of character and backbone. They are more likely to be men of low character who lack the courage to openly come against you. Instead, they find it easier to simply sit back and think malicious thoughts of your ruin. Be wise and learn to read people's spirits. Be careful who you trust.

I always guard myself well. No enemy can hurt me!

December 12

Warriors confront the evil that most
people refuse the acknowledge.
Bohdi Sanders

The average person doesn't want to acknowledge the evil that lurks in the dark places of this world. It is much more pleasant and peaceful to just pretend that all people are doing the best that they can and have good intentions, although some may simply be a little misguided. These kinds of people prefer to think that we now live in a more enlightened society, one where there is no need for physical violence.

While that might be a nice thought that makes them all warm and fuzzy inside, it is far from the truth. We do not live in some utopian society that is much more evolved than the Trojans or Vikings, even though many prefer to see the world in this way.

There are some evil, nasty people out there who do not care about you in the slightest. They will take advantage of you in every way, without batting an eyelash or giving your life a second thought. Although every person is made of the same substance, all people are not the same.

While it might be peaceful and blissful to pretend these kinds of people don't really exist, and everyone is basically good at heart, it is dangerous to live by that philosophy. It is best to live your life in a peaceful, relaxed state, enjoying all life has to offer, but at the same time, be acutely aware that evil people do exist and you must be prepared to handle them if they target you. The warrior enjoys life, but is ready to confront the evil which most people refuse to acknowledge.

I confront evil wherever I find it; and I defeat it!

*Those who do good because they want
to be seen to be good are not good.*

Lieh Tzu

Why does the warrior seek to do what he considers right according to his code of ethics? Is it because he knows that others expect him to be upstanding and live with honor? Does he only do the right thing to impress others or when others are observing his actions? No, the warrior seeks to live by his code of ethics because deep down inside he is committed to living up to the strict standards which he has set for himself.

He is not concerned with whether or not others approve or disapprove of his actions, as long as he knows inside his spirit that he is living according to the code which he has decided to make his own. The warrior lives the lifestyle of the warrior because that is who he is, not because he wants to impress someone or he wants to brag about his ethics. He walks the path of justice because he has made a firm decision to do so.

Not everyone shares this dedication to doing what is right. Many people only do good because they want to impress others; they want to make a reputation for themselves that will help them climb the social ladder of success. They want to be seen as good, but they really have no burning desire to be good. In fact, when it comes down to it, they really don't care about justice. They care about what is best for their own goals and status. They aren't truly good, upstanding people, but only appear good. Don't be a hypocrite. Live the ideals that you subscribe to, whether in public or private.

My intentions are always honorable.

December 14

Never be easily drawn into a fight.
Gichin Funakoshi

The warrior should only fight when all other options have been exhausted. By "fight" I mean an all out, no holds barred encounter. There may be times when you find that you have to restrain someone or prevent someone from continuing on a belligerent path, but this can be done without the warrior using the full extent of his power. This is different than actually fighting, and calls for wisdom and discretion.

If you encounter some drunk who is a bit out of control, pushing and shoving someone, some simple restraint may be all that is called for, not the total obliteration of this guy.

Another example would be if your son is high on drugs and out of control, you certainly wouldn't want to hurt him, but it may take some restraint or a nice stern punch to snap him back into reality. These are just two examples of where you may have to restrain someone or pull your punches because the situation calls for a moderate response.

This is not the same as a true fight. A fight is a serious situation where you have no choices left, and where someone is going to get hurt. This kind of encounter is a grave situation and should be taken seriously. Never allow yourself to be easily drawn into this kind of situation.

Always try your best to avoid fighting and to resolve things peacefully if at all possible. You should stay in control of the situation; don't be manipulated into a fight. Be smart enough to maintain your focus on your objective and don't let your emotions get involved. Don't allow anyone to draw you into an unnecessary fight.

I am never easily drawn into a fight!

December 15

Reputation often spills less blood.
Samurai Maxim

This samurai maxim appears to be in direct opposition to the teaching that you should conceal your weapons and your abilities, but it contains truth nonetheless. There is a time and a place for everything. There are times when concealing your skills is the wise thing to do, and yet at other times it may be wise to put your reputation to use, if you have a reputation as the samurai did. You have to use your best judgment where this is concerned.

The samurai had a reputation of being great warriors who could be fierce and deadly if the situation called for it. They were known as expert swordsmen. This reputation probably saved the lives of many men during the time of the samurai. Men who may have challenged an ordinary man over some trivial offense wouldn't consider challenging a samurai over the same transgression. Therefore, the samurai's reputation saved these men's lives, considering if they had challenged the samurai, they would have probably been killed.

The same notion can be true today, but you have to be very careful when it comes to counting on your reputation. Your reputation can help you resolve escalating conflicts, but having a reputation can also backfire on you.

Your enemy may be so intimidated by your reputation that he is tempted to go to extremes in order to defeat you. We live in a different world than the samurai. Today someone may take a shot at you from across the street instead of confronting you face to face. In whatever situation you may find yourself, judgment is vital. Think before you speak or act.

My reputation is good and blesses my life.

December 16

*It is only the tranquil mind that can allow
for fair and clear judgments free of error.*
Gichin Funakoshi

For thousands of years, sages have taught us to look inside for the answers that we seek. We find this wisdom repeated throughout different cultures from the Native Americans to the earliest wisdom texts. Meditation or retreating to a space of solitary silence, has been used throughout the ages as a way to solve difficult problems and to deal with confusing situations. Silence quiets the mind and allows for clear thinking.

The opposite is also true. Chaos creates a mind full of stress, which causes indecision and confusion. In his classic book *Karate-Do Kyohan*, Gichin Funakoshi tells us that you can only think clearly and rationally if your mind is tranquil. Therefore it is vital that you learn to keep your mind calm, no matter what is happening around you. You must be able to think clearly in order to make rational decisions and sound judgments.

When panic sets in, your mind doesn't function rationally. This is when mistakes are made. Practice keeping yourself calm despite what is happening. The man, who can remain calm while others are panicked, has a distinct advantage over those who have allowed panic to control their mind. This is why warriors throughout history have used fear as an effective form of warfare. Once their enemies allowed fear to enter their minds, their thinking became flawed and they were vulnerable. Knowing this, the warrior must take heed to keep his mind calm and tranquil, and not let the same ploy be played on him.

I keep my mind tranquil and I always think clearly.

December 17

Hardships often prepare ordinary people
for an extraordinary destiny.

C. S. Lewis

Nobody enjoys going through hard times. Hard times happen to everyone sooner or later. But, if you control your mind and focus on what you can get from the situation, instead of how bad you feel or how much you hate what is happening, you can turn a bad situation into something positive.

Many times, after you have made it through a hardship, you feel more capable, more confident, and a realization that you can handle whatever comes along. The situation has made you stronger and more prepared for the next hardship. Was if fun? Absolutely not! But, was it beneficial to you in some way? This is totally up to you. You have the choice to turn the situation into a learning experience or to just survive.

Think of it in terms of training. When you first start training, it is hard. You end up sore, frustrated, and sometimes doubting yourself. But if you continue to work through it, you conquer your doubts and frustrations, and you become more skilled, stronger, and can handle even more vigorous training.

Develop the mindset that nothing is too much for you to handle. See hardships as nothing more than challenges, and be determined to meet, and be victorious in, any challenge. Be determined to benefit from every hardship. Look for a way to learn from the situation, to increase your skills in some way.

I endure all and come out victorious!

December 18

Be careful of your thoughts;
they are the beginning of your acts.
Lao Tzu

Many people think that their thoughts really don't matter as long as they don't act on the negative or inappropriate thoughts, but thoughts have energy. In the *Tao Te Ching*, Lao Tzu tells us that you need to be careful of your thoughts. Your thoughts are the beginning of your actions. Keeping your mind clear and calm is part of a warrior's training. You should strive to keep your thoughts on a level plain because your thoughts can and do affect your emotions. As I have said before, you cannot afford to allow your emotions to control your actions.

You have to be rational. Keep your thoughts rational. Keep your purpose in mind and focus on what will achieve your goals. Will getting angry help you achieve your goal? Will being upset and dwelling on what has just happened change anything? No, that is living in the past. You can only deal with your problems and decide on the right action to take by being rational and focusing your thoughts on rational solutions.

This is one reason why the warrior should study and meditate on the wisdom of the past. By keeping your thoughts on things which focus on honor and integrity, you allow these qualities to filter down to your actions. When inappropriate thoughts pop into your mind, stop them in their tracks. Don't give them a chance to develop roots and turn into actions. Controlling your thoughts is one of the hardest challenges you will have in your training, but it is vitally important.

I am careful of my thoughts. My actions are honorable.

December 19

Beware that you do not lose the
substance by grasping at the shadow.

Aesop

As a warrior, you have to see things as they really are, not just as they appear to be. The majority of people are moved by hollow appearances of things. Just look at how many people actually believe the empty campaign rhetoric spewed out by politicians each year. Rational people realize that these politicians are little more than pandering liars, but people still vote for them. It is disgraceful!

Don't be like the sheep that just go along, believing whatever is presented to them as the truth. Look beyond the shadow and see the substance that is casting the shadow.

It is easy to lose the substance by grasping at the shadow. Fish never see the hook, only the bait. You have to remain aware. Don't be conned. Don't allow your attention to be side tracked to the shadow, while the substance goes unnoticed. This is what seems to happen to the majority of the people; they focus on the shadow instead of the physical reality.

The substance of your martial arts is self-defense and character training. The shadows are tournaments, perfecting your forms, points, decorum, or anything that distracts you from your true objectives.

I'm not saying that all of these things do not have a place in the martial arts, but the warrior must never mistake these things for the actual purpose of his training. Don't be caught striving to appear to be a warrior, be a warrior. Cultivate the root and the leaves and branches will take care of themselves.

I always look at the reality behind the shadow.

December 20

So live your life that the fear of
death can never enter your heart.

Tecumseh

How do you live your life so the fear of death can never enter your heart? The answer is to live your life to the fullest, leaving nothing undone. You must live your life full throttle. Live with gusto. Be adventurous and experience what life has to offer. Really experience life and at the same time, do it all with a sense of honor and character.

If you aren't living according to your code of honor, then you will sense that you are not living life as you should. This is when the fear of death starts to enter your heart. When you know that you aren't living according to the standards that you have set for yourself, you know that you aren't prepared to meet death.

The warrior who knows that he has lived up to his code of honor and has done the very best that he could do, has few regrets and little fear of death. He knows that his affairs are in order – spiritually, mentally, and physically.

He has lived life as it should be lived. Knowing that he has done his best in every endeavor, the warrior has no regrets and therefore is satisfied with his life. This doesn't mean that he welcomes death, but only that he is as prepared for death as possible.

This only comes from being at peace with how you have lived your life. In order to achieve this, you must live a life that is mindful and focused. Live your life with honor and integrity.

I live my life as it should be lived. I never fear death.

December 21

Trust your instinct to the end,
though you can render no reason.

Ralph Waldo Emerson

The warrior has to trust his instinct, even if it goes against what everyone else thinks is right. Warriors must be able to count on their own sense of right and wrong, and be able to choose the right course of action. This only comes with time. You have to develop confidence in your own intuition. Your intuition will not lead you in the wrong direction, but you do have to learn how to listen to it.

A few years back my wife and I were both teaching school in a small school district in Missouri. We were not happy there and wanted to get back to the Rocky Mountains, but couldn't find teaching positions for the both of us in the same area. The choice was for us to stay where we were or just pick up, pack a truck, and move back to Colorado without any jobs. Now this would seem like an obvious choice to most people – keep your job. But we decided to listen to our instinct instead and stepped out on a limb.

Our instinct told us it was time to go, so we packed a truck and moved to Colorado with no job prospects. Everyone who knew us thought that this was a ridiculous decision, but we felt it was right. In the end, we both found great jobs and everything worked out for the best. We listened to that inner voice instead of all the outside voices and outside reasoning, even though what our intuition was telling us seemed to be the unwise move to make. Always trust your instinct, even when you can't figure out the logic behind it.

I trust my intuition and it always guides me right.

December 22

One sword keeps another in the sheath.

George Herbert

Many people wonder why warriors spend so much time training when they may never use that training in the real world. One of the answers is put very nicely by George Herbert, "One sword keeps another in the sheath."

Even if it appears that the warrior doesn't use his martial arts training in real life, in actuality, he does. No one really knows how many times a violent confrontation has been avoided because of a warrior's training. The confidence that comes from training and the way the warrior presents himself physically, have an effect on the psyche of thugs and ruffians.

Remember, these people always seek to prey on the weak. The bad guys do not want to get into a physical confrontation with someone who appears to be able to defend himself. They would rather bully the guy who looks as if he couldn't win a fight with a wet paper bag.

So by this point of view, the warrior uses his martial arts training and other physical training basically daily, even if he is not overtly aware of it. He never knows how many times it has actually been used to deter a predator's attention.

Furthermore, he never knows when he will be called on to pull his sword out of the sheath for real, so his sword must be kept sharp and ready. It does little good to carry a sword if you don't know how to use it or if you are no longer able to use it. You must stay ready, willing and able. Predators will know whether you are or not.

I keep my skills sharp and predators do not attack me.

December 23

There is no first attack in karate.

Gichin Funakoshi

This is a famous martial arts quote from Master Funakoshi, and one which is misinterpreted many times. I have already discussed how the first attack does not necessarily refer to the first physical punch or kick, but rather the first actual threat of danger towards you or those who are under your protection. While this is an important factor to keep in mind when dealing with predators, there is another factor which is equally important in today's society.

It seems that the majority of people in our world today look for the opportunity to sue someone else as a means of getting even or increasing their financial standing. This excessive litigation mentality, along with a lack of common sense in our justice system, has added a whole different dimension to the term self-defense. Self-defense involves more than defending yourself physically.

You have to make sure that you defend yourself in every way. One of the areas that you have to be concerned with is that you are safe from legal prosecution. For this reason, it is sometimes necessary to wait for your enemy to make the first move in order to ensure that witnesses can testify that you have acted in self-defense. Legal prosecution is something to keep in mind.

This is a judgment call which the warrior has to make and many times it has to be made in a split second. Although this is something that you should keep in mind, you cannot let this cause you to put yourself in harm's way.

I recognize when the first attack has taken place and act.

December 24

The primary cause of unhappiness is never the situation, but your thoughts about it.
Eckhart Tolle

Your happiness and your unhappiness both originate in the same place – your mind. When you begin to understand this, and to control your thoughts, you will start living the happy, contented life that you have wanted to live.

When we blame anything outside of ourselves for our unhappiness, we are giving control of our lives to someone else. We are fostering a victim mentality. The true warrior is not a victim. He (or she) controls his own life, his own happiness, and his own destiny.

You are in control, why give that power away by constantly blaming someone else? Take responsibility for everything that happens in your life. Everything in your life can be traced back to a decision that you have made, in one way or another. You either decided to take one action or another, or you decided to not take an action; both have their specific consequences.

Refuse to give in to a victim mentality. Don't blame others for the life that you have created. That is a self-defeating attitude and will never empower you. Warrior up and take responsibility for your own life.

You were created with the power to create your own world, to design your own life the way that you want it to be. If you aren't happy, don't you think it is time that you do something about that? You have the power; all you have to do is use it correctly.

I control my thoughts. Nothing disturbs my inner peace!

December 25

Even if a man has no natural ability,

he can be a warrior.

Miyamoto Musashi

Being a warrior is something that comes from inside you, something that originates in your spirit. It has very little to do with what you do for a living, whether or not you have great fighting skills, or whether or not you know your weapons. Of course, developing good fighting skills and knowing how to use weapons are a major plus, but that is not what makes you a true warrior.

My definition of a true warrior is someone who has the will to fight to protect himself, his friends, his family, and his ideals, and at the same time, seeks the perfection of his own character through a life lived with honor, integrity, and an unflinching dedication to what is right according to his own code of ethics.

Warriors should exhibit the best qualities among men. The warrior makes a firm decision to try to perfect his character and to live by a strict code of ethics. His word is his honor. His duty stays fresh on his mind. He lives life a little more seriously than most, but at the same time lives life to its fullest. He sees through the veil of appearances covering most parts of this world, but does so without looking down on those who are less perceptive.

The true warrior is able to hold his head high with honor because he knows that he lives his life to the best of his ability, with honor and integrity. The warrior is a man who shoots for excellence in everything he does. These are the things which make someone a true warrior.

I will always walk the path of the warrior.

December 26

At all times, look at the thing itself –
the thing behind the appearance.
Marcus Aurelius

The warrior must have enough wisdom to read between the lines. See reality. Don't be fooled by appearances, but rather see things as they really are. This is a rare trait in today's society. Everyone seems to be into appearances, disregarding the truth. People seem to prefer to close their eyes to reality and just be content with nice appearances as long as reality doesn't interfere with their little world. Most people are comfortably numb with hollow appearances.

The warrior is not satisfied with appearances. He has a need to know the truth, and looks beyond the superficial into the realm of reality which lies behind the illusion. He may not be able to change the deceptions that everyone else seems to be content with, but he at least has the knowledge that he is not fooled by the delusions which the public has accepted as truth.

His insight gives him the knowledge that he needs to protect himself and his family when the truth finally does come forward. He has already seen what is coming and has prepared for the day that the truth, with its consequences, finally does come to light.

Always look at someone's motives, not just their presentation. What are their underlying intentions? Look past the carefully scripted and rehearsed stage production that is presented to you. Remember the bait always looks good, but very few see the hidden trap which lies in the shadows.

I am not fooled by appearances.

December 27

To expect bad people not to injure others is crazy. It is to ask the impossible. And to let them behave like that to other people, but expect them to exempt you is arrogance.

Marcus Aurelius

There are bad people in this world, this is a fact. There are sociopaths out there who have no feelings for anyone but themselves. To expect these people to obey the rules of society and respect our laws is ridiculous. They will do harm to others and they will do harm to you, if they are allowed. These people are like the snake in the story of the Farmer and the Snake. Never expect them to be anything other than what they are.

Whether these kind of people suffer from a mental illness or have developed their flawed attitude from incidents that have happened to them in their life, the result it the same – they will hurt or kill you if they get the chance! If you try to help them, they will take whatever you give them and then put a knife in your back.

This is the cold, hard truth that so many people in today's society refuse to believe because it is not politically correct. But, as we know, the truth is the truth whether anyone believes it or not. These people are bad news and that's the bottom line.

Don't expect bad people to change their nature and treat you differently than they treat others. As Marcus Aurelius said, that is arrogance, and that kind of arrogance can cost you dearly. See the true nature of everyone and be prepared for them to act according to their nature.

I conquer everyone who comes against me.

December 28

If you have to kill a snake,
kill it once and for all.

Japanese Proverb

I have made it clear that the warrior should only use force when it is absolutely necessary. It is not something that the warrior likes to do or is looking forward to having to do, but there are times when the warrior will have no choice. When the time arises that the warrior has no other recourse besides using his martial arts skills, it is important not to hold back. If the situation is serious enough for you to have to resort to violence, it is serious enough for you to totally destroy your enemy.

Now, I'm not saying that every time you have to use your martial arts skills, you should kill your enemy. That is not what I mean by destroying your enemy. What I am saying is that if the situation is serious enough for you to use force, it is serious enough for you to make sure that your enemy cannot do any harm to you, before you consider the conflict to be finished.

If you have to use your martial arts skills, make sure you finish the job. Don't play around! This is not the playground where boys are just pushing and shoving. If that is the situation, then you have no business fighting.

The warrior only fights when there is no other choice, not for pride or to prove a point. If you have to fight, it is a serious situation, and if it is a serious situation, make sure you take care of business. Make sure that you, and those around you, are safe when the fight is done. Win!

If I have to fight, I win!

Never underestimate an adversary.

Kazumi Tabata

There is never anything positive to be gained by underestimating your enemy, no matter how insignificant you may consider him. The only thing that underestimating your enemy can possibly do is aid your enemy in his quest to hurt you. It does nothing at all for you, at least nothing positive. Like everything that you do, it does have an effect on you though; the only thing is that effect will be purely negative. Why in the world would you want to do something to help your enemy and hurt yourself?

Underestimating your enemy will have several consequences. First, as I already stated, it will give your enemy a bit of a break. When you underestimate someone, you make it possible for them to use the element of surprise against you because you are not expecting them to present a challenge. In reality, you don't know what he has in mind. It is foolish to discount the possible problems that he could cause you. Not only are you aiding your enemy when you underestimate him, but you are undermining your own preparedness.

When you underestimate your enemy, you are less likely to seriously prepare for his attack. This is only common sense. Why would you prepare to defend yourself against someone who you feel is not a serious threat? Underestimating your enemy weakens your motivation to stay ready to meet this adversary, again enabling him to use the element of surprise to his advantage. Always take every enemy seriously. Arrange things so your enemies can't hurt you, and consider each and every one of them a danger.

I never underestimate any adversary.

December 30

Wisdom is not in words;

it is in understanding.

Hazrat Inayat Khan

Wisdom can be defined as the ability to make sensible decisions and judgments based on personal knowledge and experience. Wisdom is not in words, but rather in the personal knowledge that comes from understanding the words of wisdom which you read. Personal knowledge means that you have meditated and studied those words until they have become a part of you. This doesn't happen simply by reading through something; it takes attention and thought to transform these teachings into something useful.

Personal knowledge is only one part of obtaining wisdom according to this definition. The second part is personal experience. Experience comes from being actively involved or exposed to certain events or people. You can't get experience from reading a book; you get experience from participating in the world around you. You can get personal knowledge from a book, but to completely make wisdom your own; you need to combine that knowledge with experience.

This doesn't mean that you have to go out and make all the mistakes yourself in order to gain wisdom. Experience can be gained by observing the actions and behavior of others in relation to the personal knowledge that you have learned from those who have put their wisdom in writing. Be observant and look for ways in which you can turn the words of wisdom into your own personal understanding of wisdom. Learn from every experience, as well as the experiences of others. Only then will true wisdom be yours.

I act on all the wisdom I learn and my life is blessed.

December 31

The will to win, the desire to succeed,
the urge to reach your full potential, are the
keys that will unlock the door to personal excellence.

Confucius

You have to choose excellence as an act of your will. Living a life of excellence is pretty simple – you merely choose to do so, and then you do it. The catch is, you then have to discipline yourself to actually follow through.

Every year, thousands of people make New Year's resolutions, and at the same time, every year thousands of people fail to follow through with those resolutions. You can say that you are going to start living a life of excellence every single day, but it is meaningless if you don't back up that decision with your actions and actually start integrating excellence into your life. Like everything else in life, this takes discipline and effort.

The Greek poet, Hesiod, wrote, "Badness you can get easily, in quantity; the road is smooth, and it lies close by, but in front of excellence the immortal gods have put sweat, and long and steep is the way to it."

Making a decision to live a life of excellence, and living a life of excellence are two different things. Just like writing down your New Year's resolution and actually following through with it, are two different things. Like Hesiod wrote, it takes a lot of work and effort to become a man of excellence.

I have the will to win and I live a life of excellence.

IF

If you can keep your head when all about you
Are losing theirs and blaming it on you;
If you can trust yourself when all men doubt you,
But make allowance for their doubting too;

If you can wait and not be tired by waiting,
Or, being lied about, don't deal in lies,
Or, being hated, don't give way to hating,
And yet don't look too good, nor talk too wise;

If you can dream - and not make dreams your master;
If you can think - and not make thoughts your aim;
If you can meet with triumph and disaster
And treat those two impostors just the same;

If you can bear to hear the truth you've spoken
Twisted by knaves to make a trap for fools,
Or watch the things you gave your life to broken,
And stoop and build 'em up with worn-out tools;

If you can make one heap of all your winnings
And risk it on one turn of pitch-and-toss,
And lose, and start again at your beginnings
And never breathe a word about your loss;

If you can force your heart and nerve and sinew
To serve your turn long after they are gone,
And so hold on when there is nothing in you
Except the Will which says to them: "Hold on!"

If you can talk with crowds and keep your virtue,
Or walk with kings - nor lose the common touch;
If neither foes nor loving friends can hurt you;
If all men count with you, but none too much;

If you can fill the unforgiving minute
With sixty seconds' worth of distance run -
Yours is the Earth and everything that's in it,
And - which is more - you'll be a Man, my son!

Rudyard Kipling

The Quotes

January 1
Rise from the ashes of the old year
like the phoenix and become the
person you truly want to be.

January 2
Beware of an old man in a profession
where men usually die young.

January 3
Don't fear the enemy that attacks you,
fear the fake friend that hugs you.

January 4
A journey of a thousand miles
begins with one step.
Lao Tzu

January 5
Discipline is choosing between
what you want now and
what you want most.

January 6
I refuse to lower my standards
to accommodate those who
refuse to raise theirs.
Steve Gamlin

January 7
There is no greater danger than
underestimating your opponent.
Sun Tzu

January 8
Warriors are not always the
fastest or the strongest men.
Warriors are those who choose
to stand between their enemy and
those that they love or hold sacred.

January 9
Don't ever think that the reason
that I am peaceful is because
I forgot how to be violent.

January 10
Our obligation to our own family or
clan is greaterthan our obligation to
the faceless multitude.
M. F. Bradford

January 11
Be slow of tongue and quick of eye.
Cervantes

January 12
I prefer peace, but if trouble must
come, let it comein my time, so that
my children may live in peace.
Thomas Paine

January 13
Courage doesn't always roar.
Sometimes courage is the quiet
voice at the end of the day saying,
"I will try again tomorrow."
Mary Ann Radmacher

January 14
The fire of anger
only burns the angry.
Chinese Proverb

January 15
Never send a sheep to kill a wolf.

January 16
Project strength to avoid conflict.

January 17
Wise men do not argue with idiots.
Japanese Proverb

January 18
Deprived of all else, one remains
undisgraced if still endowed
with strength of character.
Tiruvalluvar

January 19
Those who know the
least obey the best.
Farquhar

January 20
There is much to be considered
before the sword is drawn.
Baltasar Gracian

January 21
When you react, you let
others control you. When you
respond, you are in control.
Bohdi Sanders

January 22
When you think you're
safe is precisely when
you're most vulnerable.
Seven Samurai

January 23
Announcing, "I'm offended," is
basically telling the world that you
can't control your own emotions, so
everyone else should do it for you.

January 24
When I am silent, I have
thunder hidden inside me.
Rumi

January 25
Be polite, be courteous, show
professionalism,and have a plan
to kill everyone in the room.
General James Mattis

January 26
The society that separates its scholars
from its warriors will have its
thinking done by cowards and
its fighting done by fools.
Thucudides

January 27
True humility is not thinking
less of yourself; it is
thinking of yourself less.
C. S. Lewis

January 28
Blood makes you related;
loyalty makes you family.

January 29
The greatest enemies, and the ones
we must mainly combat, are within.
Cervantes

January 30
Fear is not real. It is a product
of thoughts you create. Do not
misunderstand me. Danger is
very real. But fear is a choice.
After Earth

January 31
There are nine hundred and
ninety-nine patrons of virtue
to one virtuous man.
Henry David Thoreau

February 1
Don't let who you were, talk you
out of who you're becoming.

February 2
Have the courage to say no. Have the
courage to face the truth. Do the
right thing because it is right.
W. Clement Stone

February 3
The difference between who
you are, and who you want
to be, is what you do.

February 4
If you find yourself in a fair fight,
your tactics suck!

February 5
Don't ever mistake my
silence for ignorance, my
calmness for acceptance, or
my kindness for weakness.

February 6
Expect anything from anyone.
The Devil was once an angel.
Drake Graham

February 7
Complaining about a problem
without proposing a solution,
is called whining.
Theodore Roosevelt

February 8
It is not only what we do,
but what we do not do, for
which we are accountable.
Moliere

February 9
Do not allow anger to rob you of your
rational mind or your inner peace.

February 10
We do not rise to the
level of our expectations.
We fall to the level of our training.
Archilochus

February 11
If you don't stand for your
principles when they are being
tested, they are truly your principles.
They are just your wish list.
Bohdi Sanders

February 12
You must unlearn
what you have learned.
Yoda

February 13
The true warrior fights not because he
hates the one in front of him, but
because he loves those behind him.

February 14
I do what is mine to do;
the rest does not disturb me.
Marcus Aurelius

February 15
Nobody is born a warrior, in
exactly the same way that nobody
is born an average man. We make
ourselves into one or the other.
Carlos Castaneda

February 16
If you can't handle the flames,
don't wake the dragon!
Bohdi Sanders

February 17
Where you recognize evil,
speak out against it and give
no truces to your enemies.
The Havamal

February 18
The things you think about determine
the quality of your mind. Your soul
takes on the color of your thoughts.
Marcus Aurelius

February 19
If I call you brother, it is because
you have earned my respect.

February 20
It is better to sleep on
things beforehand than lie
awake about hem afterwards.
Baltasar Gracian

February 21
Attack where he is unprepared.
move when he does not expect you.
Sun Tzu

February 22
The best defense against evil men is
good men who are skilled at violence.

February 23
It is better to be a warrior in a garden,
than a gardener in a war.

February 24
I would advise you not to trust either
(men or women), more than is
absolutely necessary.
Lord Chesterfield

February 25
You all wanted to deem my flaws
as unworthy. Now you will see that
even angels fall, but a warrior will
never crawl beneath your feet.
Lorna Evol

February 26
Sometimes giving someone a second
chance is like giving them another
bullet for their gun because they
missed you the first time.

February 27
As long as it is realized and accepted
that warriors must comprehend
right and wrong, and strive to do
right and avoid wrong, then the
way of the warrior is alive.
Taira Shigesuke

February 28
Doing nothing is also an action;
not making a decision is
making a decision.
Bohdi Sanders

March 1
I don't love the bright sword for its
sharpness, nor the arrow for its
swiftness, nor the warrior for his
glory. I only love what they defend.
J. R. R. Tolkien

March 2
If you underestimate your
enemy in battle, odds are
you won't live to see another.
Into the Badlands

March 3
Love everyone.
But never sell your sword.
Paulo Coelho

March 4
A good instructor teaches students
how to fight; a great instructor
teaches students how to live.
Ricardo Almeida

March 5
I won't be wronged. I won't be
insulted. I won't be laid a hand on.
I don't do these things to other people
and I require the same from them.
John Wayne in The Shootist

March 6
A warrior is worthless unless
he rises above others and stands
strong in the midst of the storm.
Yamamoto Tsunetomo

March 7
Many people give up just
before they reach their goal.

March 8
You must be the change you
want to see in the world.
Gandhi

March 9
Always stand for what's right,
even if you have to stand alone.

March 10
A wise man fights to win, but
he is twice a fool who has
no plan for possible defeat.
Louis L'amour

March 11
Honor is that which no man can give
you and no man can take away.
It's a gift a man gives to himself.
Rob Roy

March 12
The quality of a person's life is in
direct proportion to their commitment
to excellence, regardless of their
chosen field of endeavor.
Vince Lombardi

March 13
Make a least one definite move
daily towards your goal.
Bruce Lee

March 14
Haters will see you walking on water
and say it is because you can't swim.

March 15
Success is going from failure to
failure without loss of enthusiasm.
Winston Churchill

March 16
Repetition is the mother of all skills
Edgar Sulite

March 17
Loyalty means I am your friend
whether you are right or wrong.
But I will tell you if you are wrong
and I will help you get it right.

March 18
Don't take my kindness
for weakness; the beast in
me is sleeping, not dead.

March 19
There are only two forces in
the world, the sword and the spirit.
In the long run, the sword will always
be conquered by the spirit.
Napoleon Bonaparte

March 20
Always make certain that you are
in a better position than your enemy.
Soho Takuan

March 21
Civilize the mind,
but make savage the body.

March 22
Control the situation in such
a way that nobody knows
how you control it.
Vasiliev Vladimire

March 23
Don't blame your behavior on
someone else. You are 100%
responsible for your actions.

March 24
Out of suffering have emerged the
strongest souls; the most massive
characters are seared with scars.
Khalil Gibran

March 25
Don't do something permanently
stupid just because you're
temporarily upset.

March 26
A wolf eats a sheep but now and then;
ten thousands are devoured by men.
An open foe may prove a curse,
but a pretend friend is worse.
John Gay

March 27
A lion does not have to prove
it is a threat. You already
know what it can do.

March 28
Vicory is reserved for those
who are willing to pay its price.
Sun Tzu

March 29
A man cannot be too careful
in the choice of his enemies.
Oscar Wilde

March 30
If a battle cannot be won,
Do not fight it.
Sun Tzu

March 31
It is madness for sheep
to talk peace with a wolf.
Thomas Fuller

April 1
Double the fear in your enemy's
heart, and you will halve the
chance that he will ever put
a sword in his hand.
Vlad Tepes

April 2
Every time you train, train with
the motivation and purpose that
you will be the hardest person
someone ever tries to kill.
Tim Kennedy

April 3
The ultimate aim of the martial
arts is not having to use them.
Miyamoto Musashi

April 4
He who is not prepared now, will
not be prepared when needed.
Colonel Phil Torres

April 5
Today is victory over yourself
of yesterday; tomorrow is
your victory over less men.
Miyamoto Musashi

April 6
Surround yourself with those
on the same mission as you!

April 7
There will come a time when
you think everything is finished.
That will be the beginning.
Louis L'Amour

April 8
Expect the best, but
prepare for the worst.

April 9
What I do have are a particular set of
skills, skills I have developed over a
very long career, skills that make me
a nightmare for people like you.
from the movie, Taken

April 10
We can fight the sword or we can
fight the man swinging the sword.
Which one breaks more easily?
Spartacus

April 11
Be like water! Don't get set into
one form; adapt it, and build
your own, and let it grow.
Bruce Lee

April 12
A tiger doesn't lose sleep
over the opinions of sheep.

April 13
My forefathers were warriors.
Their son is a warrior. I am
the maker of my own fortune.
Tecumseh

April 14
It's not the size of the
dog in the fight; it's the
size of the fight in the dog.
Mark Twain

April 15
You wear the belt;
it does not wear you.

April 16
An able man shows his spirit by
gentle words and resolute actions;
he is neither hot nor timid.
Philip Dormer Stanhope

April 17
Knowledge will give you power,
but character, respect.
Bruce Lee

April 18
The truth is that strength lies in the
interior of the warrior; in his heart,
his mind, and his spirit.
Miyamoto Musashi

April 19
I choose this life. I know what
I'm doing. And on any given day,
I could stop doing it. Today,
however, is not that day.
Batman

April 20
Practice not your art and
it will soon depart.
German Proverb

April 21
When nothing can be done about
the way things are, the wise stop
worrying about the situation.
Lao Tzu

April 22
In peace do not forget war.
Japanese Proverb

April 23
Warriors are not what you think
of as warriors. The warrior is
not someone who fights.
Sitting Bull

April 24
We cannot become what we
want by remaining what we are.
Max DePree

April 25
Muddy water, let stand,
becomes clear.
Lao Tzu

April 26
It is better to be a tiger for one day
than a sheep for a thousand years.
Tibetan Maxim

April 27
If you are forced into a position in
which you must either hurt or be hurt,
be sure to make your move before
someone else does.
Francesco Guicciardini

April 28
It's okay to lose to opponent,
must not lose to fear.
Mr. Miyagi

April 29
If it is not right, do not do it;
if it is not true, do not say it.
Marcus Aurelius

April 30
He who dares not offend,
cannot be honest.
Thomas Paine

May 1
Justice is a kind of pact,
not to hard or be harmed.
Epicurus

373

May 2
Walk a mile to avoid a fight;
but when one starts, don't
back down an inch!

May 3
The more you sweat in training,
the less you bleed in battle.
Navy Seal Maxim

May 4
Do not let your power be seen;
be blank and actionless.
Han Fei Tzu

May 5
Make your enemy think that your
normal force is extraordinary, and
your extraordinary is your normal.
Sun Tzu

May 6
Someone out there is training.
Law Enforcement Maxim

May 7
Protecting yourself is self-defense.
Protecting others is warriorship.
Bohdi Sanders

May 8
Power of the mind is infinite
while brawn is limited.
Koichi Tohei

May 10
A warrior's heart is like a sword;
it must be cleaned daily.
Billy Shearer

May 11
One must make the warrior
walk his everyday walk.
Miyamoto Musashi

May 12
Do not be tricked into thinking
that there are no crocodiles just
because the water is still.
Malaysian Proverb

May 13
He is victorious who knows
when and when not to fight.
Sun Tzu

May 14
Don't trouble a quiet snake.
Greek Proverb

May 16
If an art is concealed, it succeeds.
Ovid

May 17
When irate, clear-minded men never
show it then and there. Holding it in,
they watch for an opportune moment.
Tiruvalluvar

May 18
The man of true valor lies
between the extremes of
cowardice and of rashness.
Miguel de Cervantes

May 19
Never walk away from home
ahead of your axe and sword.
You can't feel a battle in your
bones or foresee a fight.
The Havamal

May 20
In seeking to save another,
beware of drowning yourself.
Sir Francis Osborne

May 21
One who is good at battle
does not get angry.
Lao Tzu

May 22
Abandoning the ego is
the secret of right living.
Taisen Deshimaru

May 23
Remember how lucky you are to
live in a time of peace and plenty,
but prepare for worse times.
Code of the Samurai

May 24
Try not! Do, or do not.
There is no try.
Yoda

May 25
By keeping your weapons in order,
your enemy will be subjugated.
Nagarjuna

May 26
Let us not look back in anger,
nor forward in fear, but
around us in awareness.
James Thurber

May 27
Style does not matter,
what works is what is important.
Mitsusuke Harada

May 28
The warrior is not led by others; but
by remaining true to his convictions.
F. J. Chu

May 29
Never get angry except on purpose.
Japanese Maxim

May 30
When the victory is yours,
tighten your helmet cords.
Japanese Proverb

May 31
There are people in every era
who, however adverse the
environment, are not corrupted,
and do not become degenerate.
Masaaki Hatsumi

June 1
Discipline, not desire,
determines your destiny.
Bud Malmstrom

June 2
I have seen the best karate.
All that really matters is what
kind of human being you are.
Masami Tsuruoka

June 3
The path of the warrior is lifelong,
and mastery is often simply
staying on the path.
Richard Strozzi Heckler

June 4
Never imagine that you are safe after
you deal a blow to your opponent.
Yagyu Tajimanokami Menenori

June 5
The wise live among people, but are
indifferent to their praise or blame.
Chuang Tzu

June 6
Hide your purpose.
Baltasar Gracian

June 7
Courtesy should be apparent
in all our actions and words
and in all aspects of daily life.
Masutatsu Oyama

June 8
When the enemy presents
an opportunity, speedily
take advantage of it.
Sun Tzu

June 9
Think, feel, and act like a warrior.
Set yourself apart from the rest of
society by your personal excellence.
Forrest E. Morgan

June 10
Strength is defeated by strategy.
Philippine Proverb

June 11
In order to progress in life,
one has to improve every
day in an endless process.
The Hagakure

June 12
Life is a succession of here and
now, here and now, unceasing
concentration in the here and now.
Taisen Deshimaru

June 13
Be strong when you are weak, brave
when you are scared, and humbled
when you are victorious.

June 14
Avoiding danger is not cowardice.
Philippine Proverb

June 15
It is no honor for an
eagle to vanquish a dove.
Italian Proverb

June 16
Man is only as strong as his
convictions and beliefs.
Kensho Furuya

June 17
Don't follow the advice of others;
rather, learn to listen to the
voice within yourself.
Dogen

June 18
Noblemen discipline themselves to
be dignified at all times…Sharpen
your mind and show your dignity.
Matsura Seizen

June 19
Cultivate the root.
Confucius

June 20
Even when you have to kill a man,
it costs nothing to be polite.
Winston Churchill

June 21
In dangerous times
wise men say nothing.
Aesop

June 22
Behavior influences consciousness.
Right behavior means right
consciousness. The actions of
every instant, every day, must be
right…every gesture is important.
Taisen Deshimaru

June 23
Certain good qualities are like
the sense: people entirely lacking
in them can neither perceive
nor comprehend them.
La Rochefoucauld

June 25
Pretend inferiority and
encourage his arrogance.
Sun Tzu

June 26
Cowards die many times before
their deaths, the valiant never
taste of death but once.
William Shakespeare

June 27
You must not show your weak points,
either in the martial arts
or in everyday life.
Taisen Deshimaru

June 28
The more quickly brought to anger,
the more quickly brought to death.
Chinese Maxim

June 29
The wise man adapts himself
to the circumstances.
Confucius

June 30
Honor is not black and white.
Forrest E. Morgan

July 1
The world is a dangerous place,
not because of those who
do evil, but because of those
who look on and do nothing.
Albert Einstein

July 2
Don't protect people who don't
deserve it. Your job is to protect the
good. Observe one's true character.
Masaaki Hatsumi

July 3
To be prepared beforehand for any
contingency is the greatest of virtues.
Sun Tzu

July 4
The shepherd hunts the
predators who attack his sheep.

July 5
True Budo has an overwhelming
emphasis on the development
of moral character.
Glen Morris

July 6
A wise man, in great or small matters,
must act with due consideration.
Sakya Pandit

July 7
Adversity is a mirror
that reveals one's true self.
Chinese Proverb

July 8
All men make mistakes, but a good
man yields when he knows his course
is wrong, and repairs the evil.
Sophocles

July 9
Brave hearts do not back down.
Euripides

July 11
To be prepared is half the victory.
Cervantes

July 13
To subdue an enemy without
fighting is the greatest of skills.
Sun Tzu

July 14
The true warrior ponders the future
without discarding the past while
living in the present.
F. J. Chu

July 15
The important thing is to be always
moving forward, little by little.
Masutatsu Oyama

July 16
Dignity is not circumstantial.
Kotoda Yahei Toshisada

July 17
Trained fighters, much more than
average people, have an obligation
to employ their skills judiciously,
to govern themselves and their
emotions at all times.
Peter Hobert

July 18
You must be deadly
serious in training.
Gichin Funakoshi

July 19
Focus on your one purpose.
Japanese Maxim

July 20
This is certain, that a man that
studies revenge keeps his wounds
green, which otherwise would
heal and do well.
Francis Bacon

July 21
Though we are powerful and
strong, and we know how to fight,
we do not wish to fight.
Cherokee Saying

July 22
Opportunity is rare and a wise
man will never let it go by him.
Bayard Taylor

July 23
Never interrupt your enemy
when he is making a mistake.
Napoleon Bonaparte

July 24
Tomorrow belongs to
those who prepare today.
African Proverb

July 25
If you are a serious warrior, you'll
become a student of anatomy.
Forrest E. Morgan

July 26
Whoso would be a man
must be a nonconformist.
Ralph Waldo Emerson

July 27
Your greatest weapon
is in your enemy's mind.
Buddha

July 28
We are what we repeatedly do.
Excellence is not an act, but a habit.
Aristotle

July 29
He who lives without discipline
dies without honor.
The Havamal

July 30
He who is an ass and takes himself
to be a stag, finds his mistake
when he comes to leap the ditch.
Italian Proverb

July 31
The wise hawk conceals his talons.
Japanese Proverb

August 1
Don't teach undesirable people.
Masaaki Hatsumi

August 2
Let not the fruit of action
be your motive to act.
The Bhagavad Gita

August 3
You can also commit
injustice by doing nothing.
Marcus Aurelius

August 4
In critical times, one must be devoted
utterly to the cause of justice.
Gichin Funakoshi

August 5
Individuals create karma;
karma does not create individuals.
Bodhidharma

August 6
We should know what our
convictions are, and stand for them.
Carl Jung

August 7
Let the wise man take
refuge in his silence.
Baltasar Gracian

August 8
Things are not always what
they seem; the first appearance
deceives many; the intelligence
of a few perceives what has
been carefully hidden.
Phaedrus

August 9
The Universal Way is not just
a matter of speaking wisdom
but one of continual practice.
Lao Tzu

August 10
Shun any action that
will diminish honor.
Tiruvalluvar

August 11
The success of very important matters
often depends on doing or not doing
something that seems trivial.
Francesco Guicciardini

August 12
Even if the stream is shallow
wade it as if it were deep.
Korean Proverb

August 13
In whatever position you
find yourself, determine
first your objective.
Marshall Ferdinand Foch

August 14
Take away the cause,
and the effect ceases.
Miguel de Cervantes

August 15
To be prepared for war is
one of the most effective
means of preserving peace.
George Washington

August 16
A man can compromise in his actions
without compromising his principles.
Bohdi Sanders

August 17
Make yourself a sheep,
and the wolf is ready.
Russian Proverb

August 18
It is foolish to try and live on past
experiences. It is a very dangerous, if
not fatal habit, to judge ourselves to
be safe because of something that we
felt or did twenty years ago.
Charles Spurgeon

August 19
He does not guard himself well
who is not always on his guard.
French Proverb

August 20
The master warrior is a
man of character, a man
of wisdom and insight.
Forrest E. Morgan

August 21
Deal with a dangerous situation while
it is safe. Eliminate what is vicious
before it becomes destructive.
Lao Tzu

August 22
Whatever you think, be
sure it is what you think.
T. S. Eliot

August 23
Having the idea is
not living the reality.
Rumi

August 24
If you live in the river you
should understand the crocodile.
Indian Proverb

August 25
Those who play with cats
must expect to be scratched.
Cervantes

August 26
Be your friend's true friend.
The Havamal

August 27
Snakes follow the way of serpents.
Japanese Proverb

August 28
To generalize is to be an idiot.
William Blake

August 29
Don't easily trust anyone on this
earth because there are all kinds.
Bruce Lee

August 30
Hold yourself responsible
for a higher standard than
anyone else expects of you.
Never excuse yourself.
Henry Ward Beecher

August 31
Hated by Many –
Confronted by None!

September 1
Doing it halfway is no good;
you have to do it all the way,
give yourself wholly to it.
Taisen Deshimaru

September 2
When you step beyond your own
gate, you face a million enemies.
Gichin Funakoshi

September 3
In the midst of men who hate us,
let us live without hatred.
The Dhammapada

September 4
But here we may wonder
what he would do if nobody
knew anything about it.
The Code of the Samurai

September 5
The angry man will defeat
himself in battle as in life.
Samurai Maxim

September 6
Do not seek to follow in the footsteps
of wise men, seek what they sought.
Basho

September 7
The hunter can make many
mistakes, the hunted, only one.
Native American Maxim

September 8
Your reality check must be done long
before you actually find yourself
confronted with a life and death,
kill-or-be-killed situation.
Dirk Skinner

September 9
Gratitude is the sign of noble souls.
Aesop

September 10
To respond immediately to an angry
person is like throwing fuel on a fire.
Spanish Proverb

September 11
Trust in today's friends as if
they might be tomorrow's enemies.
Baltasar Gracian

September 12
If you wanna live life on
your own terms, you gotta
be willing to crash and burn.
Motley Crue

September 13
Embrace the snake
and it will bite you.
Bulgarian Proverb

September 14
Do not forget great kindness,
even for a single meal.
Emperor Wen Di

September 15
Men flourish only for a moment.
Homer

September 16
People hate those who make
them feel their own inferiority.
Lord Chesterfield

September 17
It is easier to prevent bad
habits than to break them.
Benjamin Franklin

September 18
When you arise in the morning, give
thanks for the morning light, for your
life and strength. Give thanks for
your food and the joy of living. If
you see no reason for giving thanks,
the fault lies in yourself.
Tecumseh

September 19
Ikken hisatsu – one punch kills – is
the essence of karate. Put everything
– your whole life – into one punch.
Masami Tsuruoka

September 20
Thatch your roof before
rainy weather; dig your
well before you are thirsty.
Chinese Proverb

September 21
Defeat is a state of mind; no one
is ever defeated until defeat has
been accepted as a reality.
Bruce Lee

September 22
Never separate yourself
from the Way of the Warrior.
Miyamoto Musashi

September 23
If your temper rises,
withdraw your hand;
if your hand rises,
withdraw your temper.
Gojun Miyagi

September 24
Treat every encounter as
a fight to the finish.
*The Eight Essentials
for Novice Swordsmen*

September 25
When the world is at
peace, a gentleman keeps
his swords by his side.
Wu Tsu

September 26
It is not only what we do,
but what we do not do, for
which we are accountable.
Moliere

September 27
To see what is right and
not to do it is cowardice.
Confucius

September 28
A man's word is his honor.
Okinawan Proverb

September 29
Don't appear just; be just.
Aechylus

September 30
You cannot talk to a frog in a well
about the vast sea; he is limited to his
area of space. A summer insect has
no knowledge of snow; it knows
nothing beyond its own season.
Chiu Shu

October 1
One should have learning on the left
and the martial arts on the right.
Hojo Nagauji

October 2
How often do we supply our
enemies with the means of
our own destruction.
Aesop

October 3
Warriors aren't born, and they
aren't made. They create themselves
through trial and error and by
their ability to conquer their
own frailties and faults.
Philip J. Messina

October 4
You cannot step twice
into the same river.
Heraclitus

October 5
Carelessness is a great enemy.
Japanese Proverb

October 6
To spare the ravening leopard is
an act of injustice to the sheep.
Persian Proverb

October 7
The best armor is to
keep out of range.
Italian Proverb

October 8
It is truly regrettable that a
person will treat a man who is
valuable to him well, and a man
who is worthless to him poorly.
Hojo Shigetoki

Every action we take,
everything we do, is either a
victory or defeat in the struggle
to become what we want to be.
Anne Byrhhe

October 10
We ought to do everything
both cautiously and
confidently at the same time.
Epictetus

October 11
Tomorrow's battle is won
during today's practice.
Samurai Maxim

October 12
Rely not on the likelihood of the
enemy's not coming, but on our own
readiness to receive him; not on the
chance of his not attacking, but rather
on the fact that we have made
our position unassailable.
Sun Tzu

October 13
Instead of worrying, a
strong man wears a smile.
Japanese Proverb

October 14
No matter what the warrior is doing,
he must conduct himself in the
manner of a true warrior.
Bushido Shoshinshu

October 15
To stand still is to regress.
Gichin Funakoshi

October 16
Never do anything against conscience
even if the state demands it.
Albert Einstein

October 17
Highly evolved people have their
own conscience as pure law.
Lao Tzu

October 18
It is not the oath that makes us
believe the man, but the man the oath.
Aechylus

October 19
The superior man is watchful
over himself even when alone.
Chung Yung

October 21
It is no easy thing for a
principle to become a man's own
unless each day he maintains
it and works it out in his life.
Epictetus

October 22
The superior man does not give
up good conduct because the
inferior man rails against him.
Hsun-Tzu

October 23
Let them know a real man,
who lives as he was meant to live.
Marcus Aurelius

October 24
A successful samurai should put his
heart in order first thing in the
morning and last thing at night.
The Hagakure

October 25
The warrior is always in training, and
to some extent, at some level of
consciousness, training is
always on his mind.
Forrest E. Morgan

October 26
Outside noisy, inside empty.
Chinese Proverb

October 27
All warfare is based on deception.
Sun Tzu

October 28
Knowing is not enough,
we must apply.
Willing is not enough,
we must do.
Goethe

October 29
The superior man seeks what is right;
the inferior one, what is profitable.
Confucius

October 30
Each action of the warrior is
performed from a place of
fundamental wisdom. It is completely
different from the ordinary behavior
of a fool. Even if it looks the same,
it is different on the inside.
Takuan Soho

October 31
Great winds are powerless to
disturb the water of a deep well.
Chinese Proverb

November 1
Do nothing to make you
lose respect for yourself.
Baltasar Gracian

November 2
The pebble in the brook secretly
thinks itself a precious stone.
Japanese Proverb

November 3
When the time comes that
foes pose as friends, keep a
friendly face but banish their
brotherhood from your heart.
Tiruvalluvar

November 4
Kill the spider and you
will destroy the cobweb.
Maltese Proverb

November 5
Trust in God, but tie your camel.
Arabian Proverb

November 6
Depend on others and
you will go hungry.
Nepalese Proverb

November 7
Great spirits have always
encountered violent opposition
from mediocre minds.
Albert Einstein

November 8
The warrior backs up his words
with conviction and action.
Tony L. Jones

November 9
A hundred lifetimes may not be
enough to rectify the mistake
made in one short morning.
Chinese Proverb

November 10
A promise is a debt.
Irish Proverb

November 11
Victorious warriors win first and
then go to war, defeated warriors
go to war first then seek to win.
Sun Tzu

November 12
Perfection is attained
by slow degrees; she
requires the hand of time.
Voltaire

November 13
The steadfastness of the wise is but
the art of keeping their agitation
locked in their hearts.
La Rochefoucauld

November 14
Those skilled at making the enemy
move do so by creating a situation
to which he must conform.
Sun Tzu

November 15
It is you who must make the effort;
the sages can only teach.
Ralph W. Sockman

November 16
Surprise defeats strength and speed.
Glenn Morris

November 17
For when moral value is considered,
the concern is not the actions, which
are seen, but rather with their inner
principles, which are not seen.
Emmanuel Kant

November 18
The man of principle
never forgets what he is,
because of what others are.
Baltasar Gracian

November 19
Deliberate Often – Decide Once.
Latin Proverb

November 20
A wise man, in great or small matters,
must act with due consideration.
Whether attacking a hare or
an elephant, the lion has
no time for indecision.
Sakya Pandit

November 21
Efforts and enemies, if left
unfinished, can both ravage you
like an unextinguished fire.
Tiruvalluvar

November 22
When you see a rattlesnake poised to
strike, you do not wait until he has
struck before you crush him.
Franklin Delano Roosevelt

November 23
He who plants a forest in the
morning cannot expect to saw
planks the same evening.
Chinese Proverb

November 24
No weapon is sharper than the mind;
even the finest sword is inferior.
The Masters of Huainan

November 25
The wise pursue understanding;
fools follow the reports of others.
Tibetan Proverb

November 26
He is the best man who, when making
his plans, fear and reflects on
everything that can happen to him,
but in the moment of action is bold.
Herodotus

November 27
What lies in our power to do,
it lies in our power not to do.
Aristotle

November 28
Even in the sheath the
knife must be sharp.
Finnish Proverb

November 29
Lay down for yourself, at the outset,
a certain stamp and type of character
for yourself which you are to
maintain whether you are by yourself
or are meeting with people.
Epictetus

November 30
Hear all sides and you will
be enlightened. Hear one side
and you will be in the dark.
Wei Zheng

December 1
Because a human being is
so malleable, whatever one
cultivates is what one becomes.
Lao Tzu

December 2
In the beginner's mind there are
many possibilities, but in the
expert's mind there are few.
Shunryu Suzuki

December 3
Only one who continually
reexamines himself and
corrects his faults will grow.
The Hagakure

December 4
If you calm your own mind and
discern the inner mind of others, that
may be called the foremost art of war.
Shiba Yoshimasa

December 5
Truth is not a matter
of personal viewpoint.
Vernon Howard

December 6
Don't follow any advice, no matter
how good, until you feel as deeply in
your spirit as you think in your mind
that the counsel is wise.
David Seabury

December 7
Do not let trifles disturb
your tranquility of mind.
Ignore the inconsequential.
Grenville Kleiser

December 8
Think like a man of action,
act like a man of thought.
Thomas Mann

December 9
Take a deep breath of life and
consider how it should be lived.
Don Quixote's Creed

December 10
A hero in old age never
lets go of his principles.
Cao Cao

December 11
My enemy is not the man
who wrongs me, but the man
who means to wrong me.
Democritus

December 12
Warriors confront the evil that most
people refuse to acknowledge.
Bohdi Sanders

December 13
Those who do good because
they want to be seen to
be good are not good.
Lieh Tzu

December 14
Never be easily drawn into a fight.
Gichin Funakoshi

December 15
Reputation often spills less blood.
Samurai Maxim

December 16
It is only the tranquil mind
that can allow for fair and
clear judgments free of error.
Gichin Funakoshi

December 17
Hardships often prepare ordinary
people for an extraordinary destiny.
C. S. Lewis

December 18
Be careful of your thoughts;
they are the beginning of your acts.
Lao Tzu

December 19
Beware that you do not lose the
substance by grasping at the shadow.
Aesop

December 20
So live your life that the fear of
death can never enter your heart.
Tecumseh

December 21
Trust your instinct to the end,
though you can render no reason.
Ralph Waldo Emerson

December 22
One sword keeps
another in the sheath.
George Herbert

December 23
There is no first attack in karate.
Gichin Funakoshi

December 24
The primary cause of unhappiness
is never the situation,
but your thoughts about it.
Eckhart Tolle

December 25
Even if a man has no natural
ability, he can be a warrior.
Miyamoto Musashi

December 26
At all times, look at the thing itself –
the thing behind the appearance.
Marcus Aurelius

December 27
To expect bad people not to injure
others is crazy. It is to ask the
impossible. And to let them behave
like that to other people, but expect
them to exempt you is arrogance.
Marcus Aurelius

December 28
If you have to kill a snake,
kill it once and for all.
Japanese Proverb

December 29
Never underestimate an adversary.
Kazumi Tabata

December 30
Wisdom is not in words;
it is in understanding.
Hazrat Inayat Khan

December 31
The will to win, the desire to succeed,
the urge to reach your full potential,
are the keys that will unlock the door
to personal excellence.
Confucius

INDEX

Guicciardini, 223

R

About the Author

Dr. Bohdi Sanders is a multi-award winning author and a Martial Arts Hall of Fame inductee. His book, *Modern Bushido*, hit #1 on Amazon and hit the top 10 for a total of 105 weeks. Seven of his other books have been best-sellers and were also ranked in the Top 10 on Amazon. Dr. Sanders has been a martial artist for over 32 years and has trained in Shotokan Karate, Krav Maga, Ninjutsu, and Jujutsu. His books have been endorsed by some of the today's top martial artists as highly motivational and inspirational.

Dr. Sanders also holds national certifications as a Personal Fitness Trainer and a Certified Specialist in Martial Arts Conditioning through the International Sports Science Association. He is also a certified Usui-Tibetan Reiki Master and is a certified Master of Acupressure. He is the author of:

- *Modern Bushido: Living a Life of Excellence*
- *Men of the Code: Living as a Superior Man*
- *Warrior Wisdom: Ageless Wisdom for the Modern Warrior*
- *Warrior: The Way of Warriorhood*
- *The Warrior Lifestyle: Making Your Life Extraordinary*
- *Defensive Living: The Other Side of Self-Defense*
- *Wisdom of the Elders: The Ultimate Quote Book for Life*
- *Martial Arts Wisdom... and more.*

Dr. Sanders' books have won several national awards, including:

- #1 New Release in Philosophy on Amazon: *Men of the Code*
- #1 on Amazon's Best Seller List: *Modern Bushido* 2013
- The Indie Excellence Book Awards: 1st Place Winner 2013
- USA Book News Best Books of 2013:1st Place Winner 2013
- IIMAA Best Martial Arts Book of the Year 2011
- U. S. Martial Arts Hall of Fame: Author of the Year 2011
- U. S. Martial Artist Association: Inspiration of the Year 2011
- The Indie Excellence Book Awards:1st Place Winner 2010
- USA Book News Best Books of 2010: 1st Place Winner 2010

Other Titles by Kaizen Quest

Other Titles by Kaizen Quest

Other Titles by Kaizen Quest

Other Titles by Kaizen Quest

LEGACY

Through the Eyes of the Warrior

Al Dacascos

Foreword by Mark Dacascos

Full List of Titles by Kaizen Quest

- *Modern Bushido: Living a Life of Excellence* by Bohdi Sanders

- *BUSHIDO: The Way of the Warrior* by Bohdi Sanders

- *LEGACY: Through the Eyes of the Warrior* by Al Dacascos

- *Men of the Code: Living as a Superior Man* by Bohdi Sanders

- *WARRIOR: The Way of Warriorhood* by Bohdi Sanders

- *Defensive Living: The Other Side of Self-Defense* by Bohdi Sanders

- *Wisdom of the Elders: The Ultimate Quote Book* by Bohdi Sanders

- *The Warrior Lifestyle* by Bohdi Sanders

- *Warrior Wisdom* by Bohdi Sanders

- *Secrets of the Soul* by Bohdi Sanders

- *Martial Arts Wisdom: Quotes, Maxims, Stories* by Bohdi Sanders

- *As a Man Thinketh* by James Allen

- *The Mastery of Destiny* by James Allen

Please Take a Couple of Minutes and Review BUSHIDO!

Reader reviews are very important to authors in today's fast-paced world and I value your opinion. Reviews are the lifeblood of the author. Posting a quick review on Amazon and on Facebook, and other social media, really helps authors out.

If you have enjoyed *BUSHIDO: The Way of the Warrior*, please consider taking just a couple of minutes and reviewing it on Amazon and on your social media pages. Also, please tell your friends about *BUSHIDO*. I would sincerely appreciate it.

Bohdi Sanders

Looking for More Wisdom?

If you are interested in living the warrior lifestyle or simply in living a life of character, integrity and honor you will enjoy The Wisdom Warrior website and newsletter. The Wisdom Warrior website contains dozens of articles, useful links, and news for those seeking to live the warrior lifestyle.

The newsletter is also a valuable resource. Each edition of *The Wisdom Warrior Newsletter* is packed with motivating quotes, articles, and information which everyone will find useful in their journey to perfect their character and live the life which they were meant to live.

The Wisdom Warrior Newsletter is a newsletter sent directly to your email account and is absolutely **FREE!** There is no cost or obligation to you whatsoever. You will also receive the current news updates and new articles by Dr. Bohdi Sanders as soon as they are available. Your email address is never shared with anyone else.

All you need to do to start receiving this valuable and informative newsletter is to go to the Wisdom Warrior website and simply sign up. It is that simple! You will find The Wisdom Warrior website at:

www.TheWisdomWarrior.com

Also, be sure to find posts by Dr. Sanders on Facebook. Dr. Sanders posts enlightening commentaries, photographs, and quotes throughout the week on his Facebook pages. You can find them at:

www.facebook.com/The.Warrior.Lifestyle

www.facebook.com/TheGentlemanWarrior/

www.facebook.com/bohdi.sanders

Don't miss the opportunity to receive tons of FREE wisdom, enlightening posts, interesting articles, and intriguing photographs on The Wisdom Warrior website and on Dr. Sanders' Facebook pages.

Sign Up Today!